PEACE AND CONFLICT SERIES
Ron Milam, General Editor

PEACE & CONFLICT SERIES

ALSO IN THIS SERIES:
Rain in Our Hearts: Alpha Company in the Vietnam War, by James Allen Logue and Gary D. Ford

Crooked Bamboo: A Memoir from Inside the Diem Regime, by Nguyen Thai; edited by Justin Simundson

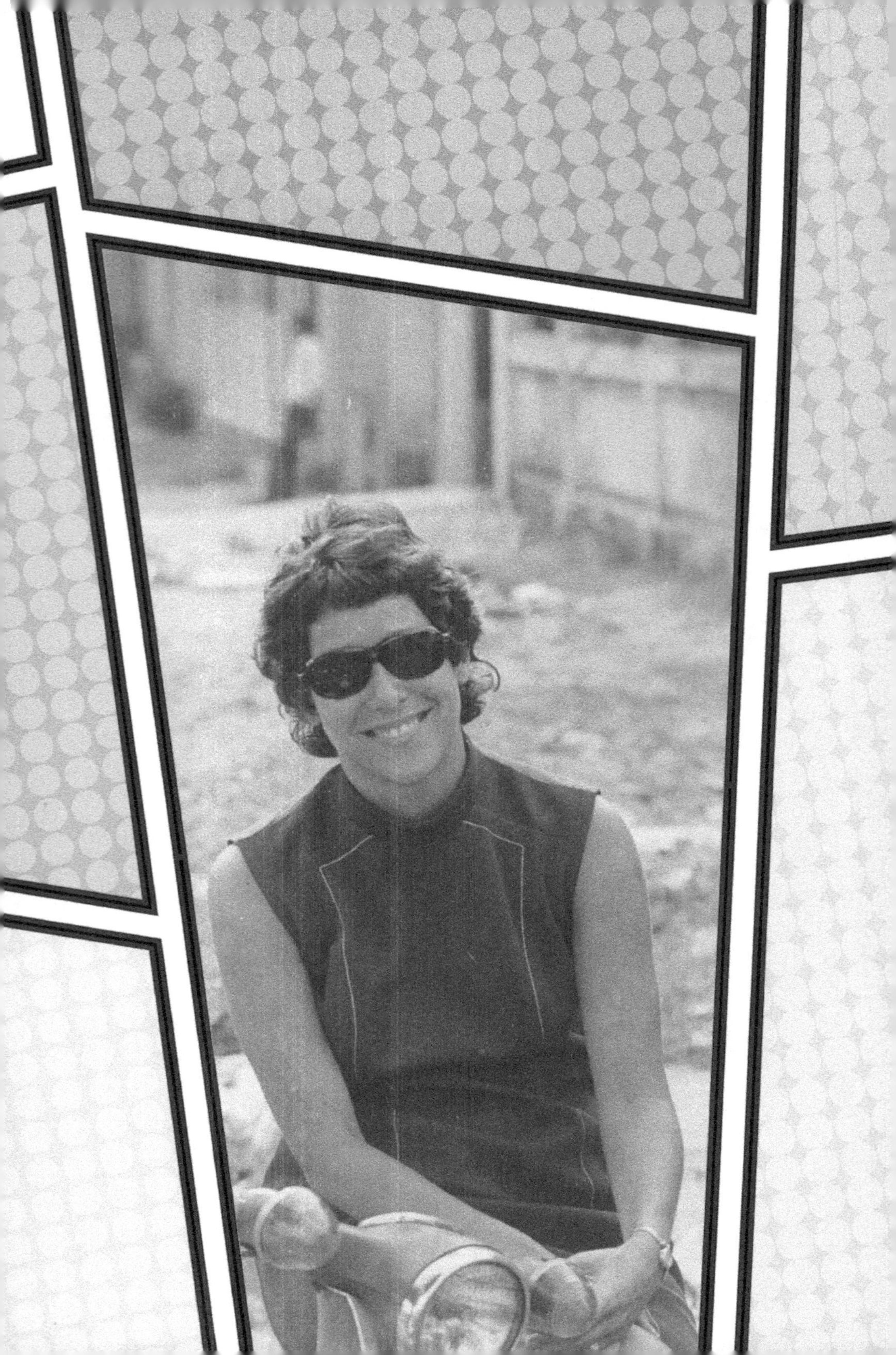

GIRLS DON'T!

A WOMAN'S WAR IN VIETNAM

INETTE MILLER

TEXAS TECH UNIVERSITY PRESS

Copyright © 2021 by Inette Miller

All rights reserved. No portion of this book may be reproduced in any form or by any means, including electronic storage and retrieval systems, except by explicit prior written permission of the publisher. Brief passages excerpted for review and critical purposes are excepted.

This book is typeset in EB Garamond. The paper used in this book meets the minimum requirements of ANSI/NISO Z39.48-1992 (R1997). ♾

Designed by Hannah Gaskamp
Cover design by Hannah Gaskamp

Library of Congress Control Number: 2020946962

ISBN: 978-1-68283-077-2 (cloth)

ISBN: 978-1-68283-247-9 (paper)

First paperback edition 2025

Texas Tech University Press
Box 41037
Lubbock, Texas 79409-1037 USA
800.832.4042
ttup@ttu.edu
www.ttupress.org

For Sam and Daniel.
Sons, who deserve the story of their parents' youth.

And

For Buddy and Harmon.
Brothers, who blazed the trail I tried to follow.

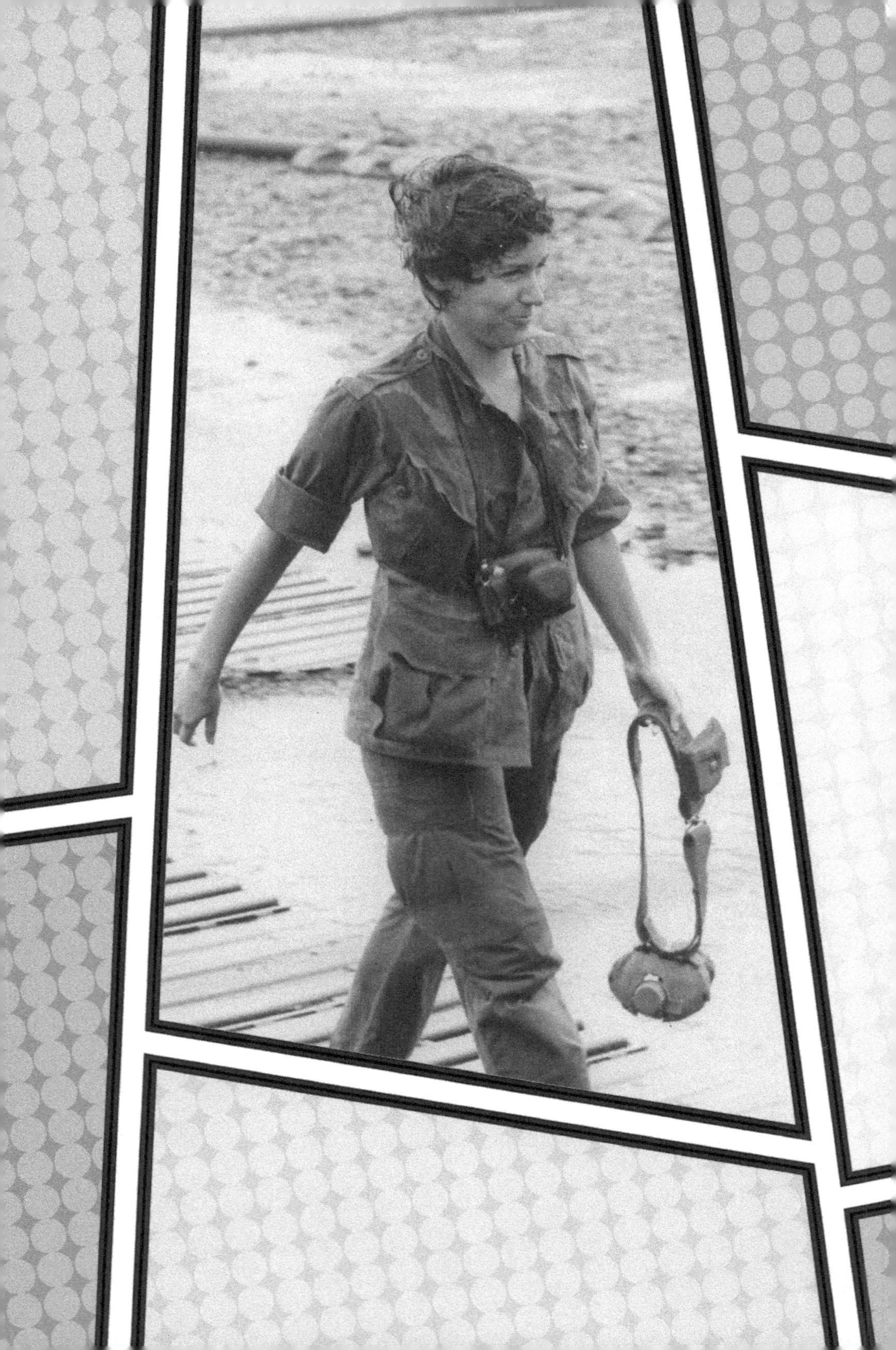

> "Ten people were in that bunker, and each and every one had a different account of what took place."
>
> RICHARD FARRELL
> AWP *Writer's Chronicle*

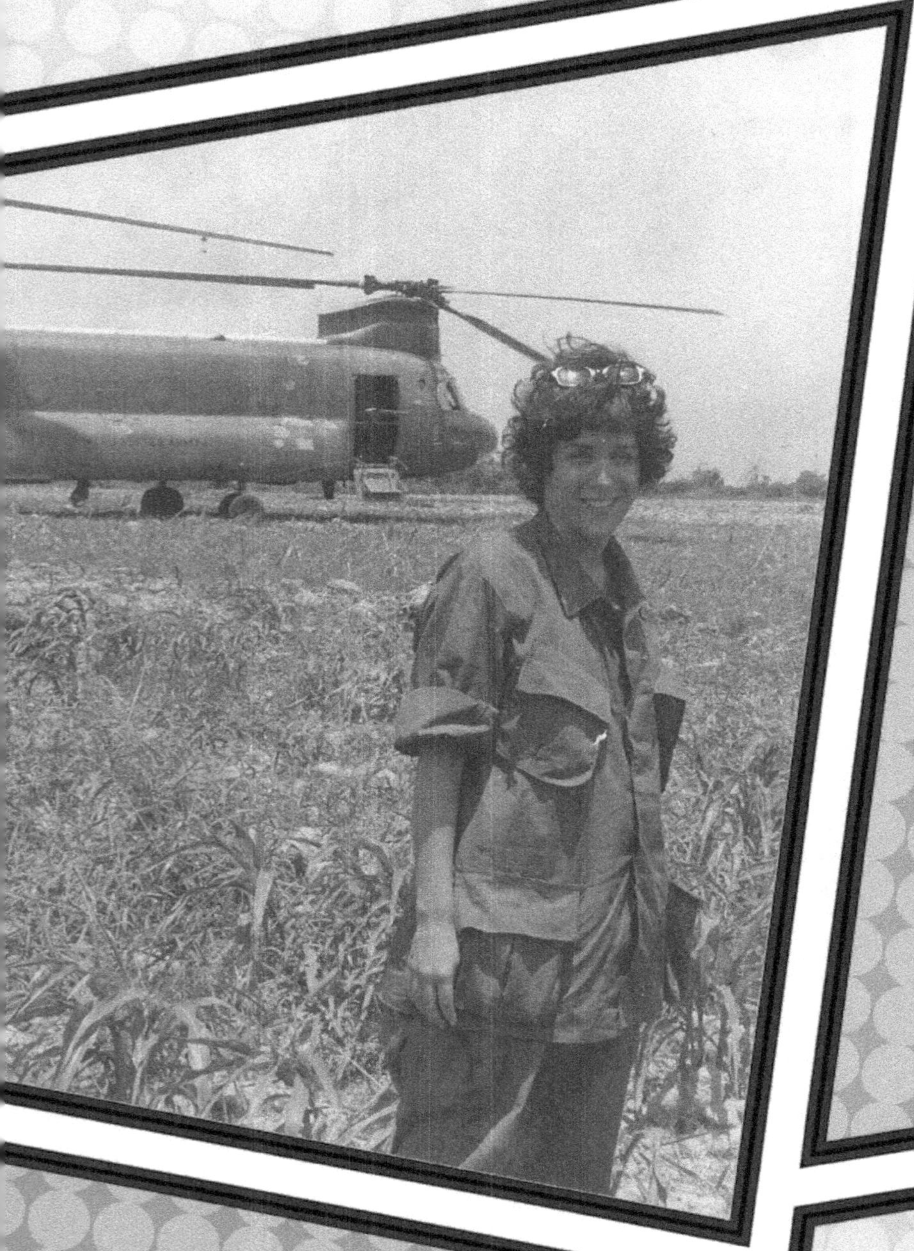

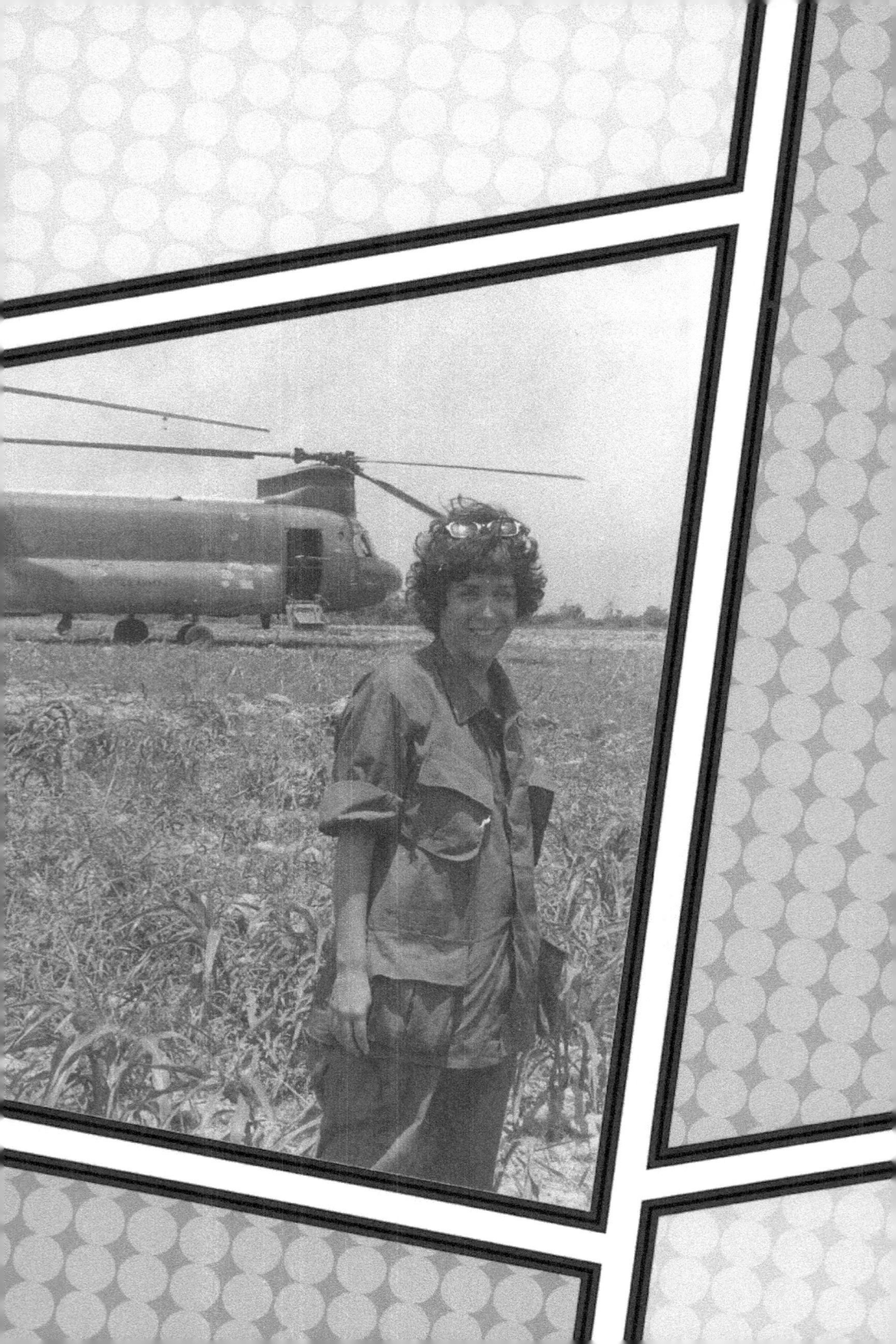

CONTENTS

CHAPTER 1
3   **RISING AND FALLING**
MARCH 1971

CHAPTER 2
17   **STARTING OUT**
THE YEAR BEFORE: JANUARY 1970

CHAPTER 3
31   **ARRIVING**
FEBRUARY 1970

CHAPTER 4
47   **DIVING IN**
MARCH 1970

CHAPTER 5
63   **LIVING MARRIED**
APRIL 1970

CHAPTER 6
79   **LEARNING THE ROPES**
LATE APRIL 1970

CHAPTER 7
99   **DIGGING IN**
MAY 1970

CHAPTER 8
111   **TAKING RISKS**
JUNE 1970

Contents

133 **CHAPTER 9**
FACING DEMONS
JULY 1970

149 **CHAPTER 10**
DRIVING RAINS
AUGUST 1970

169 **CHAPTER 11**
TESTING LOYALTIES
SEPTEMBER & OCTOBER 1970

189 **CHAPTER 12**
COMING UP FOR BREATH
NOVEMBER 1970

203 **CHAPTER 13**
FINDING MIDDLE GROUND
DECEMBER 1970

217 **CHAPTER 14**
CLAIMING HIGH GROUND
JANUARY 1971

241 **CHAPTER 15**
COMING FULL CIRCLE
FEBRUARY 1971

257 **CHAPTER 16**
RISING AND FALLING (REDUX)
MARCH 1971

263 **CHAPTER 17**
AFTERWARDS

267 **WITH GRATITUDE**
269 **INDEX**

GIRLS DON'T!

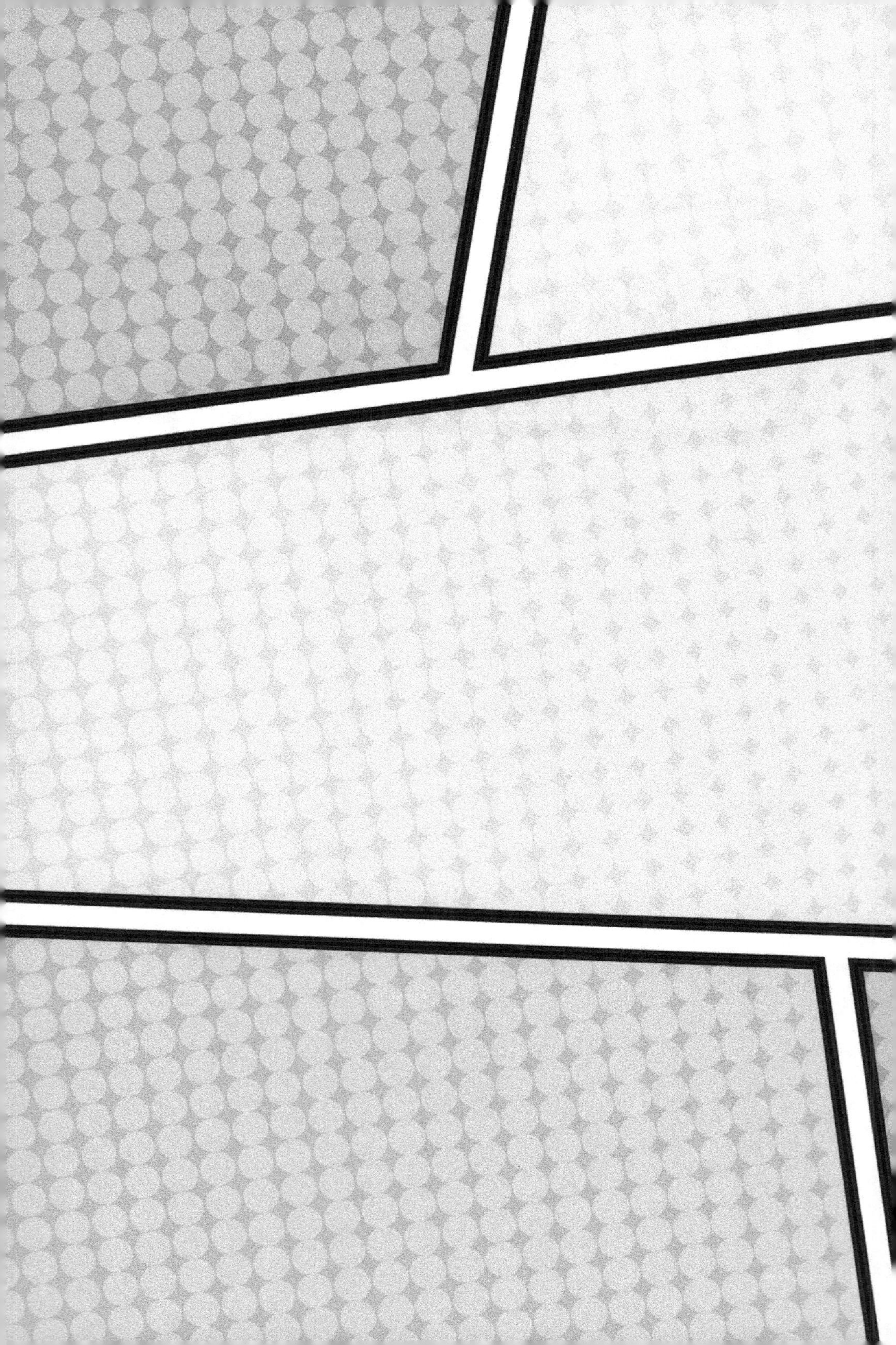

CHAPTER 1

RISING AND FALLING

MARCH 1971

—QUANG TRI, VIETNAM

When I was in my early twenties, just a year out of college and with precisely that amount of experience in paid daily journalism, I sent myself to war. To Vietnam, the war that was tearing America apart and redefining what it meant to be female in an era of divisions as deep and agonizing as those we're enduring today. I justified my choice publicly with a degree of self-inflating logic: "It's the best story around." But there was so much more to it than that.

The chopper pilots in this Central Highlands village were men. I was a woman. It was that easy. For days, while fifty of my correspondent colleagues sat in the Quonset hut we shared in Quang Tri waiting for a press chopper, waiting for word of what might be happening over the border in Laos, I sat a half-mile away in a little room near the base hospital where Huey medical evacuation pilots took turns flying into trouble.

The Medevac pilots could get me where I needed to go. I knew I could make friends among them. In a couple days, I had friends—men, who'd never been to college and were a good four or five years younger than me. These were kids who flew several-million-dollar pieces of machinery at an age when they might typically be mastering their mother's Chevrolet. They were guys who piloted helicopters, lifted bodies in one piece or several out of the bald spots on precariously cleared mountaintops—landing zones (LZs)—with just enough trees scraped off to touch down.

Each and every LZ was just another meaningless piece of turf—claimed today, gone tomorrow. But today it had a name, LZ Liz maybe, after somebody's mama back in Tennessee. Today it was worth fighting for; tomorrow, maybe not.

I had allies among these pilots, and they didn't mind it a bit if I chose to come with them on their endless missions to places of dire unimportance. But their job—to get our boys back to a hospital where eighteen-year-old lives stood a chance of sucking breath for another day, and limbs might be severed or reattached—was critical.

They didn't mind at all if I came along, sitting in the middle of their open-sided Huey—loosely sandwiched between the tail gunners in back, the pilot and copilot up front—dangling my legs over magnificent, mountain *forests*. "Jungle," I thought of my alternate word choice, makes them sound foreign—degrades their splendor.

They were exquisite forests, teeming with life: exotic flowers, ancient trees, shrubs, and animals still thriving after a schoolchild's lifetime of strafing—dropping chemical and mechanical explosives on top of them. They were remarkably resilient. There had been (but I'd never seen them) tigers too, elephants, incredible crawling and flying creatures. These were landscapes brimming with vitality.

The skies were always crystal blue, like a chlorinated swimming pool. I'd swing my legs over the side into the imaginary water. Huey Medevacs moved slowly, barely moved across the unblemished blue. They sat nearly immobile in the sky, hung there really, the engine's hum and the rotors' whir disappearing into a background of uniformity. It felt like floating on my back in the country club pool—that prosaic.

Sometimes I'd lean out over the Ho Chi Minh Trail, as visible from the sky as a dirt road through a county fair. From the best seat in the house I watched the B-52s dive in and drop their lethal cargo, trailing billows of smoke. It felt like watching a movie—that engrossing and that removed.

But going in to pick up the bleeding, suffering kids was different.

The young pilots liked my choosing to ride along with them. I was that extreme rarity, an American girl. I just might be their good luck charm. But they couldn't figure out *why* I'd want to and, initially at least, it quieted them.

Without exception, they'd offer: "Take this with you—take it!" and press a weapon in my hand. They didn't understand. "No, thanks"; I was a witness, never a combatant. *Bao chi*—a journalist. My only hope for quick release depended on my captors' recognizing me as an observer, not a participant. It was neither my plan nor my job to fight this war.

The men wanted to take care of me; they offered their protective arms. Then and now, I've had trouble submitting to that care. But, increasingly, I'm grateful for the offer.

Over the course of two solid days, my fifth and sixth in Quang Tri, I flew eight ninety-minute round-trip medical evacuations with the same pilot. Mike and I had gone in and out of obscure landing zones that were buried invisibly inside impenetrable vegetation. We'd carried back dozens of wounded young soldiers curled up against their pain, gripping their tenuously attached legs, bleeding profusely against my fatigues. I watched my faded olive-greens darken as the clothes absorbed their blood.

I never reached out to hold a hand or stanch a wound. (I had not become the nurse that would have been one of two acceptable "fallback" occupations of parental expectation.) I held back everything but words.

We ferried the wounded to the base hospital in Quang Tri. In the same breath that we touched down (blades still spinning), doctors and nurses swarmed the helicopter and got to work. Mike grabbed a cup of coffee in a paper cup; we headed out again.

During a lull at the end of a very long first day, the warrant officer pilot let me play with the controls. "Fly a chopper," he offered by way of diversion from the obliterating intensity of his task. So I climbed up next to him, bumped the copilot from his seat, and pushed then pulled on the stick in my left hand—made that hulking machine rise or fall to my touch. It was pretty silly, but I felt exuberant, powerful—a flying machine responding to my hand.

At the end of our first day, I was about to walk the distance to the Quonset hut across the base. Mike looked hard in my eyes, his dark ones measuring mine and asking me more than his words articulated.

"You want to go up with me tomorrow? I'll understand if you don't."

He'd *understand* if I didn't want to spend another day clenching my stomach taut as a vise when we flew into mountaintop

LZs—where smoke grenades announced if it were safe or not to touch down—then flew out again and into another and out again, never completely releasing my breath.

Understand, that twice that day he'd headed into blazing hot LZs—artillery shells popping, automatic M16s and AK-47s in full chorus—then was abruptly warned off by the blood-red flare streaking the sky that told us, "Get out of here!" as we closed in to land. Both times Mike veered abruptly, evasively, and headed back into the clear blue sky. The wounded would have to wait for another chopper, another time.

So he'd understand if I didn't want to wake up tomorrow and continue these stomach-churning crapshoots with fate, didn't want to nuzzle next to endless streams of high school athletes dripping pieces of their guts onto my boots, my hair, and my hands.

He'd understand.

"Yeah, Mike, I'll go up with you tomorrow. What time do you want me here?"

This was my job, and I thought I was particularly suited to it. I was paid to observe history, mull its implications, and record it. But I would have done it for free. In the Medevac chopper I felt completely alive, exhilarated, probing my personal limits.

We flew out the next morning, when the sun broke the horizon. Nighttime was the domain of the indigenous armies. The Viet Cong and the North Vietnamese weaved through the overgrown, unlit paths like they were the back alleys of a neighborhood schoolyard. After dark, American and South Vietnamese soldiers hunkered down in defensive position, but the Viet Cong moved about freely. Our task—the Medevac mission, bright and early the next morning—was to scrape up the devastation from the past night's firefight.

Mike accomplished his perilous job without a hitch. No two LZs were the same, but no two were very different either. No two bloody boys' faces were exactly the same, but no two were entirely different either. Uniformly, their eyes brimmed with pain, fear, or a dull obliterating shock. Their mouths turned down at the edges; their lips pressed firmly against tears. I worked hard not to add my anguish to theirs.

I pretended that flying with dead and dying men in a helicopter over a guerilla war wasn't some god-awful aberration from everything life had predicted for me, and for them too. I acted as though this was what we'd all expected. Sometimes a groan escaped their best effort to quash it. Over their heads hung, like the black cloud over that remembered *Li'l Abner* character, some palpable sense of shame—ashamed that they'd screwed up and found themselves in bandages in a Medevac, but relieved too, and shamed also by their relief. Their friends were still hunkered down in that remote LZ, target practice for indigenous fighters.

I scrunched down next to two or three body bags each mission and three or four roughly bandaged boys. I distracted myself with idle chatter, with them or with Mike, ten feet in front of me, through a headset he'd handed me.

"You guys take some heavy fighting?" I asked.

"Nah, I fucked up." The soldier spoke with no facial expression, voice modulation, or affect. He asked me who I was—and then, what I knew. Always the grunts hoped the journalists knew more, knew better.

"Where to now?" I asked Mike through my headset.

He answered with a question. "Everything okay back there?"

"Yeah, everything's okay."

The dead body of what I imagined was some unknown woman's favorite son pressed hard, already rigid against my hips and thighs. I pulled my knees up tight to my chest, minimizing the points of contact. But I refused to feel queasy. I was good at idle conversation. Good too at damping down feelings. I'd been bred to both. Ironically, my mother would be proud.

Mike and I shared two exhausting days of medical evacuation missions and we'd come to know some important things about one another, none of them communicated with words. I knew that he was solid, tempered, tested, and that I could depend on him with my life. He knew I wasn't going to pass out, throw up, or otherwise come unglued. Between us, there wasn't a drop of bravado. That had been wrung out. We were both one-year veterans of this war; we no longer needed to fake it.

In the beginning, correspondent and soldier alike, we pretended to be braver than we knew how to be. But a year later, there was a peculiar kind of honesty, a warped sort of confidence—one I suspected we might have trouble applying elsewhere.

After the second day of it, under an almost full moon, I sat curled in the dark across from my pilot inside the midsection of the chopper where body bags had been lying earlier. The mud and the blood had been mopped up. The two of us studied the big, bright familiar-like-home sky.

I was a married woman, just a year married and very much in love, listening to this man I'd known for two days tell me his story. When he'd reached out to hold me, I just said, "No."

Mike's story. He read a letter from his wife tucked in his shirt pocket. Inevitably, back in Arizona, there was another man—a man "who doesn't fly choppers in Vietnam! Who hasn't left his wife alone!" Her hurt and her rage bellowed.

Mike spoke little after that; I answered almost nothing. But after two days nesting against severed limbs and still-warm young bodies—rigid chest and choked-off breath—I allowed myself to feel something. I recognized a full year's sorrow damped down inside of me. I felt hollowed out and barren: sons without mothers, mothers without sons, kids drafted to kill other kids.

Words never did it, then or after. A generation's youth sweated in the muggy countryside of Vietnam and were silenced—if not by death, then by an experience for which there were no suitable words and very few willing listeners. We were condemned—all of us—to a lifetime searching for the right ones, words and listeners both. Condemned, finally, to the habit of silence. In the pitch-black chopper, I was cured for a single moment of my deep yearning to explain.

I was up in Quang Tri when *Time* reported this in early March:

> Since the Laotian operation began on February 8, the loss rate of US helicopters had quadrupled. So far, during the Laos operation, Communist gunners have knocked out no fewer than sixty-one American helicopters, about ten percent of the fleet originally committed.

A week later that number was up to seventy-three. When the South Vietnamese ground troops failed to accomplish their mission, the American helicopter pilots picked up the slack. Our losses were heavy.

General Do Cao Tri, the personable, pipe-smoking South Vietnamese success story, who'd laughed when he'd told me last June, "I like being a hero," was summoned to work his magic on the Laotian operation. Two-and-a-half hours later, Tri, the nation's most decorated hero, was dead. His body was pulled from the wreckage of yet another downed helicopter.

Paradoxically, it was privilege—the reward of friendship—that got me on my own doomed Huey chopper in the first place. Mike, on his day off, saw to it that I secured a place on the first chopper out the next morning, while most correspondents languished waiting for the official press chopper, or the promise of one.

Two other reporters made the cut, men, whom our lanky pilot agreed to take on: a tall, beefy, network TV correspondent I knew and an older British newspaper reporter I did not.

This slightly older pilot was savoring his authority and refused to tell us precisely where we were headed. There was plenty of room inside and we three sprawled across the metal floor. We talked some about jumping off at the LZ, maybe getting a story and coming out the next day.

Through the headsets, our pilot told us that he was "short." Just six days more and his personal war was history. "I've flown these babies for a year and I've never once never taken fire. You're in good hands." He wasn't bragging; that wasn't done. He was reassuring us civilians.

I'd been here for over a year as well. I too was relatively unscathed in any place you could wrap a bandage. The truth of the matter—steeped in incongruity—was that I loved the exhilaration, felt more alive than I'd ever felt, and wished I could find a way to make the feeling last. I was on shakier ground about what I might expect after the war.

With the pilot's good luck, and mine, we could all rest easy.

And easy it was. Dust off, like every other, almost routine. I'd had ample grist for the *Time* mill this week: sending off stories I'd pecked out in Quang Tri via any colleague headed for Saigon. The return message had been: "Good work. Watch your ass!"

Dust off was a whirl of blades and wind. Standing alongside, it was dust in the eyes and hair plastered flat. Inside, it was a torrent of engine noise and gentle rocking. First, we hovered a few feet off the ground, staring into the stinging eyes of the people standing nearby. Next, we were gazing at the roof line. Finally, we were skimming the tops of the Quonset huts over dirt fields and pulling slowly away from the tediously camouflaged military-base architecture into the forever green countryside—into the forests and away (it felt) from everything man and machine had touched.

We headed over the indistinguishable national border from Vietnam into Laos with our pilot doing a travelogue, now eagerly sharing our whereabouts. There were sharp-peaked jagged mountains in all directions, deep green to the tops. The sky was clear and there wasn't another plane or helicopter in sight. There were no sounds in all of the world but ours.

We lofted slowly, meditatively, over the peaks, over trees I could almost brush with my toes, but this time I didn't try. I was inside talking with the Brit and the ABC reporter about the war—of course, always, the *war*.

What they'd heard: "They're going to pull out all air support. The air losses aren't worth it."

What I'd heard: "No. They'll send in American ground troops."

The stuff of journalistic ardor: rumors, gossip, the balderdash of politics. No matter who held the information, we offered one another what we had.

I was the primary source this time and that felt just fine. I was the one among three who'd been in Quang Tri for a week—in and out of Laos on the choppers—the one-year veteran. I was more confident of my place in the journalistic pecking order than I'd been earlier.

"What're our losses?" the ABC correspondent, disoriented without a cameraman, asked me.

"Not heavy," I said. I knew, because I'd counted.

"How's ARVN (Army of the Republic of Vietnam) troop morale?"

"Bad, very bad," I answered decisively, because I'd seen that too first-hand.

They accepted what I told them and solicited more.

This was a considerably more relaxed flight for me than in the past days. Schmoozing with reporters broke through that edgy isolation. Yesterday, I'd been trapped inside my head with solitary thoughts and fears, because between warriors and correspondents, there was a huge gap of experience.

The soldiers, who were consistently in awe of my *choosing* to go to war, didn't get it. They didn't get that I began with an advantage they would never have: I could fly in and fly out at will.

Hopping off the chopper when we got to the LZ was nothing new. We'd keep our heads down and run, "Like a bat out of hell for cover." I'd done that all year, exactly as a senior correspondent had instructed me last March.

We weaved now among the peaks, not dipping too low into the valleys. The vegetation was thick, lush, and visually impenetrable. But we stayed high so I didn't have to think about what might be hiding where I couldn't see it. We flew for a half an hour, maybe less. There were no seats in the middle of the Huey, or any other form of restraint, so we three wobbled around on the cool floor of the chopper. The sides were wide open. Finally, in the distance, a peak showed gray dirt and rock markings, distinctive for its lack of trees. It was our destination.

From our earliest sighting through a very slow approach, the clearing grew larger, and what initially looked like an empty stretch of rock began to take on life. Life, in the form of figures moving across the bare surface: first, like cockroaches on a kitchen floor, then dollhouse-sized humans, and finally armed South Vietnamese soldiers in olive green.

Now, we three journalists sat against one another on one of the open sides, leaning out and down over the clearing that was about a forty-foot-square landing site. We hovered above the LZ, waiting for the appropriate colored smoke grenade—green smoke announcing it was safe to land. We saw it and headed in to touch down.

Typically, with Medevacs, it happened fast. The chopper touched down lightly, the rotors and engine still revved—a momentary easy target for any trigger behind the impenetrable tree line. The intention was to keep that moment as brief as possible.

Routinely, we'd touch down, the tail gunners poised for action; the men on the ground threw body bags and shoved stretchers with wounded into the open midsection where I sat. The ambulatory wounded scrambled in. Within three minutes, tops, we were airborne and taking the boys back to the base hospital.

This time we got the okay signal, saw the green flare, and we three reporters prepared to spring out, wired to exit. But the chopper never grazed ground. As the crew settled into routine, ready to grab the wounded and take off, we heard a staccato, explosive burst of artillery. I was unnerved. A year of relatively uneventful Medevac transport had lulled me into the balmy fantasy that enemy snipers absolved American choppers with big white crosses from the sins of the war.

I heard just a few words.

The pilot shouted, "Stay put! We're taking fire!"

And from the ground, "Clear out!" And then, more emphatically: "Get the hell out of here!"

The men on the ground scattered and disappeared. The wounded were pushed, dragged, or carried away on their stretchers. Four body bags lay in a heap on the ground. The gray rock was still and empty. We were hovering now at a sickeningly low and torpid pace like a hot air balloon tethered to the ground.

We were rising imperceptibly, maybe thirty-five feet off the ground, pulling away from the mountainside, and I was focusing out of the open side at the thick jungle—no longer a benevolent forest—in front of me. Then I saw it, like a camera flash into open eyes, a quick burst of light from inside the trees. First, there was a world of trees and vines and ferns, then there was the flash of artillery fire, and finally I felt it connect: a hit, a lurch—the helicopter, my pulse rate.

We five—two pilots, three reporters—looked sharply around at each other, expressionless, taking count. The two gunners, facing backwards, were instantaneously in action, laying automatic fire over anything that might consider moving.

We felt another jolt. Somebody yelled: "What the hell!" Then the worst.

CHAPTER 2

STARTING OUT

THE YEAR BEFORE: JANUARY 1970

I was three-and-a-half years old when I pulled up my skirt and peed next to Howie Appelfeld in the back alley. I had watched him whiz—thrilled at the discovery. I pulled down my panties and returned the compliment. I squatted over the cracked concrete—not low enough to miss the white cotton briefs at my ankles. I pulled them up wet. We laughed, and then we laughed some more.

Afterwards, I bragged to my mother: We peed together!

"For shame!" my mother hissed. "Girls don't!"

There was an inevitability about my pull to Vietnam. Of course, I was a journalist by temperament—curious, impassioned, pushy, and a storyteller by predisposition—making a beeline for the best story around. But more to the point, I was the aspiring younger sister of two hotshot older brothers, firmly expected to know my place and be a *girl*.

The fact is, I loved the girl things: the clothes, the hair, the dolls, and the rest. But I was a pretty capable softball player, too, who could lay a decent double to triple if I timed the slide right. No one could tell me I couldn't play drums in the school orchestra—but they did that, and more. By the time I was fourteen, the die was cast. I was angry.

My father, who'd been my affectionate advocate in childhood, was pretty disgusted at how things turned out. His third child was supposed to be a girl, doted on and adored, prepared to attract. That wasn't on my agenda. Mine ran toward proving myself in what seemed, in that confused and distorted time, the preferred and superior male world.

I was a tall, exuberant girl with a mop of curls who wanted to be my brothers' brother—to claim the privilege that went with that. *Tomboy* didn't speak to the issue. Tomboy was a cute, feminine adaptation to male interests. Nor was it an absence of attraction to boys and men. It was political, at the basest emotional level—the source, I imagine, of most politics. I loved what the boys got to be. I hated what the girls were confined within.

I went to Vietnam, finally, because that's *not* where girls were expected to go. I was seeking my lifeblood in a place, ironically, of abundant death—but seeking it, nonetheless.

The first time Bob set eyes on me—three-and-a-half years before Vietnam—I was dancing the cha-cha with the ship's hired social director aboard the USS *Aurelia*, headed from the New York harbor to Rotterdam for a junior year of college in Florence, Italy. Ours was a slow, ten-day crossing, and we saw the upscale *Queen Elizabeth* glide past us three times between the United States and Europe.

"One of the kids pointed you out dancing with this European man on an empty dance floor," Bob told me later. "'She's with us!' I didn't know what to make of you."

I had spent the summer months teaching ballroom dancing in mandated spike heels at Arthur Murray's, with sleazy dance instructors pressing their arousal into the tango. It was a job. My parents were incredibly fine dancers.

The first time I noticed Bob, my roommate was laughing at his antics, confessing she found him "funny and sweet." I knew at once she was right on both counts. It was a couple days after we'd arrived in Florence. But it took four months to turn romantic.

Bob was everything my family was not. He was like a foreign language I'd never imagined speaking but found surprisingly easy to understand. Bob was easy.

My family struggled for supremacy; each generation leapfrogged off the last. Gladly, my parents bent their backs for the children to push off—we would do the same for ours. But Bob and his family were generationally and personally content. No hum of activity or scurrying up mountainsides there.

Bob was a laid-back, small-town, West Coast boy whose idea of an ideal woman ran toward his mother: shy, intelligent, even-tempered, devoutly Catholic, and a nurse. I was—on the other hand—an ambitious, passionate Baltimore girl who had fasted every Yom Kippur since I was nine. I expected a man to be rich, powerful, and Jewish—on no account, Bob. We expected for ourselves that which our families expected for us. We were that young.

If Bob was not what I'd imagined for myself, he was undeniably kind, honest, smart, and funny. With Bob, I got integrity. I used to call him "ingenuous" and say that he could not lie, even in his own best interests. With Bob, I got sweetness, almost feminine, the kind I could not allow myself. With Bob, I got calm. He didn't struggle against the spinning planet and its inhabitants as I did. He accepted what was.

From me, Bob took high-voltage energy and sunshine. I was the perfectly effervescent audience to his wry humor. I was the imaginative, ever-prodding risk taker.

The fit was easy. Except for the family things (and we *were* that young). We weren't either of us what the other's family required. What was required made for a very rocky, difficult, three-and-a-half-year courtship.

My parents opposed Bob from the get-go. That he wasn't Jewish would have been enough. Jewish was who we were, without break, traceable to the Patriarchs—and to the Matriarchs, too. My betrayal was complete.

But with Bob, there was more. His values were internal: art, philosophy, music, religion, introspection. My family's values were external: second-generation immigrant ambition, status, money, how things looked. They didn't *get* Bob, dressed in his red wool vest with worn Levi's.

Throughout the courtship, I was sure that if I chose Bob, I'd be forced to relinquish family. My parents cut me no slack.

In January, three-and-a-half years after we'd met—five months after he'd been drafted—Bob called me from Fort Gordon, Georgia, to tell me I'd never see him again.

"I got orders to Vietnam. I'm going AWOL."

They were those kinds of years, 1968 and 1969. If you lived them, no words are necessary. If they are dry recorded history, I will try to explain.

Early in college, in long braids and white lipstick, I ran through tear gas. I'd been a student at both the University of Wisconsin and, later, at the University of California, Berkeley. Both were iconic names conjuring demolished buildings and extreme violence in the name of peace.

I marched: on streets, sidewalks, city parks, campuses, on both coasts and in the heartland. I signed hundreds of documents of public and private protest. There were limitations here, too, on what a woman could do to renounce the war in Vietnam. *I* could not refuse to go; I could only honor those men who did.

I made heroes of the guys who'd tossed their draft cards into burning trash cans. I didn't miss a single anti-war Moratorium at the Washington Monument. I wore black armbands. I didn't *know* anyone under thirty who did not oppose and contest that war.

In fact, because we were educated and therefore privileged, neither Bob nor I knew a single man who'd been drafted and sent to fight. Our friends found excuses. On physicians' letterhead exempted for bee-sting allergies, poor eyesight, below normal weight. On psychiatrists' stationery, a future orthopedic surgeon was discarded as psychotic. They were safely in the Reserves or the Coast Guard; in Army language school studying Russian; on alternate duty as conscientious objectors; in jail. There were teaching exemptions, and architects-who-build-hospitals exemptions, and married-with-children excuses. Everyone had his story.

"I'm not going," Bob told me by phone within hours of getting his orders. But now, we both knew, it was a little too late. Before induction, before they'd buzzed off his straight brown shoulder-length hair and full-faced, ragged beard—before he'd agreed to three months of Basic Training and two more of Advanced Infantry Training—*then* he could have refused.

For five months, we simply denied the inevitable. We kidded ourselves that Bob's training, courtesy of the US Army, was not in preparation for Vietnam. We seized every rumor: *some* GIs, *somewhere*, had been sent to Germany. Right!

Bob had postponed giving into the draft. After graduation in 1968, he hitchhiked across the country, stood in lines on skid row grabbing temp jobs in Denver, Chicago, and Cody, Wyoming. He switched draft boards, delayed, stalled—and refused to make a decision. Finally, it was decided for him. He was served notice, "Greetings: Report for induction into the US Army—September 2, 1969."

He met the Army's bus in Annapolis, Maryland. He looked, standing there in front of the post office, like the pale Irish half of his maternal gene pool—nothing like the darker Italian one. He was five feet ten and called himself "husky." He'd played football in high school and college but had ambivalent feelings about that sport. It had been one year since he'd taken his diploma in history.

When the bus pulled off, I was crying but not resigned.

"I'll visit!" I shouted into his open window. And although there were abundant rules prohibiting visitation during Basic Training and he was three states away, I did.

Now, however, Bob's belated refusal to serve meant a military tribunal—no longer civilian legal guarantees—and an Army prison. He had ten days to report to Oakland, California—or refuse—for his flight to Saigon.

On the phone, Bob, never given to hyperbole, said quietly: "I'm taking off. You won't see me again."

I hung up and felt stone-cold panic. I snatched up the phone and begged my boss for time off. He offered me a week to sort out my needs. I sat, cried, and wrote obsessive diary entries. I spent my grief and days off inside a little carriage house that I'd rented behind a stately, antebellum mansion beside a rose garden in Annapolis. I took Bob's words at face value. I would not see him again.

I picked hard at an old wound, already scabbed over. He *should* have been a conscientious objector—a former altar boy who'd studied eight years under the nuns, then another eight under the Jesuits, the apple of a devout mother's eye. He entered a Christian Brothers' monastery as a novitiate, days out of high school. "I believed I had a vocation. I thought I was meant to serve God."

He had loved every moment of it: the routine, the silence, and the prayers.

"But I didn't have it," he tried to explain the inexplicable. "I couldn't be a Brother."

Yet Bob did have the qualities compatible with monastic life. It was what drew me to him from the first: gentleness, decency, and a depth of faith. Refusing to take a human life was not just a matter of church doctrine for him. He agonized over the indecent war. It was a struggle for his soul. Doubtless, he would die before he would kill.

I'd been pacing the tiny space between living room, bedroom, and suck-in-your-stomach kitchen for four days. I jumped when I heard a knock on the door. I bolted out of the bentwood rocker I'd bought at a yard sale the week before, looked up at the door, then through its foggy glass panels.

"Oh, my God!"

Bob's wide, ruddy face was on the other side, not peering back at me at all, totally self-absorbed. He was dressed head to foot in olive green, bundled against the January winds in an Army-issue topcoat, clutching an enormous duffel. His face was impenetrable.

I yanked open the door and fell into his substantial arms. Then I pulled him inside, in front of my living room fire.

"I don't . . . don't know what to do," he stammered.

I wrapped my arms around his massive back and held on. His comforting bulk filled up the black hole of his last phone call. I, for once, didn't have words to ladle on top of his silence. I was silent with him.

It was Wednesday. There were seven days left of the ten-day leave. Bob had passed the first three days in a fog of uncertainty, at bus stations and skid row hotels.

We layered sweaters, coats, scarves, and gloves against the sharp, January wind and rain. We layered, too, our three-and-a-half-year history together, protection against the violent storm.

We walked along the edge of the Severn River, tracing the curving paths of the paradoxically pastoral Naval Academy campus—once, twice . . . unconsciously repeating our circuit. We wiped rain off our faces with the free hands that were not looped around each other's waists. Then we stepped off campus and took a turn around the sidewalks of the funky, charming, racist village—still undiscovered by the Washington affluent and fashionable—that was Annapolis then.

On that first day, I still believed in the power of logic. I drew up lists, plotted alternative courses of action, and generally behaved as though we had an array of choices. From the moment Bob appeared at the front door, his dilemma had become mine—*you* had become *we*.

We walked through long silences and listened to the rain pound the river and pelt out a cadence on the awnings over the village sidewalks. Intermittently, there'd be an abrupt explosion of words, sometimes his, sometimes mine.

Bob: "I hate the fucking war!"

"Who doesn't?"

"I can't do it!"

"So don't. We'll go to Sweden." I pitched option number one. Sweden—traveling Europe again—it sounded good to me.

"Sweden!" He dismissed it. He was less angry than dazed. "What would I do in Sweden? I don't even speak the language."

Without hesitation, I ticked off the next one on the roster.

"Canada then; Canada would be easy." That option didn't excite me like a return to Europe, but different enough—okay.

Starting Out

"Easy. Sure. I could never come home again, not even for my parents' funerals. What kind of choice is that?"

He batted away at my list. I'd half expected him to. It was considerably easier for me to be glib. We had dissimilar agendas, disparate voices yapping at our heels, very different things to prove.

Neither of us slept much that night or the next one. They were confusing nights of blurred distinction between ardent touch and fear. We were working overtime to silence the demons.

On the third day we again slid over wet sidewalks, marched off four- or five-mile circles. Bob mopped off his glasses. I shook water from my long curls. We stopped and perched on the stone abutment that separated the Naval Academy's grassy campus from the river. I sat securely on top, dangling my legs over a huge rock. He hopped from stone to stone, scrambling precariously close to the edge, tempting fate to lessen his choices.

"Don't, Bob! It's slippery!"

We'd run out of logic, and options.

"It's looking grim," he said from the rim of the rock ledge. Slowly, he climbed down and sat near me. He sighed softly. "I keep seeing my dad's face."

It would have been appropriate for Bob to refuse either the draft or Vietnam. But he did not do either finally, because being a man and fighting a war were part and parcel of being his father's eldest son.

His father couldn't hear too well because of time spent under fire on an Aleutian Island chain in the Pacific—and he sometimes limped. World War II had harmed Bob's father. But it had accounted too, for the marriage to his mother. She'd been an Army nurse. The *war* had been family. *The* war had made his father—and countless other men—"who I am today." That heritage of national service passed to the oldest son either through the genes or across the salad plate.

Bob agreed to be a soldier, then prayed with all his heart that he'd never be sent to Vietnam. He agreed for a single reason: he wanted his father to love him. But his father was a man incapable of speaking or acting that love, so Bob never knew if his decision made one whit of difference.

He did know, and found an ironic comfort in the fact, that the very first US draft lottery some months later nailed him—or *would have* nailed him. If he had not already agreed (for his own subtle, anguished reasons) to submit, fate would have fingered him anyway. His birthday, September 14, was the first scrap of paper drawn from the spinning barrel.

Late Friday, our third day together, we gave up the outdoors and came inside my little house to get warm and dry. When Bob shoved the stuck front door open, he shouted his last words on the matter: "Between a rock and a hard place, no room to maneuver."

I didn't buy it. I would not let other people's expectations write my script. I was twenty-three years old and decisively unwilling to hand it over.

We'd been inside for ten minutes. Bob had stoked the fire; I'd put on a pot of coffee. We were in the bedroom tugging off wet clothes, changing into dry ones.

At Christmas the month before, when Bob was on leave from Fort Gordon, we'd visited his parents in California. I'd been sitting at their breakfast table studying their morning newspaper. A blurry snapshot of a girl my age smiled up at me from Saigon. The girl, it said, had flown to Vietnam for a single month and mailed stories home to her hometown paper. I stared at the black-and-white photo of the young blonde in jungle fatigues. She looked cocky, with one leg lifted onto a statue of three Vietnamese combatants. I thought: If she can, I can. It was that simple. But I'd filed away the thought—until now.

Now I sucked in my breath, pulled my erect shoulders a bit straighter, let loose a nervous giggle and blurted.

"Look, I'm a reporter." (For a year, I'd cut my reportorial teeth on Naval Academy cheating scandals, integration-purposed busing protests, even book burnings—at the Annapolis *Evening Capital*.) "The war is the biggest story around. Let's get married and do the war together."

It was an outrageous suggestion, and I hadn't even known it was inside my head until it was out of my mouth. Sweden? Canada? Vietnam! Now *that* was adventure!

Bob looked stunned. He leaned back against my dresser and searched hard for something inside my eyes. I looked back at him with a full-face smile. He looked away at the floor and he stayed still like that for a very long time.

"Umm . . . " He exhaled and hummed the sound. Then he looked up, smiled his slanting grin—just a slight notch in his full face, but his eyes were twinkling.

"Okay. Let's do it!"

"Well?" I couldn't hold back a laugh. "Aren't you going to propose?"

I sat down primly on the edge of my mattress, hands in my lap, beaming and waiting. This time Bob didn't hesitate. He knelt on one knee on the hardwood floor at the foot of the bed. He cleared his throat, and he asked. "Will you marry me?" His soft blue eyes grabbed hold of my dark ones with complete earnestness.

"Gladly." I hugged him.

"So how do we do this?" he asked.

"Fast," I answered.

He didn't miss a beat. "Doing anything Tuesday?"

Bob phoned the news to his parents in California. They had expected, we were amazed to hear, an engagement ring at Christmas.

Girls Don't!

"We'll be there," his mother said.

We took the news to my parents at Friday night dinner and they too seemed less shocked than resigned. Contrary to either of our intentions, all four parents had been anticipating a marriage.

For me, marriage and the war were the identical decision. I had never considered the one before I'd considered the other. Marriage felt less a foreordained track to my mother's conventional life if it took me to war. The war made a certain sense to me if we were married. I walked that tightrope.

My mother managed, "Why don't you wait until he gets back?"

"And hope that he doesn't?" I retaliated for a litany of recent hurts.

My father was silent and grim.

"Following Bob to Vietnam." Each mother, independent of the other, said those exact words. In some weird twist of shared traditional values, they condoned a wife who followed her man.

We were married under the *chupah*. The Catholic boy who agreed to the war agreed, too, to trounce the wine glass. After three-and-a-half years of diddling, it took us four-and-a-half days to put together a wedding on January 27, 1970. Just that long to get a license, find a rabbi, hire a caterer, fit a gown, and buy rings.

The wedding was an odd mix of form and nonconform. I was barely speaking to my mother for a half dozen accumulated slights and reasons, but I wore white satin to the floor. Bob had a tuxedo, a Basic Training buzz cut, and a face burnt red where a full beard had shaded fair skin before induction. All parents were present.

Bob's father, who when not raging at his children around the dinner table was engagingly handsome and cunningly charming. He had navy-blue eyes, thick black lashes, and curly salt-and-pepper hair, and he wooed my mother and father by calling the bride and groom "headstrong kids." All the grown-ups nodded their

Starting Out

agreement.

Bob's mother—this gray-haired matron and the only verifiably *religious* person in the mix—had suspended her yearnings for a Catholic Mass and simply supported her son.

"You're good for Bob," she told me afterwards. "He needs a little push. Just be careful you don't push too hard." She wore a pale blue, long-sleeved knit dress—the color of her eyes and Bob's. She was soft-spoken, always.

Here she found her words swallowed up by the effusive Millers. "We think the world of Inette," she told my mother, who failed to hear her.

"When she makes up her mind," my mother answered to no one in particular, "there's no talking her out of it."

My mother—who would never, ever go gray and worked hard at being a size four petite—had refused to buy a mother-of-the-bride dress for this slapdash affair. But she was perfectly warm and gracious to Bob's parents.

My father, like my mother, had given up the fight when the battle was over. They, it turned out, didn't want to lose me either. And although I fully failed to appreciate it at the time, they were plenty worried about me in Vietnam.

So they were all there.

The fourth-choice rabbi was there, too. The first three had refused to join a Catholic and a Jew on four days' notice—and this rabbi threatened to back out when I appealed to him for a ceremony in English. "So Bob can understand."

"It is," he insisted angrily, "a *Jewish* wedding."

It was an imitation formal wedding: little rented gold chairs with red cushions arranged in my brother's living room; the "Wedding March" on the stereo; an incorrigible uncle seated at the food table dipping into the covered chafing dish throughout the vows. It was a pretense of the affair my parents had intended for their only daughter—a shoddy imitation, neither here nor there. Not Golden Gate Park hippie nuptials, the worst of their nightmares: free verse, free tokes, bare feet, and guitar. But not the Miami Fontainebleau Hotel with three hundred guests and a full orchestra either.

The day after the wedding, Bob flew with his parents back to Oakland for the first leg of his flight to Saigon. I hunkered down for three weeks of paperwork: visa applications, work permits, and assorted bureaucratic permissions—left to figure out how I'd get myself to Saigon.

I never doubted I would.

In the years before I arrived in Vietnam, there had been the *Tet Offensive*, *Vietnamization*, stark cold political ambition. In the years after I'd left, there were the *killing fields*, the failed truce, and the lost war.

But when I was there in 1970 and 1971, there remained a mist of illusion. It seemed that the war was ending, but it still had five years to go. It seemed the war was being turned over to the South Vietnamese Army, but it never was, except ultimately to the North Vietnamese. It seemed we had turned some corner in accepting our colonial limitations, but we had not. It seemed that "the light at the end of the tunnel" burned brighter—but it was illusory.

In the mists of 1970 and 1971, the Viet Cong waited us out in the jungles of South Vietnam. The Khmer Rouge became patriots of another cause in Cambodia.

In the mists of 1970 and 1971, my boyfriend and I got married, defied every recorded prohibition against American military wives in Vietnam, and went to war.

CHAPTER 3

ARRIVING

FEBRUARY 1970

I thought it remarkable. *Anyone* could have taken the Pan Am flight I took to Saigon in mid-February 1970, but, of course, not everyone did. People go where they need to go.

I paid $585 of my savings from a $125 a week small town reporter's salary for the flight from Baltimore to San Francisco to Saigon, with refueling stops in Honolulu and Guam. From San Francisco, the flight took twenty-two hours. I was twenty-three years old. I'd been married twenty-one days.

I remember, still, the astonishing fragrance off of the gardenia, ginger, and plumeria garden at the Honolulu airport. It was night-time, and it pinched my nostrils with an almost sickening sweetness. It was just about the last sweet thing I smelled for fourteen months.

The man sitting next to me on the flight to Saigon said he was a retired engineer, working a civilian job for the US government.

But Bob and I had been warned to tell no one we were married. The US military strictly forbade dependents. Even generals' wives were exiled no closer than Thailand. I was prepped and paranoid. The milquetoast guy next to me could be an informer.

So when he asked, I said, "I'm single." Not such a big lie; just one day and night together married, the rest spent in inoculations and intense letters to one another across the abyss. I was prepared to be single. All documents were in my name.

The plan. I'd be met by a friend of a friend who would help me find housing. I was not prepared to be met instead by Bob, stationed an hour away in Long Binh—dressed now in baggy combat fatigues, looking skinny and tan at the other end of the customs counter. He was smiling shyly at me.

"Think fast!" my brother Harmon used to yell at me, then reveal a hidden hand and heave a hard fastball at my stomach.

I grabbed my suitcase, walked up to my husband, thrust out a hand to him, and said, "It's nice to see you again, Bob." We shook hands. "My good friend, Bob," I introduced him to the engineer.

I was—in the language of the day—*blown away* by Bob standing at Ton Son Nhut airport, tropical sunlight streaming through the pores of the building, huge ceiling fans beating at the thick hot air. But I was confused; he was not part of the plan.

I don't know what Bob made of the handshake. Surprise, surely? But Bob could be depended on not to blow it. The friend of a friend was *not* there; Bob was. I had no other names, maps, or travel guides. I needed a room for the night. The engineer knew a cheap residential hotel a mile from downtown. We took a cab together: my seatmate, my husband, and me.

I got a room, simple and clean. Bob closed the blinds on the incredible heat in the mustard-colored room and we held each other. I remember very little of the holding. I heard Bob's story in a daze of jet lag.

"I don't know why I did it. I know we agreed not to say anything, and my sergeant is a real tough-ass—a greaser who never cracks a smile. But I told him: 'My wife's a journalist; she's coming to Saigon tomorrow. Can I have a pass?'"

"Private," the sergeant had answered, "there are no passes in Vietnam."

But he put Bob on a bus headed for Saigon the next morning, picking up soldiers at the airport. He warned Bob to be back on the bus when it returned that afternoon. And then he volunteered, "I'll see if I can get you transferred to Saigon."

"Holy shit," Bob answered.

In that first strange twist of fate, it turned out that the sergeant had a Korean wife he'd married when he'd been stationed there. He had a soft spot for family life.

I had Bob for just a few hours. I threaded my hand through his bent arm and we walked for the first time in downtown Saigon. The smell of urine was oppressive. The heat felt like a concrete wall bearing down on me. My contact lenses tore at my eyes in the filthy air. Armed men and massive coils of rusted barbed wire barred the entrance to official buildings. I wondered whether you had to crawl through the spirals to get inside.

We kept touching one another—couldn't stop ourselves really—testing the physical reality of where and what we were: the Republic of South Vietnam and married. Then, in a blink he was gone.

I spent my first night alone, face down on the floor of the mustard-colored room. Minutes after I'd climbed between the crisp sheets, gunfire exploded outside my street-level windows. I mistook the first explosion for an automobile backfire—the only sound anything like it in my suburban repertoire.

But then I got it. The staccato shots sounded like they were exploding next to my head. I held my breath, slid off the mattress, and tried to squeeze myself against the cool tile floor under the bed frame. I couldn't fit. But I stayed like that: flat on my stomach, hip against frame, cowering for hours afterwards. Sometime in the middle of the night, I crawled back in bed and slept.

I arrived in Saigon with $500 in my pocket and thirty days to find a job.

The man responsible for getting me into Vietnam, Phil Evans, had been my boss for the past year—the executive editor at the Annapolis *Evening Capital*. Formerly with the *Baltimore Sun*, he'd set out with the ambition to create a first-rate newspaper for the Baltimore-to-Washington suburban stretch. With a tight budget, he'd sought talented young reporters—short on experience, long on zeal. It was an entirely idealistic and ennobling first job. I got hooked.*

Phil hired me and recognized my knack for reporting before I did. He trained me, nurtured me, and then, when I asked him, wrote me the letter that told the South Vietnamese Embassy that I was a war correspondent for the *Evening Capital*. His letter bought me a thirty-day work visa.

More than that, Phil could not do. "We can't keep a war correspondent," he told me. "We're too small; we can't afford the insurance on your life. We'll buy what you send us, $25 a story."

I would have to find a job, then. But first, I needed a place to live.

I had one person's name and number in my purse when I arrived. Bill Dowell had been an Army intelligence officer in Vietnam. He'd returned, this time, as an NBC Radio correspondent. He'd served, the first time around, with the husband of my newspaper colleague in Annapolis.

I'd expected Bill to meet me at the airport. He'd miscalculated

---

* Forty-nine years later, in June 2018, that newsroom, home to my very first reporting job in Annapolis, was the site of the brutal murder of five journalists.

the twelve-hour difference between San Francisco and Saigon and met my plane a day early. He'd already found me a home.

On day two in Saigon, I met Bill for breakfast at the spare and spacious Brodard's. Café au lait and a hard French roll with butter and jam, he suggested. Bill was tall, thin, and gangly, with curly blond hair and an affable, uncomplicated manner. He was just about my age.

Bill was the kid in high school you'd regale with stories about the boys you loved. He'd listen for hours to your angst. He'd never ask you out, and you wouldn't have accepted. He was worth more than that—a good male friend. I couldn't have stumbled on an easier comrade.

He told me to climb onto the back of his motorcycle, and I did. Then he told me to get off it and climb on again. This time, sidesaddle—as the Vietnamese women did. Damn, I thought, but didn't say out loud. He expects me to ride like a girl!

"Are you serious?" I asked him. He was. In Saigon, I never saw a woman ride behind a motorcycle driver any other way.

We drove first through downtown Saigon's office, apartment, and government buildings. Only one building, a hotel, stretched to ten stories. Then we headed up a major North-South boulevard for more than a mile. It was impossible to count the number of traffic lanes, for the helter-skelter of motorcycles, bicycles, trucks, and what looked like rickshaws crammed onto every inch of asphalt.

We drove past a large, open-air vegetable market, an ornate Buddhist temple with an impressively wide and steep staircase, a walled French high school, and an endless array of minuscule shops. I was mesmerized, my senses were one hundred percent alive.

We turned down a series of increasingly smaller rock, then dirt, roads, and eventually wound through a maze of earthen paths that were no more than two-arms'-width across. We skimmed past free-range chickens, toddlers in t-shirts with naked bottoms, and huts built from beer-can sheet metal stamped Pabst Blue Ribbon.

The smells were organic, rich and fetid at the same time: rotting vegetables, stagnant waterways, human and animal excrement. Life: I savored it all from the back of a motorcycle, baked under a tropical sun.

If in the past I had found Rome and Zurich foreign, I was now reassessing. European cities were familiar indeed by comparison. Nothing around me was in any way recognizable to my Western sensibilities.

We stopped, finally, at what seemed to be the edge of the Earth—a sprawling white stucco house dead-ending at a filthy tributary of the Saigon River. The rambling house wrapped around a concrete courtyard where nothing grew. Laundry dangled on crisscrossed clotheslines; a decrepit rowboat lay grounded at the water's edge.

I was introduced to Mrs. An—a round-face, beaming thirty-nine-year-old woman. Tiny but plump, she wore an *ao dai*—a lovely high-necked yellow silk dress slit from ankle to hip over loose black satin trousers. Her skin was smooth as glass. She had a gold tooth in the front of her wide smile, and she bubbled with life. She didn't speak a word of English. I couldn't answer her with a word of Vietnamese. Bill translated her French.

Mrs. An unlocked the door to a room that opened onto the courtyard facing the squalid river. It was a large square room, maybe fifteen feet by fifteen, and behind it a bathroom. The room was dominated by an enormous platform bed and a huge ceiling fan hanging below a fluorescent light.

The bathroom was idiosyncratic, with a large concrete shower stall and no place for a curtain. The sink stood under the shower head. There was only cold water.

The main room had wall hooks for clothing, a small desk with a wooden chair, and a night table but no lamp. There was the screen door I'd entered, installed just that day in anticipation of my American needs, and a window. The window had screens and shutters, but no glass. The walls were whitewashed stucco; the floor, concrete tile. It was clean, bright, airy, and totally inviting. I could imagine myself and my few possessions inside these walls.

Mrs. An and I talked turkey. We bargained a rent price in piastres; what I'd thought would be $110 a month, I later came to realize was only $25. The confusion had less to do with my inability to calculate than with my ignorance of the multilevel currency system—the black market. There were piastres, the native currency. There was military payment currency (MPC)—the only scrip GIs were authorized to use. And there was "green": what we call dollars. Each had a different and ascending value.

The official exchange rate had nothing to do with the actual value of the dollar. Green was officially forbidden in Vietnam, but it was how American civilians survived the economy. It was worth a great deal more than piastres to Vietnamese looking for an economic future somewhere other than the unstable Vietnam.

So, within two days of arrival, I had a home. It would not have been everyone's idea of home, and when I met other correspondents, I was shocked by their maids, their multi-room flats with air conditioning, and their proximity to their downtown offices.

My home was a different story, and at first I thought it might be a grave mistake. I was way outside the mainstream. Yet in time I came to regard it as a retreat. I came to love being part of the family.

Mrs. An had five children; only the last was a son. She counted me as simply another young woman under her roof. Nhung, the second oldest, was a high school senior. She spoke excellent English. We came to care for and depend on one another in unexpected ways.

Girls Don't!

The next order of business was transport.

By the end of my first week I'd bought an ancient Honda 50 for $125. It was the smallest but most ubiquitous motorbike in Saigon. I was crazy about it: old and not terribly powerful, but a motorcycle nonetheless and *red*.

At first I was totally paralyzed by the vehicular anarchy on the streets, the unregulated frenzy. I'd never driven a motorcycle and I was definitely not a natural. But necessity being the mother of invention, I learned. On my Honda I was no longer the pedestrian victim of the packed-out streets. Shifting, steering, balancing, checking tires and gas tank—I was part of the pack.

There were no traffic rules in Saigon. Apocryphally threaded through traffic mythology were stories of men shot for going through red lights. But, the storyteller would reassure, that had less to do with traffic law than with boys with time—and rifles—on their hands.

The only rules, it seemed, were evolutionary ones—survival. And it worked only if you were willing to be daring. After a terrifying initiation—skinned knees and scraped paint—I joined the ranks of the reckless. For a few cents, I had a tank full of gas. I was mobile and it made all the difference in the world.

With my letter from Phil, I moved slowly through the bureaucracy. First to the ersatz Vietnamese press office, an older yellow French Colonial building where I brandished my letter and they affixed one of my two dozen mug shots to a Vietnamese press card. My wedding photos featured wavy dark hair halfway down my back. My mug shots three weeks later showed a tiny cap of dark fuzz. I was looking a whole lot like my oldest brother, Buddy.

"Short and easy," is what I told the hairdresser I needed for war. I'd hoped Bob would like the haircut when he saw it. When he did see it, he repeatedly rubbed his hand across my head. But he didn't say—then, or ever—what he liked about me, or did not like. Forever, I had to guess.

The Vietnamese press pass was worth less than the paper it was printed on. It was the polite formality, I came to understand—like so many—before the authentic one in this American-occupied nation. I squared my shoulders and headed to JUSPAO, the Joint US Public Affairs Office, a tall, concrete, modern structure, and got the real card.

Theoretically, you could work in Vietnam without an American press pass, but in fact it was your ticket onto all military transport. US military airplanes and helicopters were the only actual way around the countryside—there weren't alternative civilian flights to base camps or jungle landing zones. No reporter could cover the war without one.

When the US military chose to punish a correspondent for reporting what it would rather he did not (like the infamous American massacre at My Lai), they lifted the card. Representatives of small, radical presses were easier to disenfranchise without political fallout than establishment ones.

The American press officer asked my blood type, then typed it onto my press card. I didn't have a clue; I'd never donated blood. I didn't want to stall the accreditation process, so I winged it: "O positive." And that's what I carried into combat all year.

Ten full years later, when I gave birth to my first son, I discovered I was O negative. An emergency transfusion in Vietnam would have finished off what any war wound had begun. But it didn't happen.

With the press card, I was official. Days later, I was formally briefed at MACV (Military Area Command, Vietnam): Saigon's Pentagon. It was a large, low, undistinguished building, and every doorknob and window had been shipped across the ocean from the United States. What passed for landscaping wasn't much, just a few palm trees, a scraggly lawn.

Girls Don't!

Inside: offices, dining rooms, movie theaters, and other amenities for the American generals and their staffs who ran the war. Enormous cargo ships brimming with middle-American necessities docked daily just outside of Saigon. Thus, MACV's furnishings managed to replicate standard-issue law office decor and equipment.

Outside: American buildings stood in stark contrast to the surrounding Vietnamese ones. And there was no mistaking them for French. They were a far cry from either clustered village huts or the graceful French Colonial villas. There was an exponential trailer park quality to MACV.

I bridged the considerable defenses of the building with my press pass. I was briefed for several hours by an assortment of burly colonels in a pristine boardroom. I was handed maps, folders, and the official version of the American war in Vietnam. My ignorance was limitless, but I was bent on not letting on.

At the time, I could not have distinguished the flat fertile Delta region from the rugged mountainous Central Highlands; Navy captains (who commanded ships) from Army captains (who took commands from almost everyone); fast, sleek Cobra gunship helicopters from huge ponderous cargo-carrying Chinooks. I had prepared myself for reporting the war in Vietnam in two ways: getting shots and shopping. So I was more than inclined to smile agreeably, laugh at the men's jokes, and nod knowingly while I listened. I did not ask questions.

My behavior was in direct contrast to that of the single other correspondent being briefed alongside of me. Gloria Emerson was a *New York Times* reporter who had waged a ten-year war of her own to convince the *Times* that they could send a woman to Vietnam. *She* had prepared. She was tall, slender, and imposing: black hair against alabaster skin, thirty-eight at the time. Fresh from paying her dues reporting fashion in the *Times*' Paris bureau, she'd been given her shot.

She barreled questions at the lieutenant colonel. *She* never smiled. She was dubious; she implied we were not being told the truth. I was completely in awe of this woman: her erudition, her take-no-bullshit demeanor. A week or so later, Gloria overheard me telling a press attaché at JUSPAO that I was broke and looking for work. She grabbed my arm, pulled me aside, and whispered with enormous passion.

"Don't *ever* let a man know you're broke."

I was astounded and touched by her concern, but her words were wasted on me then. I didn't yet see men as predators or adversaries; I saw them as standard bearers. I wanted to be one of them.

So I was official. But what I was not was employed. I had twenty-six days left on my visa to find a job. My timing wasn't great. Toward the end of the previous October, before our leap into marriage or our move to Vietnam, President Richard Nixon appeared on network TV and announced the first withdrawal of 50,000 American troops from Vietnam. The American commitment had peaked at 550,000 men.

Nixon's message was clear: the war was ending. Absolutely no one doubted the truth of it. That he turned out to be wrong, either optimistic or deceitful—that the war would not end for five long years—felt impossible.

Bob's gut reaction in October and in the months afterwards was, "Hell, I'm going the wrong way."

For me, too, in my two-week job search, it looked like the wrong place at the wrong time. The days passed and the pressure to find work—or be forced out of the country—intensified.

I walked through relentlessly hot downtown streets alternately in one of the three polyester dresses or the one synthetic pantsuit my mother bought for me on our last shopping frenzy.

"Drip dry for Vietnam," she said. We'd had no time to shop for a trousseau, so we shopped for the war instead. Crowded into

Loehmann's communal, mirrored dressing rooms, surrounded by overweight old women in their bulging undergarments, we debated my wardrobe needs.

"*Mom*—I'm only taking one suitcase."

"You'll need something nice for evening," she countered.

I now slogged, sweating profusely in polyester, to the Associated Press office, the largest news agency in Saigon and the one most likely to lay on extra help. Hunched over his typewriter when I arrived, veteran AP reporter George Esper saw me, stood up, leaned across the counter between us, and chatted amiably. But still he said. "The war's ending, our correspondents are being reassigned. I'd like to help you, but nobody's hiring."

He was fairly prophetic. That's what I heard at the UPI office and the Reuters apartment, at *Newsweek*, at the radio networks—and more. It looked pretty bleak, but I refused to countenance self-doubt. If I tolerated a single qualm, I would drown in an ocean of them. My parents' objections were alive and galling.

I wrote a first-person, first-impressions story for Phil. He bought it—$25 on receipt. Then, I went to *Time*.

Bureau Chief Marsh Clark had been in-country for more than a year. He'd been to Beirut before; he went to Jerusalem after. He made light of the wars he'd known. He said that *Time* didn't much value his life if his assignments were any indication.

Marsh was decidedly middle-aged to my young eyes, and balding. He was average height and trim, a bit past his physical prime, I would have said, a little slack. He looked very much like someone who had *lived*, and because he made me conscious by comparison that I had not, I was a little scared of him. But he was low key and receptive. He smiled at me, laughed easily, and invited me onto the terrace of the Continental Palace Hotel for a *citron pressé*. Lemonade, it turned out.

I told Marsh my story, pretty much all there was to tell, and it was a very good thing I did. Because somewhere in the telling—the marriage, the husband, the newspaper job, Phil's letter; the radical edge at the University of Wisconsin, the year hitchhiking around Europe, the un-peaceful marching for peace at Berkeley—something clicked.

I did not try to impress Marsh. He seemed to invite the truth. I chuckled as I spilled out words over lemonade, waved my hands to punctuate the telling, and lurched with encouragement from story to story—as I still do.

Marsh heard me out.

"I guess that's it," I laughed. "My story."

He laughed back. "You tell an engaging one."

We had a refill. He told me his story. His first wife, back home with the kids, didn't buy that they were no longer married. He'd flown to a Third World country to get the divorce after he'd met Pippa. His second wife was younger, British, and with him now.

Marsh was a good old Republican from a staunchly conservative, heartland, political family. He adhered strenuously to the patriotic Time Inc. view of the war. But he was a man capable of being amused by the liberal anti-war correspondents who might come his way. Was he easygoing? He was completely without pretense, although not perhaps without vanity. But he was without any barrier to my reaching him. I was very lucky to have known Marsh Clark.

Marsh said this. "Inette, there were a dozen correspondents here last month. They've been pulled back to New York. We're down to just three, and a freelance photographer. I know this war isn't over. I've got a big budget to hire if something breaks. If you can do it, you'll get your chance. Call me," he said, "see if I've got something for you."

I called Marsh every day for two-and-a-half weeks. It made me uncomfortable to keep bothering him. I stopped in, too, every couple of days. "Sorry, nothing's cooking," he said each time.

I was down to my last $50. I agreed to write a vile, unwholesome story for the US press office and then swore I'd never do it again. It paid $125. I'd been assigned to report on the sugarcane industry in Vietnam. Then I sat down and sweated out a fictional story, typed on the portable Olympia I'd lugged from Annapolis, about an industry that the war had obliterated. It was fresh with willing quotes from prevaricating American bureaucrats. My fingers balked; I hated the lies and hated myself more for agreeing to them.

Then I wrote another story for Phil—first-person again—"American girl with a Vietnamese family." I sold the same story with photos to the *San Francisco Examiner* and the Cleveland *Plain Dealer*.

I wrote, in part:

> I am adjusting to icy cold showers and not being able to drink the tap water. I sweep the tile floor constantly, picking up the quarter inch of dust that gathers during a hot Saigon day. There is my faithful once-a-week malaria pill ritual to lessen the risk that one of about thirty mosquito bites I scratch weekly is disease carrying. Predictably, I curse the roosters that wake me each morning.
>
> But when I'm at my lowest physical and mental ebb, in walks Mrs. An, who scolds me for not eating properly, or excitedly describes her plans to make me a Vietnamese dress. And I surrender again to the comfort of people caring about me so far from home.

Feature stories were what I did most naturally and perhaps best, but I knew full well that within the profession only *hard* news (politics, crime, and war) was respected. Hard news was, by definition, male; feature stories were female. I was determined to be respected.

I had just eight days left on my visa. I was reading Graham Greene's *The Quiet American* in my whitewashed room. It was noon, hot, and my Honda was parked at the door.

"*Ba Eenayt*, telephone!" Mrs. An pronounced my name and added always the polite *Ba*, for "Mrs." I went into her cool, dark part of the house. An accented Vietnamese voice spoke English on the other end of the phone. He said: "Hold please for Marsh Clark."

Then Marsh: "Inette. I need you. Pack a bag and get down to the office within an hour. You're flying to Phnom Penh."

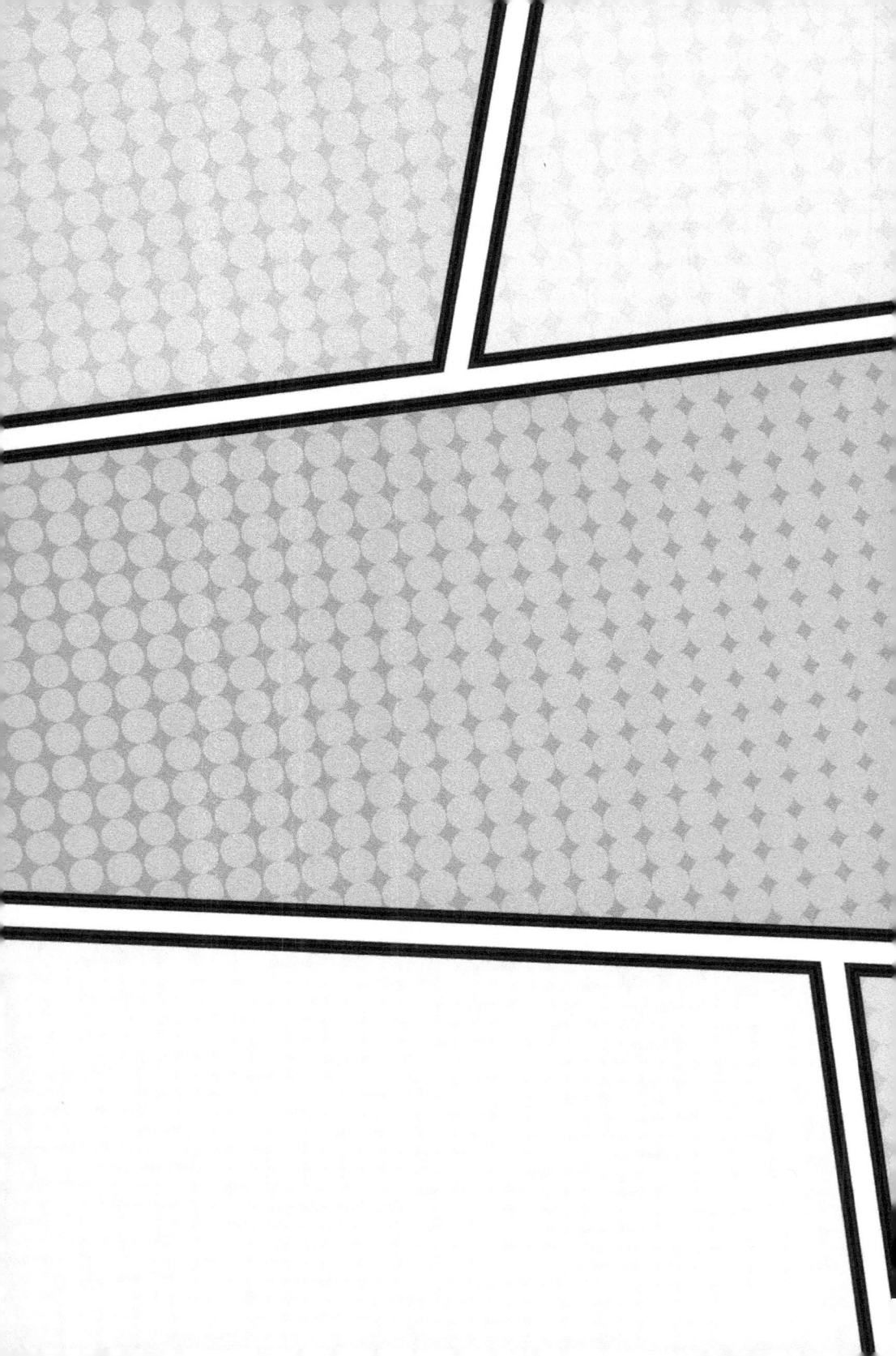

CHAPTER 4

DIVING IN

MARCH 1970

I had no idea where Phnom Penh was, but I didn't tell Marsh that. The unlikely spelling was revealed only after he'd piled fourteen inches of *Time*'s Cambodian back files into my arms.

Marsh issued instructions.

"Student riots erupted yesterday in Phnom Penh. There is no precedent. Prince Norodom Sihanouk holds the reins of his country tight. Riots don't happen there. But Sihanouk has been in Paris for six months, officially for health reasons; more likely, he's partying. Students trashed the NFL [National Liberation Front/Viet Cong] embassy there and *Time* needs someone to find out what's going on."

For two years, Marsh said, Sihanouk prohibited Western reporters from entering Cambodia. He kept a blacklist of the Western correspondents who were based in Southeast Asia.

"You're too new in country to be on the list. You can get in for us. Want to go?"

I didn't hesitate. "Sure I want to go."

I had no idea what I was agreeing to and my stomach responded like it always did to a hit of adrenaline: it balled up in a knot tight enough to bind a docking ocean liner. "Sure," I said. Like leaping off a diving board—it simply didn't do to stand on the edge and think about it.

"You'll fly to Bangkok," he said, and handed me a plane ticket already issued in my name. "There are no diplomatic relations between Cambodia and Vietnam—haven't been for years. You'll get your visa in Bangkok. David Greenway will brief you. He's our Bangkok bureau chief, our Cambodia expert. He'll tell you what you need to know. Read the files on the way over. You'll need to take pictures. Do you have a camera?"

"Yeah, I do." I reached into my bag and pulled out my Kodak Instamatic, the technical equivalent of the original box camera. Marsh didn't break a smile.

"You'll need a 35 millimeter; take the office Pentax. My driver will take you to Tan Son Nhut. Okay?"

"Okay."

"Oh, yeah," he stretched out his hand across the desk. "Here's your expense money. That should be enough."

I took the thick white envelope without counting and stuck it into my swollen leather purse next to the office Pentax. I carried a large canvas tote bag in my right hand, an oversized purse on my left shoulder—nothing more. I turned to leave.

"Uh, Inette." Marsh looked up at me and for the first time grinned. "Good luck."

I'd flown United and TWA back and forth from Baltimore to the University of Wisconsin for years—and of course, Pan Am to Saigon. But Royal Thai Airlines was another story. We were handed silk fans with the airline's purple logo, warm wet washcloths, exotic papaya drinks, and unknown but glorious foods. (Ten years' worth of *Time* stories out of Cambodia nested in my lap.) Everything about the flight felt wondrous—not least of all my arrival in Bangkok.

One man stood out of the mass of Thai faces behind a velvet rope barrier and signaled me with a roughly drawn placard: "Miss Miller, *Time* Magazine." It seemed I had arrived.

Bangkok was not so much exotic as overbearing. Through my driver's car windows it appeared crowded, brimming with faux American-style buildings, enormous traffic circles, and garish billboards screaming advertisements for unfamiliar foreign films. Barreling through dense, smelly traffic fumes, I instantly judged it glitzy, loud, and without a trace of Saigon's more subtle, if diminishing, charms.

Thailand had never been a French colony. Bangkok grew up emulating, not the genteel landscaped elegance of the French Colonial era, but the brash, mercantile, bigger-is-better twentieth-century America. At least, that was my first take.

The Thai driver who'd held the placard took me directly to the *Time* office. David Greenway was tall, slim, handsome, and very Ivy League. I was starting to deduce that *Time* correspondents traditionally arrived on board with Harvard, Princeton, or Yale diplomas, a tradition that was only just beginning to change.

David was setting things into boxes when I arrived, preparing for his departure from Southeast Asia. He was packing up two years of frustration, I gathered—sitting with abundant expertise on the border of a nation he knew well but couldn't enter.

"Thailand and Cambodia no longer have diplomatic relations," he told me. "The Indonesian Embassy is playing intermediary, issuing visas. My driver will take you there after lunch. Tell them you're an American government secretary in Saigon, a tourist for a week's sightseeing in Phnom Penh. Smile, bat your lashes, be charming. That's all. Don't say another word."

I balked. I'd come a long distance to avoid feminine means to ignoble ends. Now Greenway challenged me to play the game. My throat constricted around the knee-jerk words I was repressing. Easily I might have called him on his chauvinistic bullshit, and saying those words would have gone a way toward dissolving the plug in my throat. But I swallowed hard and said nothing.

"Afterwards the driver will take you to your hotel, the Erawan. We tried to get you into the Imperial, but it was booked. Sorry, it's second best; it doesn't have a swimming pool. Here's your assignment. You're to go to every foreign embassy whose language you speak. What do you speak?"

"I speak Italian; high school French and Spanish."

"Good. Don't forget the Australians, New Zealanders, and South Africans—the British Commonwealth. Go to all of them. Tell them who you are. Then get the press attaché—better yet, the chief political officer—to tell you what they know. What are the riots about? What do they mean? But outside of the embassies, play like a tourist, *look* like a tourist. Remember: you are not supposed to be there. You can be arrested for being there. Get it?"

I nodded.

"You have four days until the magazine closes. Your story needs to be in New York by Friday. When you're done, come back here to file it. Obviously there's no way to file it from Cambodia. I'll be in the States by then. I'm finished here. I just hung around today because Marsh asked me to fill you in. We'll have a room waiting for you at the Imperial when you return. Questions?"

"When do I leave?"

"Tomorrow. Anything else? No? Well, have fun. I wish it were me."

Diving In

The Indonesian Embassy was as dark as a tomb. I smiled easily at the officials and no one doubted my intentions. I got my tourist visa in minutes and headed for the hotel.

The Erawan was incredible. My first stay alone, ever, in an opulent hotel. It was memorable—pampered solicitude in a room of my own. Had David said "second best"? In that elegant hotel room, on the queen-sized bed, under the silk brocade bedspread, I dreamed dreams of Bob.

The Friday before, after three weeks without a glimpse of him, I'd grabbed a bus from Saigon to Long Binh and spent an afternoon at my husband's place of business. Long Binh was an environmental nightmare: square miles of jungle flattened to brown dirt, metal prefab construction, nothing growing—green only *outside* the wire fences. In a world turned upside down, asphalt and brown dust were safe; green living things were deadly.

Bob and I had hugged hello and then leaned against a camouflage truck behind Bob's base office holding hands. The hot sun baked my face. Bob's whiskered head was shaded by his fatigue cap. The US Army kept its men and women on a short leash; we had neither an unsupervised moment nor a private spot to visit in.

Obviously, I was an anomaly. Bob was required to stay within sight of his barracks office. Our options were limited to a forty-foot radius of parked jeeps and open-back trucks.

"New dress?" Bob asked, noting my red, white, and blue mini. I had hesitated to buy it back in Loehmann's dressing room, fretting that mid-thigh might be too short for Vietnam. My mother dismissed my qualms. Her only consideration: "You have the legs for it."

"New uniform?" I teased Bob.

We were exposed on that parking lot to every passing observer, GI or Vietnamese laundress. We held back words we didn't want overheard. We were embarrassed holding hands among men who had no one to touch. When we tired of standing, we slid into the driver and passenger seats of the olive truck we'd been leaning against and talked just a little more freely.

"Is your transfer coming through?" I asked.

"I'll be the last to know."

"When do you have to go on duty?"

"I've got an hour and a half."

I reached out and squeezed his thigh below windshield level. He grasped my neck with his long straight fingers and stroked under my hairline. There was nothing more between us than those furtive touches. The Army forbade.

Bob and I had slept together in cheap hotel rooms from Athens to Amsterdam, but when our junior year abroad was over in 1967, I was still a virgin. There was really no question that I would be.

"Don't let a boy touch you," was what my mother offered by way of enlightened sex education. My mother—never a woman of few words—on this matter offered just these. That, and how to thread a Kotex through a sanitary napkin belt. Virginity intact—a master stroke from my mother. I never came close—until Bob—and even then it was two years groping in the dark.

Bob came to the same place by a different route. The Church forbade. It was, for him, a convoluted ethical, intellectual treatise played out in his head. He played out a good number of things in his head.

"It has to do," he told me, "with not abusing another person's body or everlasting soul."

I chose not to understand. It had, for God's sake, to do with an "everlasting soul." Who took such things into consideration? But Bob had been eight years with the nuns, eight with the Jesuits and part of a year in a monastery. He knew about eternal Hell.

Diving In

So the sumptuous Erawan Hotel was thick with my yearning. I was still quite innocent of hurt or inhibition. I was like a young jock rolling under the lavender brocade: all synapse and soaring sensation, awake to the slightest touch. But on that queen-sized bed, there was no one to touch me.

Up earlier than I needed to be the next morning in Bangkok, I quieted my nerves with sit-ups and stretches. I flashed my passport at the airport and flew the puddle jumper—just a hop and a skip—into Phnom Penh.

It was springtime, or what I recognized as such. I allowed myself to be the tourist I'd told the customs official I would be. The colors are what I remember. I hadn't yet learned the names of the vivid, lustrous flowers, and now I can barely grab a blurred memory of them. But every strip of earth in that lovely city was filled with blooming neon color.

The street corner markets too—cotton batik in fuchsia and lime, in frothy patterns I'd never before seen. I bought two large rectangular swatches and I kept them for twenty years. I used them first for beach cover-ups when they could wrap easily around my hips, and afterwards, for small tablecloths.

Everything in Phnom Penh felt gentle. The sun was quieter and softer than in Saigon or Bangkok, undoubtedly because abundant shade trees branched over sidewalks. The streets and sidewalks themselves were quiet, with none of the bustle of financial Bangkok or occupied Saigon. Occasionally, cars or mopeds waded by, but it was an effortless stroll across every downtown street. It was a town more than a city—a wholly inviting place—and I wish with all my heart it had stayed that way.

The people too were different. Their faces were rounder, fleshier, and less angular than those of the Vietnamese. Singularly at odds with Saigon were the willing smiles and the trusting eyes—as different as a curious three-year-old from a sullen teen. It was starkly visible. *These* were a people sheltered from carnage—and *those*, a people who'd lost their virtue to war.

I read the *Time* stories, and they told me that whatever Prince Norodom Sihanouk was or was not, whatever he had or had not done for his people, he had kept his nation out of war. Stuck in the unenviable predicament of being the next-door neighbor to a nation perpetually at war, Cambodia held tight to its neutrality.

"That's neutrality!" Certain US military advocates challenged a nation that permitted the Viet Cong to rest comfortably within its jungle borders. But that was a distinctly partisan view.

At first sight, I fell in love with Phnom Penh. Like a remembered lover, I see her still through my very young eyes. I was privileged to have been among the last outsiders to visit that tremulously lovely, ephemeral city before it all changed. And it changed in the blink of an eyelid, far faster than anyone had ever suggested that Saigon had.

I stayed, as instructed, at "the only place to stay" in Phnom Penh, the Hotel Le Royal. But of course there were others less elaborate. The Royal was an aging, pale yellow behemoth, with an ornate wrought-iron gate, a cavernous lobby, terra-cotta tile floors, and a courtyard swimming pool serviced by the bar and restaurant. It was the very essence of French Colonial architecture, and it appeared to be one of those art forms that improved in its deterioration. The French built, it seemed to me, with an eye to the day they wouldn't be there to keep up the paint and the trim, yet intending the aesthetic would last.

I stood outside the National Liberation Front (Viet Cong) embassy—now the shell of an embassy. It was a distinguished building still, white stucco with an imposing front porch and an upper balustrade and balcony. It clashed vehemently with my images of the clandestine nature of Viet Cong jungle warfare and their underground political tunneling into the government of South Vietnam. Who could imagine a guerilla army on the diplomatic circuit: fine wines, hors d'oeuvres, black pajamas, and truck-tire sandals? It spoke of Sihanouk's tenaciously courted neutrality.

Strewn over the landscaped gardens were the remnants of the previous day's turmoil: sofas, chairs, lamps, desks hurled off the upper balcony and splintered across the railings. The flower beds were flattened under the contents of scattered file drawers.

I squinted up at the second story of the building. The sun was directly in my eyes. I pulled out the office Pentax, focused it as Marsh had instructed me, and snapped. No good. The sun was glaring off the lens. So I stepped off the sidewalk into the street and walked twenty paces to the left of the building. Better. I pulled the heavy camera to my eye, twisted the focus, snapped, and snapped again.

I was concentrating hard on the undertaking. I didn't hear a thing before I felt a hand on my shoulder. I jumped and whirled around. I was facing a small, solemn policeman who was speaking French. "Mademoiselle," he nodded. "What are you doing? Why are you taking pictures of this place?"

He looked up, gesturing toward the embassy, and I seized the moment to drop the Pentax into my oversized purse and pull out my Instamatic. "This?" I asked, waving the tiny Kodak in the air. "I am an American tourist taking pictures of your beautiful country." I pieced together some stilted high school French.

"You cannot take pictures here," the officer frowned.

"No?" I answered. "I did not know. I am sorry."

"Au revoir, Mademoiselle."

"Au revoir, Monsieur."

I walked slowly, methodically around the neighborhood, ogling buildings and snapping random Instamatic shots. Shadowing me conspicuously about twenty-five feet behind trailed a plainclothes crony of the police officer. I was being followed and I was scared. I set one foot carefully in front of the other; the effort took all I had. I focused fully on appearing calm. Inside, I quivered.

My plan had been to begin the embassy rounds after I snapped the photos of the previous day's riot site. Now I dared not. I pulled out my tourist map and headed for the river. I sat and munched some bread and cheese I'd picked up earlier at the market. I tried to look tranquil; I was hyperventilating and the dry bread was clogging my throat. The middle-aged shadow was sitting on the embankment behind me.

Okay, so I'd be a tourist: the Royal Palace, Sihanouk's ancestral home. That would be innocuous. I got in line behind a dozen other tourists. The tour guide polled language preference: one couple spoke French, one German, the others Cambodian. I kept silent. She settled on French. She led us first through the palace grounds and then inside.

I'd been on dozens of palace tours in Europe and this one was typical: tour-guide jokes and responsive laughter; gasps at furnished opulence; jockeying for position.

But this one was also different. I was hiding out from the Cambodian police in the Royal Palace. On my first day, I'd screwed up and called attention to myself. I hadn't yet done what I was there to do.

The tour lasted an hour. As usual, there was a crescendo, the most spectacular sight saved for last. We respectfully approached the Royal Throne Room. Our guide had told us the history of the lineage, gestured toward the throne itself, which she whispered had been touched by no hands other than the royal family's, even when dusted. No photos were allowed here.

We circled next to the throne, standing at arm's distance. It was slightly elevated on a platform. I recall the tour guide reaching her most reverent pitch—but the woman's words dimmed, my head heated up, perspiration beaded across my forehead, and my squashed fears constricted my breath. The scene in front of me lost focus. I tried hanging my head over my chest—I pretty much knew where this dizziness ended, and I was trying to stave it off.

It was no good. Nothing I did slowed the spinning. The warmth flooded my face; there was a blur of words and images, then a free fall into blackness. My hands broke the fall as they slid along the royal armrests.

I blacked out face down on the seat of the royal throne.

Before I came to full consciousness, I felt their fingernails. Their fingers dug into my arms and they yanked me, none too gently, none too kindly, off the throne and across the room to an entirely different chair.

Now the story is absurd, and hilarious. But at the time I was mortified. I exited the palace with profuse apologies to the pretty young guide. I stepped tentatively outside the gates after I scrutinized the streets and sidewalks for police. I saw none and headed back to the hotel. Enough for one day.

After eight sound hours of sleep and a hearty breakfast, I was ready to take on my assignment. I'd spent a year chasing news stories in southern Maryland: redneck book burnings, Naval Academy cheating scandals, and school integration battles. Today I was a reporter again, and I knew exactly how to be one. There would always be a limitless list of questions I'd be too polite to ask on my own behalf but that I'd willingly demand on behalf of "the public's right to know." I was idealistic. I believed with all my heart: If I don't get the story, nobody will—the public depends on me. It was very personal.

So even if the stakes were a little higher in Phnom Penh, where I was the only Western reporter walking the streets, the job was the same. I looked over my shoulder. If I were being followed, I saw no evidence of it.

It was another splendid, tranquil day and I headed to the section of town where the massive embassy villas lined several avenues. Each building was architecturally distinct, but all were variations of a graceful, pastel stucco theme. Each had a flag prominently displayed. All were surrounded by exquisite flower gardens, sculpted into a variety of geometric configurations and color schemes. Some had gates with guards; some did not.

It never occurred to me to make appointments. I thought it best, given the unknown nature of my reception, to show up on the embassy doorstep. I saw no reason to make it easier for anyone to say "No."

At the British Embassy, in my crispest English, I told the guard that I wanted to speak with the political attaché and I was admitted immediately through the heavy doors. There was another layer. The receptionist demanded to know my business. I said only, "I'm with *Time* magazine." Those were the magic words and I was admitted. It was heady stuff.

An attractive political attaché—with a recognizably custom-made pinstripe suit (in the *tropics*) and wireframe glasses—stepped out into the reception room, shook my hand, and invited me into his office. He stood over me, about six foot three to my five foot seven.

I settled into a Queen Anne sofa, he into a wing chair. An inviting tea with scones and assorted breads was set before us.

"From *Time*, I'm told?" he asked after we'd exchanged names.

"Yes, from the Saigon bureau." I sipped and nibbled.

"And what of David Greenway? I've known David for some time."

"Ah, yes," I answered. "David sends his regrets. He's on his way to the States, transferred to the New York office."

"I'm sure that's a great relief for him. And you, Miss Miller," he continued. "I'm surprised to see a lady posted in Saigon."

Diving In

"Well," I hesitated, just a breath, to register his idea of a woman's place. "Times change—even at *Time*, even in Saigon."

"Yes, of course. But then, how may I help you?"

He did help me. I asked for his educated guess of what was going on in that capital city.

"A cousin of the prince, I think. An ambitious act by a royal relative in the vacuum of power of the prince's prolonged absence. He won't last. The prince will return and handle his family. Did you know there are more royal relatives here than foreign diplomats? It's a bees' hive at the palace. Tell your people in New York that this is a tempest in a teapot. Nothing to waste another thought on."

"You're sure of this? The riots . . . "

"Oh, heavens, Miss Miller, riots? Hardly. Just family spats, like our royal family back home."

Over the next two days, I scoured every embassy where I had a prayer of communicating—eight, maybe ten. I was barred from none, although most often my queries were intercepted by the press officer, not his boss.

I sat in a number of handsomely decorated embassy offices and sipped endless cups of coffee or tea. A few others asked after David. Most registered some degree of surprise that a woman was covering the war for *Time*. I struggled to harness my defensiveness. I wanted to rebut their ignorance, and I was still too young to know that the rebuttal lay in the action, not the words.

Uniformly, I was offered explanations that scoffed at the notion of riots and insisted that peace was an airplane flight from Paris. I was much assured that the prince was beloved. Effusive taxi drivers and hotel clerks bolstered the embassy perceptions. This was not a regime seriously threatened by rival factions. The prince was the firmly embedded spiritual father of the nation, profoundly cherished.

By Friday, I was back in Bangkok with my story—and my roll of film. *Time* Saigon correspondent Bob Anson, just two years my senior, met me at the office and later at the Imperial Hotel (with pool).

"No swimsuit?" he said. "Buy one. Put it on your expense account."

I looked askance at him. The idea that news organizations were noble places—poor and struggling—was already rooted in my soul. "No way."

"Come with me," he said firmly. "If you don't pad your expense sheet, you'll make the rest of us look bad." He was teasing me. I swallowed hard and felt like the twenty-three-year-old kid I was. I followed him to the lobby gift shop; I bought a white satin bikini.

I filed my very first *Time* story from the Bangkok office telex machine (years before laptops or cell phones), with Anson showing me the ropes. He told me it was first-rate.

"You can *write*, Inette. Good, *Time* is a writer's magazine. But expect this. Every word you write here will be rewritten in New York. You'll report some battle you've witnessed, write it up pretty, and then New York will send it down to the Pentagon correspondents for the generals' take on what happened. What you saw—and what they *heard*—are two different things. You can't get attached to what your story looks like in the magazine or you'll go crazy. Keep the original file for your resume."

For a year, I'd been the kind of earnest reporter who regularly threatened to quit or pull my newspaper story if an editor messed with my intentions. I'd fought over length, space, place, and principle. Anson spoke an alien language to me. I struggled now to accommodate his game rules. I *wanted* to work for *Time*. But truth was truth wasn't it? That could never be rewritten.

Diving In

Bob was giving me my first shot of *Time* reality—a Republican magazine, I knew. It had a devoutly pro-war stance, he said. Anson, too, was young, distinctively *not* Ivy League, an anti-war thorn in Marsh Clark's side—and proud of it. I was awed by Anson's assurance.

I'd spoken at length to assorted embassy people in Phnom Penh. None refused me. Everyone was gracious—flattered, in fact, that *Time* solicited their opinion. They were far more eager, I noted, than my sources had been at the 50,000-circulation *Evening Capital*. Size definitely had its perks. My job had been easy: willing sources and absolutely no divergence of opinion.

What I sent to the *Time* New York office from Bangkok and what I later broadcast from Saigon, on NBC and Westinghouse Radio interviews, was this:

"Heads will roll," I said that they said, "when Prince Sihanouk returns to Phnom Penh." The diplomatic circuit agreed, I wrote, that the riots were a peculiar aberration in the way things were done in Cambodia. "An impotent henchman getting uppity," I recorded the speculation, "a shortsighted move by a royal relative reacting to the prince's absence." No English-, French-, or Italian-speaking diplomat could imagine otherwise.

I returned to Saigon, sought-after for interviews. I had been the only Western correspondent to enter Cambodia in years. It was exhilarating, a quantum leap in stature, but I knew my broadcast skills were clumsy. My 35mm film was shipped by carrier to the New York office. My story and pictures were praised in New York. Marsh was thrilled. "You've got yourself a job."

Three days later, every opinion I'd dutifully reported from Phnom Penh was upended; all my written words were thoroughly discredited.

The wires buzzed. An American-inspired coup d'état dumped Prince Norodom Sihanouk in absentia. His government was history. Royal relatives fled the country, and the US generals had, in Lon Nol, the Cambodian leader they wanted.

The student riots (we understood only years later) were the handiwork of the CIA, and so the Phnom Penh diplomatic corps could be fairly faulted with neither its ignorance nor its honesty. I'd reported their truth, but the truth had shifted.

Americans no longer needed visas to cross the Cambodian border from Vietnam. We didn't even need permission to march our troops or fly our bombers into the pristine Cambodian countryside. Cambodia was no longer neutral. With Sihanouk gone, it seemed that no one was looking after Cambodian interests. That nation and its people were torn in a dozen competing directions. The Vietnamese, long detested by Cambodians as militaristic, were marching through the country as if they owned it. It was a very different war. Prince Norodom Sihanouk was unable to return to his country for twenty years.

Nevertheless, I got to keep my job.

CHAPTER 5

LIVING MARRIED

APRIL 1970

Bob's "tough-ass staff sergeant with a soft spot for families" was true to his word. After six weeks of paperwork, Bob—who'd been randomly trained in Georgia to be an MP—was transferred to the only active military police unit left in Saigon. He grabbed seventeen hours for himself sandwiched between the old unit in Long Binh and the new one in Saigon. He figured nobody needed him before the morning and he pronounced himself military-free for a few precious hours.

More than two months after our one-night honeymoon, we celebrated our homecoming over a white tablecloth, a dim candle, and a carafe of house wine at a tidy neighborhood bistro. French restaurants were as ubiquitous as Vietnamese or Chinese, and most were inexpensive. We savored veal and new potatoes, salad and hard-crusted bread, crème caramel and espresso.

"So that's how you've been living, while I've been eating C-rations?" Bob squeezed my arm between his thumb and fingers.

In truth, until that night, I'd found all food tasteless in the oppressive heat and filthy air. My clothes already hung a size too large.

After dinner, we ambled in the general direction of home. On this particular sultry night, neither of us saw a reason in the world to hurry. Bob was in Saigon for good; so was I. We each imagined this would be the first of a string of lovely sensuous nights together. We took our time.

Typically, patience was a quality foreign to me. If I were heading somewhere, I'd just as soon be there. For Bob, on the other hand, anticipation was not a cruel punishment. He could live with uncertainty, wait it seemed forever—for clarity, for results, for me.

We walked home from the bistro through the dark streets, sometimes wandering dirt paths inhaling the pungent smells, poking through the night-slowed traffic, touching wherever our fingers fell, stopping to kiss gingerly where no one could see us; neither of us reared to—nor comfortable with—a public show of affection.

Outside my door, I introduced Bob to Mrs. An as *"mon mari."* Increasingly, I spoke to her in reclaimed French. She smiled approval. A married woman meant something.

Inside the door I wrapped my arms around Bob's shoulders and he pulled me snug against him. The fit was recognizable, exactly right from the first hug on a boat crossing the Mediterranean. We had the same length legs. Bob made up the four-inch difference entirely in his torso. Neither of us could be called thin—too much skeleton and muscle for that—but we were both now taut.

I missed playing with Bob's familiar beard. He was working on redeeming his lost mustache. Army regulations now permitted lip hair.

Living Married

"Oh, babe. How have you been?" he whispered into my ear and led me to the oversized platform bed.

The next morning, Bob reported for duty at the 54th MP Battalion and found out the sorry truth.

"Hello, soldier! We're shipping out in twenty-nine days. Start packing."

"Huh?"

The 54th—his entire unit—was being pulled out of Saigon and reassigned north. Worse yet—and it could get worse—I Corps, snug up against North Vietnam, was the legendary *boonies*. He would be expected to lead convoys through the jungle, be the *point* man, drive the first jeep and take the first fire.

When we spoke again a few days later, his initial nausea had subsided. He said only, "Long Binh is looking mighty fine." Now it was my turn to feel sick.

It was just plain bad luck, neither intention nor malice, that Bob had been transferred to the only remaining MP unit in the city and that that unit was scheduled to pull out in less than a month. Who knew? Not the staff sergeant, not Bob, not me.

I Corps was the place where, even during a lull in the war, there wasn't much quiet. I Corps was the military sector where more American soldiers had died than in any other part of Vietnam.

A month was a lifetime in Vietnam. In truth, there was nothing but now. And *now*, I chose not to think of Bob's future. Now, Bob had twelve-hour, nighttime shifts. He went on duty at 7 p.m., went off at 7 a.m.; he slept away the morning and early afternoon in a distant barracks. He awakened sometime after lunch, groggy and disoriented, showered before dinner, and reported for duty. He had Saturdays off for us.

During his twelve-hour shifts, Bob stood guard over American military installations scattered across Saigon. Every post was different. But at every post he was the sole American military presence standing at attention, M16 semi-automatic rifle at ready. Sometimes he'd stand in front of the American Embassy or, less illustriously, in front of the PX warehouse or some obscure office building with every sign of American ownership *except* a flag. Always, he'd be alone.

The MP guard post was a classically indefensible position and the boys knew it. Regularly, in broad daylight, young Vietnamese men (younger than Bob) on small shabby Hondas (indistinguishable in a street teeming with them) sidled up to American buildings and with a good, strong arm hurled a homemade plastique explosive into the face of the MP standing out front.

The MP's scattered remains were just a fragment of the devastation a single bomb delivered. Often it took out the first couple floors of a building and its human and material contents too.

The young motorcyclist with the good right arm typically faded into the crowd and was never apprehended. I doubt anyone tried. To what end? There were innumerable true believers on the other side of the war, physically indistinguishable from the Vietnamese on our side.

That, of course, was the crux of this war: identifying the enemy in any downtown café or gas station was impossible. The risk to an ambitious nationalist on a motorcycle was infinitesimal.

There was never even the pretense of a defense for Bob or his fellows. Their positions were token—symbolic. Some had a chicken-wire cage; most had nothing. "Sitting ducks," Bob called his unit.

"Tomorrow's burger," his fellow MP agreed.

Macabre gallows humor was how scared draftees diffused their terror.

But there was a historical explanation for this meaningless watch. During the Tet Offensive in 1968—when the Viet Cong had supremely undermined American confidence and effortlessly infiltrated what, until then, we'd considered secure American-held cities—there'd been one unsettling discovery among many. Every single American-trained Vietnamese Army guard standing watch over American buildings in Saigon disappeared before the fighting began. They dropped their rifles—pickings for the enemy's arsenal—and faded into the street crowd.

And these were *ours*. These were the "friendlies," as we imprecisely called them. When push came to shove, they were long gone. Tet was the cold shower on American expectation that we were building a South Vietnamese fighting force to replace ours.

The morning after, the Vietnamese guards were back to their posts with stories. The usual Monday morning stories. "My child was sick." "I hurt my arm." "I never left my post."

After Tet, Bob's MP unit took up the slack. It had been two years since Tet, and when Bob's unit was gone the task would fall to the Marines.

I was torn. I hated the war and detested the military on principle—more posturing than integrity. I had long empathized with the Vietnamese people, and now they had names and faces. I loved Bob; I despised that he was military. I loved my work: the access, the discovery, the being in the thick of things.

But I wished with all my heart there'd been another way for both of us. Of course, there was not. It had taken Gloria Emerson ten years to convince an establishment news outlet that a woman could cover this war. I was here, ironically, by virtue of Bob's status—although vigorously forbidden by the military.

Bob's life sucked. I couldn't do a thing about that.

For several days that month, Bob stood watch in front of American cargo ships docked near Saigon. The ships delivered goods earmarked for the PX and officers' clubs: refrigerators, sterling silver flatware, steaks, Idaho potatoes, Sara Lee cakes. Bob watched it leak out past him. Surreptitiously in the night, he saw the money change hands. He counted any number of private entrepreneurs in US Army uniform haul off their ill-gotten wares for sale on the Vietnamese black market.

"Theft, it's SOP—standard operating procedure," Bob told me, who was wide-eyed and innocent. "Everyone takes a cut. They're brazen; they don't even hide it."

On Bob's day off, three weeks after his transfer, we strolled downtown and examined the cluttered sidewalk market. There were Cannon all-cotton beach towels; turquoise-and-silver Navajo jewelry; and just about anything that a young couple starting out in Kansas City might need to furnish their first apartment. I was amazed, but I was not outraged. Between us, Bob was the moral arbiter.

"Shiiiit! I recognize this stuff," he snorted his disgust. "Another wealthy top sergeant." Bob anguished over keeping silent while his government was ripped off by its own. He'd flip between rage—nightmares filled with savage possibilities that included the rifle he carried—and sullen impotence and defeat.

On a good day: "I'll go to MACV—make those suckers hear me." On a lesser day: "Riiight! Like they'll listen to some righteous draftee."

His nation was being ripped off. There was still that loyalty. But it was the same nation that had yanked him out of his post-collegiate reverie and insisted he fight this war. It was a government that was dropping napalm on kids and flaunting its political might in somebody else's hometown. It was not clear to Bob on which side the immorality was greater. It wasn't clear, either, who would listen—who wasn't part of the problem, who could imagine a solution.

Bob's mind was incisive, and his heart was pure. But his carry-through was circumscribed. After guarding the ships and resolving his irresolution with inaction, he settled into loathing himself for his passivity.

After standing watch over the ships, Bob was sent to guard the swollen, ugly US Embassy building—and from that post, to a military arsenal near Ton Son Nhut airport.

Alone on a dark stretch of barren roadway in front of a square cinderblock building, Bob stood, or sometimes sat, grimly imagining the contents of the building he guarded. He jumped alert, weapon-to-chin, at each unsavory sound and every cracking branch. I have this image down pat because I saw him there often.

But the first time I saw Bob in his full MP regalia, I laughed. Part warrior, part intellectual. He looked to me like a character who'd stepped out of the Sunday comics. His oversized helmet met the top edge of his horn-rimmed glasses. He had a gun on his hip, a rifle strapped over his shoulder, a huge MP patch on his arm—and the ever-present, curved-stem briar pipe jutting from his lips. He didn't look sufficiently malevolent to be military police.

I wasn't always in town, but when I was, I worked largely during daylight hours. For a stretch of night, after 8:00 or 9:00 but before 1 a.m.—after which the citywide curfew outlawed civilian vehicles from the streets until 6 a.m.—I'd drive my Honda across town and sit guard duty with Bob at that desolate outpost. It was as cozy a domestic scene as I'd experienced since we married.

"Here, you hold the bag," he'd say, and pass me the one-pound bag of M&Ms from the PX.

"Okay. Want some?"

He'd take whatever I poured into his hand and toss them in his mouth by the fistful. But I'd pick through them one by one for the red ones, the yellow, green, or brown ones—never orange, if I could help it, preferably not tan.

"You know they all taste precisely the same," he'd say.

"You're absolutely wrong," I'd answer. Then switching gears,

"Are you here tomorrow?"

"Uh huh, at least through Friday."

Always, sitting at that post, I brought along a small red transistor radio that I'd been gifted for my bat mitzvah ten years before. My father dispatched it to me when I'd asked.

Bob and I'd tune into the only station whose language we understood: Armed Forces Radio. We'd catch the jazz hour or folk night if we had to, but really we only wanted the rock and roll. Sitting guard duty, though, we didn't want anything too heavy—not the Dead or The Who, Bob's usual favorites.

Maybe "Lady Madonna" or "(I Can't Get No) Satisfaction." It was a matter of the setting. I preferred the ebullient Beatles at that pitch-black outpost, or the irreverent Stones, when Bob cradled the M16. We kept the volume down so we could talk. So Bob could hear, too. We turned it off entirely when the lieutenant's patrol jeep made the rounds, making sure his MPs were still awake—and alive—at their posts.

"I'd like you to meet my wife," Bob told the dazed lieutenant after a sharp salute.

"Nice to meet you," I smiled broadly.

"Everything okay on post?" the lieutenant muttered. His sergeant driver gawked and blurted, "How did *you* get here?"

"Everything's fine," Bob answered them in turn. "She's a journalist. She works for *Time*."

They drove off to their next post with the lieutenant puzzling what the regulations might say about me. Sometimes the young patrol officer thought it was a hoot; others thought it was an infraction. In neither case did they press their point.

I know Bob loved those quiet nights with me. It was just a bit of benevolence in the face of the military harshness. But I think what he loved most about my sitting guard duty with him was that it stretched military regulations in a direction considered logically impossible.

He reasoned, "If military dependents can't be in Vietnam, but *you* can be because you are a correspondent, then there can be no regulation governing wives sitting guard duty with their MP husbands. It appeals to my sense of the ridiculous." (And to his eight years of Jesuitical training.)

For me, it was simpler. I loved being with Bob.

Always, if I traveled alone on foot in Saigon, I moved within a circle of two dozen kids no more than six feet distant, who stared without blinking into my face and at my body. American women were rare indeed. It was usually assumed (although they were now even rarer) that I was French.

The gawking kids, dressed in dirty tan shorts and nothing else—no shoes, no t-shirts—moved along with me every step I took until I reached some invisible neighborhood border, maybe an intersection with a larger street, where they faded away.

Where neighborhood gave way to downtown, the "streetboys"—homeless kids, hustlers, teetering on the edge of criminal—began their pursuit. "Madame, *Madame*! Good price shoeshine?" The attention got old real fast.

I stood head and shoulders above almost every Vietnamese man on the street and every woman. I was huge at five feet seven inches, a traveling circus freak. At first I tried to smile and engage the scruffy kids with the black eyes, but they wanted no part of it. They just stared. Eventually, I became a walking metaphor for American political policy in Vietnam: I looked right through them. I didn't see them at all. I wished, in fact, they would disappear.

For two years, since the Tet attack in 1968, there had been relatively few remaining uniformed American servicemen stationed in Saigon. Bob's MP unit was one. The generals and their support staff—invisible behind the walls of MACV—were another.

Uniformed GIs strolling Saigon streets were most often on leave from someplace else.

After the Tet invasion and fiasco, American policy had shifted: remove all trace of the massive American military presence—that green machine in search of hamburgers, opium, and whores—from Saigon. Remove that easy target and the obvious irritant to the indigenous population. The huge base at Long Binh (where Bob began his tour) was built thirty miles away for that express purpose.

So Bob was exceedingly conspicuous when we strolled together on Saturday nights. And I was, too. We were conspicuous like a zit on prom night. When I walked with Bob, people stared but kept their distance: a big, hulking, uniformed American GI—and a big, Western, "round eye" woman. Alone, I was uncomfortable on the streets of Saigon. With Bob, I was uneasy as well.

On our Saturdays, we leaned more toward one another and less toward the world around us. I'd hold Bob's bent arm and hang on tight.

I didn't notice these things at the time, and I'm still not sure which ones were of consequence. But I know that couples harden early on, into patterns of expectation. Sometimes we give away—assign—qualities to the other that might have been our own.

So in our young world, we agreed: *I* was the outgoing one, the socially adept one. *He* was the introspective one, the intellectual. I was the pragmatist. I grabbed up the male stuff: angry, aggressive, and ambitious. He usurped the female: sensitive, spiritual, calm.

We set patterns like these too. Even though he was entirely without mechanical instinct or desire, it was *he* who fixed the motorcycle. Even though I couldn't cook at all, *I* boiled the drinking water for the refrigerator. He walked on the outside edge of the sidewalk. Despite some obvious contradictions, we remained our parents' kids.

Living Married

It was a Saturday night almost three weeks after Bob's transfer from Long Binh, maybe nine o'clock. The streets were still alive; the sidewalks swarmed with family life. The storefronts glowed incandescent with decorative porch-size porcelain lions and blue-and-gray rice bowls. We were beginning to get the hang of this town. Figuring out a few favorite places to eat, to sit and watch the passing parade, to browse the shop windows.

In the afternoon, we enjoyed the decrepit city zoo and the neglected parks. By day, we sat in the shade. But at night, we preferred making our way around the sidewalk hazards: noodle-soup pushcarts, long strings of refugee huts, pedicab drivers sprawled in repose inside the passenger seat of their bicycle-propelled carts. We were walkers by nature, explorers on foot—together in Athens, Rome, Florence, and now Saigon. We were carving out a routine amidst the unknowable.

It was after sunset on that particular Saturday. The air had cooled enough for us to savor the walking. We meandered past mothers feeding small sons by spoon at tables and chairs scattered across every thoroughfare. Not quite Paris—short on awnings, umbrellas, and ambiance. We stepped over and around limbless Vietnamese veterans, pockmarked and diseased children. Beggars chose the downtown sidewalks where they might expect the stray foreigner with piastres to spare, never the remote dirt streets where I lived.

That night I wore my floral print, drip-dry mini-dress. Bob wore what the US Army demanded: baggy olive-green combat fatigues, combat boots, and a fatigue cap. We'd eaten dinner in a superb Chinese restaurant two miles out of downtown in the direction of Mrs. An's home. We were sated and just a little looser than usual after a couple beers. It felt like summer, this April. The sky was clear; the stars were visible above the dim city lights. I was strolling with my best beau in my mid-thigh dress. My legs were tan. Bob's smile was shining white against his brown face. He'd gotten past his usual burn, peel, red. He eyes looked particularly blue.

"I'm feeling the beer," I said. "It's stronger than I thought it would be."

"Who'd have thought of Vietnamese beer at all? It sure isn't Genesee."

"Which way?"

"Down that street." He gestured ahead of us.

"*My boyfriend's back,*" I sang out into the noisy night with no fear of drawing attention. "*My boyfriend's back and—*"

Bob joined the chorus. "*Hey la, hey la, my boyfriend's back.*"

I leaned over and put my index finger deep into Bob's young-Kirk Douglas chin cleft. "*Mama said there'd be days like this. There'd be days like this, my mama said.*" I belted out the first lines, and then I ran out of words.

"Did *your* mama tell you that you were beautiful?" I asked playfully.

"With five kids to clean up for early Mass, my mother didn't have time to notice."

We walked quietly after that. My chest was brimming with sensation. I was full of feeling that I wish now I could have zip-locked and frozen. For a fleeting moment, shoulder to shoulder, I was all and only heart. We could have been anywhere. We were going nowhere in particular.

But I had no staying power. I despised myself for breaking the mood—injecting the future into the moment—but I couldn't stop myself.

"Just ten days 'til your unit leaves," I said. "I can't help thinking."

There was a long silence during which we could both hear our feet slapping the sidewalk.

"Hell. It's about *not* thinking. 'Do what you're told, Soldier.'

When I said 'yes' to Vietnam, I said 'yes' to all of it. It sure as hell isn't multiple choice here. The only answer is 'Yes, *sir*!'"

"Bobby, I love you."

"Yeah, well."

I stopped, pulled him against me. Standing in front of a gas station with gas fumes radiating, I nuzzled his neck. He breathed in my hair, ran his hands across the small of my back.

We found a small corner park. It was just a few gnarly trees, a couple broken benches, trash and bare dirt where grass had given up the fight. We settled on a wobbly bench and leaned back. Directly across from us sat a seemingly ancient man with a wispy chest-length white beard. He was dressed in traditional *ao dai*. He looked out of another century—or *National Geographic*. He sat as though in a trance.

Bob ran his hand absently over my back, down my arm, back again. I sat curled tight under his arm, head against his shoulder, content to say nothing.

"It sucks," he said absently. "I'm a jerk for agreeing in the first place. Once you're here, you're theirs."

"Stop it. You had no choice."

"I had a choice, all right. We're living it."

"Don't do this to yourself."

"Shit, I'm scared."

I don't know how long we sat like that, maybe an hour, maybe less. Me: wishing Bob had the wherewithal to fight the gut-wrenching military. Me: knowing that his state of mind—and body—kept me firmly inside the military's clutches as well.

Bob stood up first, offered me his two hands, and lifted me to my feet.

I wrapped my hands around his left bicep—his hands were jammed deep inside his pockets—and we walked without noting direction. We walked past people squatting down on strong calves, eating; past toddlers peeing and defecating at the edge of the street; past couples riding hip to butt together on Hondas. We walked past the neighborhood pagoda with the wide, steep steps that we hadn't yet climbed.

We walked past the closed vegetable market and past shopkeepers pulling down metal security fences over display windows. It was getting late, time to think of home and Bob's body next to mine. Time for that heart-healing, military-repelling, war-denying warmth.

We had ten more days. There'd be another Saturday night—one more life-infusing night together after tonight.

Abruptly Bob yanked his arm out of my grip and fell forward. "Shit!"

He was scrambling like the Roadrunner on his sturdy legs to find a footing. One hand scraped across the sidewalk to break his fall and he pushed himself back to his feet. Glass crashed and shattered in a tight, insistent circle around us. Green glass, I noted, and thought, "Coca Cola." Panicked, we looked at one another. There was blood spurting from Bob's temple into his eyes. He paid it no mind; I followed his lead.

We turned from each other and, like rabbits caught in a headlight, scanned the nearby furniture and knickknack shops, stared out at the impassive wall of Vietnamese faces taking our measure, giving nothing away.

Only Bob had been pelted with bottles; I'd been spared. Hidden from us, someone had picked his target easily—the baggy, olive-green circus act. We stood still for a sensate second among the broken shards of glass. Then Bob grabbed my hand and ran, pulling me along. We ran halfway home before we slowed to a walk, before we said another word.

"You okay?" Bob panted.

"Yeah. Okay." I sucked for breath.

We had run a half-mile before I pulled some balled-up toilet paper from my purse; before I searched Bob's head and found two welts swelling over his ear and at the base of his neck; before I found the gaping bloody wound next to his eye.

"Does it hurt?"

"Not much."

We had run almost home before we stopped and remembered to hold our shaking bodies together.

Our last Saturday came and went. We slept like spoons, curled into loving hand-holds. We grieved the tidal wave that was separating us again, but mostly in silence. Neither of us could pry loose words that adequately summed our fear, loss, or horror at Bob's ironic dilemma: first, the merciful move to Saigon to be near me, then this—the real war, the real chance of doing harm and being harmed.

"More goodbyes," was all I mustered that last Saturday. But I knew I'd risk anything to keep him there.

"To the jungle this time," he answered.

Bob's unit was packed and ready. Three days left until the 54th hoisted its last duffle into trucks and jeeps, then onto a mammoth Chinook chopper to I Corps.

It was an early afternoon. Bob had finished up guard duty at an obscure office building the night before; he'd slept from 7:30 that morning until after lunch. He was hanging around the barracks with the other night-shift MPs.

A skinny American sergeant with thinning hair walked into the room. Without fanfare, he shouted, "Can anybody here type?"

Bob didn't need special training in the military to know that you never, under any imaginable circumstance, *volunteer*. He held his hand plastered to his hip and kept his silence. Other than the hum of irrelevant conversation, the room was still. Not one of the dozens of milling men answered.

"Hey soldiers, I *asked* you something. Can any of you MPs type?"

Bob, who from kindergarten through college had never been the one to raise his hand in class and volunteer an answer—this time, for some inexplicable reason, saw his hand shoot straight up.

"I can type," he said. "I can type."

And thanks to his mother, his gentle, Catholic, child-loving mother—who insisted on so little from her kids but who, when he was in seventh grade, insisted that her oldest son take typing—he could.

So, because with two days left until he would have led Army convoys into jungles (and maybe out again), he'd raised his hand and said "I can type," Bob got to stay in Saigon, got to wave goodbye to his fellow MPs in the 54th on their convoy out of town.

Got to spend the rest of his war in the provost marshal's office—the Saigon Military Police Station—a tiny administrative unit of fewer than twenty people. Got to face a whole other kind of angst in that converted French villa, another wartime drama altogether. But, nevertheless, got to sleep most nights curled up next to his wife.

CHAPTER 6
LEARNING THE ROPES

LATE APRIL 1970

I worked steadily in April. Marsh saw to it. He filled my empty coffers, paid me a daily stipend plus expenses. He was generous with me and with Time Inc. money. Most of my assignments could be handled in Saigon or on a day trip out and back before dark. I felt pretty sure that my assignments were circumscribed because I was a stringer (a freelancer hired in the field, rather than at corporate New York), not because I was a girl. I was resolute to give him my best.

I no longer felt like a complete outsider in the Time-Life suite of offices. I didn't have an office of my own, like Bob Anson, Burt

Pines, Jim Willwerth, or Marsh, but all doors were open and there was plenty of room for me and for Ennio Iacobucci, the Italian freelance photographer; for Dick Swanson, the *Life* photographer; for John Saar, the *Life* correspondent; and for assorted passing journalists sprawled on the overstuffed, aging sofas and cracked leather chairs in the dim front room.

The *Time* Vietnamese support staff sat at desks tucked in one corner of the reception room and in the most distant offices, here and there: the office manager, the accountant, the telex operator, the political savant and interpreter, the secretary, the black market money fixer, and more.

The others accepted me because Marsh had.

I wrote an early story about the South Vietnamese government's efforts at land reform: redistribution of large land holdings into smaller peasant plots, a futile effort to beat the Communists at their own game. It felt as thin as the US Information Office sugar industry story. But it was a beginning. Assignments always came from the New York office, but this one had the imprint of the Pentagon. No one in the office had been too enthusiastic about it, so by default it was mine.

At the imposing, baroque National Assembly Building I met the Vietnamese people's elected representatives and senators. My high school French was expanding briskly, but still barely adequate. With Vietnamese civil servants of a certain age, no other language would do. French signified a bureaucrat's stature, his distinction above the agrarian peasantry.

On Mondays, we juggled story ideas in Saigon, sent them to New York for approval, and awaited the return telex. The assignments arrived from corporate headquarters on Tuesday for a weekend deadline. Sometimes what we proposed in Saigon came back as assignment. Often, it did not. Sometimes a story idea—concocted by the generals in Washington, whispered into the

Time Pentagon correspondent's ears, and passed on to New York—bumped ours.

Although seldom spoken aloud, we had something of the last word. A breaking story took precedence over an assigned one. We could usually dig up an urgent war story to bury one we loathed. New York, of course, had the actual last word—they put the magazine to bed. So there was that persistent tension, a seesaw of equilibrium, between Corporate and Saigon.

I didn't have to fight my colleagues for the dead tree story, either. It too was mine because no one would touch it. But I knew that there was something here that the others were ignoring.

In my first few days in Saigon, I hadn't been able to put my finger on exactly what I was missing. What *wasn't* there? Later, I recognized it. I missed the birds and their sweet, poignant songs. The birds, I learned, had survived the Japanese occupation during World War II, later the Chinese, and then the French.

That they had not survived the American war had everything to do with napalm and Agent Orange and other cutting-edge chemical warfare. Defoliants had killed the birds either directly or indirectly, by denuding their leafy habitat.

I wrote:

> Slowly the mammoth deciduous trees, the tamarinds and the mahoganies planted sixty years ago by occupying Frenchmen along Saigon's magnificent boulevards, gave way too. They succumbed to these intentional chemicals free-floating from outlying villages—and they succumbed too to the unintentional pollution of US Army convoys and antiquated motorbikes. Some still stood erect in rows, leafless and dead along the major avenues—gaunt skeletons of their original brilliance. Saigon was a hotter and homelier place because of their loss.

Not a day passed when I didn't hear a version of this refrain: "You should have been here ten years ago. This place was beautiful! The French! Now, *they* knew how to build a city!"

American construction, on the other hand, tended toward bowling alleys, movie theaters, and shopping complexes built solely for the Americans required to fight the war. On completion, we put tall fences around them, stationed Marine guards at the gates, and forbade any Vietnamese—save servants—from entering. Unlike the French, we didn't plant or cultivate trees, parks, or gardens. We didn't build schools or museums. We were here to wage war.

One story led to another, my dead tree story to the history of American defoliation.

I wrote:

> To date, 4.5 million acres of Vietnamese land has been defoliated with 13.5 million gallons of herbicide. During the year ending 1968, 6,000 square kilometers were sprayed. The current number of land area now covered by flights is "Classified."
>
> The Air Force has no specific safeguard for personnel handling defoliants. In fact, Colonel Bruce M. Whitesides claims many men have rubbed defoliants on their skin and had no ill effects. "Look at that man," he pointed to one of his staff. "He's worked for years around the stuff and he has seven healthy babies."
>
> He denied any documented evidence for deformed babies or harmed wildlife. "I don't know anything about birds."

I listened, took notes, and challenged duplicity where I found it. "No documented evidence, Colonel? Let me offer some."

A version of the dying tree story made the New York cut and then a bit of my herbicide story too—but none of my recorded skepticism.

The *Time* New York office wasn't the only sieve my stories had to pass through. There was an institutionalized censorship of all press coverage. Nothing left Saigon's telex or telephone wires without the South Vietnamese Press Office monitoring it. But the censorship was arbitrary and amateurish, entirely dependent on any given bureaucrat and whether he was hungry, sleepy, or apathetic on a given day.

I followed the dying birds, trees, and incidentally contaminated human story with one we called "Another Alleged Massacre."

> Once again, as with My Lai, an obscure village coddled between mountains and jungles promises to become notorious. This time, the place is Son Thang, and the charges are based on the alleged murder of sixteen Vietnamese civilians by five young American Marines.

The Marines were incarcerated pending court martial. Their upcoming trial was the justification for my current assignment. This one was, for me, hearsay. I'd never set foot in the village; the events had taken place in February. My sources were lawyers, witnesses, and the underground American press who'd unearthed the story—a small cadre of true believers closeted in a dank, dingy apartment.

These were men I would have had a lot in common with at UW Madison, but less in Saigon where I worked for what we would *then* have called an "establishment rag." (I no longer did.) I liked them; they were warm and forthcoming. I appreciated their irreverence and their guts. Their work invited expulsion from the country. I wanted to stay in-country; I knew better than to merge my fortunes with them. But it was a temptation.

"Another Alleged Massacre" led to "Sat Cong Badges."

> The enlisted man claimed, it was Company policy—a three-day pass was issued to any man who could bring back "proof" that he had killed a Viet Cong. He said, "Ears were

the most common proof, but it was okay if you brought back a finger." The ear of the dead Viet Cong was nailed to the headquarters' door until it decomposed. "Then we threw it to the dogs." In the same company: Killing a VC with a mortar brought a $25 bonus.

Like any responsible reporter, I solicited the official response, which was: "The MACV official policy prohibits distribution of such 'unofficial' badges, but they have 'heard rumors' that there may have been violations."

So cast-off stories, or pieces of them that no one else wanted—because they had bigger fish to fry—became mine. They were small stories that spoke to my place in the office pecking order. I hadn't been hired out of New York and I wasn't salaried. I was a stringer, paid only for the days I worked. I reminded myself to be grateful. I was covering Vietnam and getting an education that came cheap, within a day's drive of the office.

In the middle of a story, typically, I'd take a long lunch break downtown, buy fruit and cheese at one of the outdoor markets, and take a quick swim in the Officers' Club pool next door to JUSPAO. Accredited foreign correspondents were automatically granted the rank and privileges of a US Army major. I could eat steak, baked potato, and salad for $4 at any officers' club—but my PFC (private first class) husband couldn't even enter one.

The officers' club next door to JUSPAO had a history. A couple years before, a passing motorcyclist had pitched a plastique explosive through the building's front door. He took out the first floor and shook the complacency out of the other four. It was fixed up like new now, but there were still eager raconteurs who needed far less prodding than the $1 scotch and soda in front of them to loosen their tongues. I'd heard the narrative enough times, elaborated always by embellishing journalists, to make it my own.

As a result, I never quite relaxed inside that building. I was always anticipating that the cool, safe interior might be violated. Each time I swam or ate there, I imagined what it would feel like on the fifth floor when the first floor caved in on itself. So I was looking one direction when the blow came from an altogether different one.

Of all the markets in Saigon, it was hard to beat the Central Market, the granddaddy of all outdoor vendors in Vietnam. It hawked everything I might imagine and a fair sprinkling of things I couldn't have begun to dream up: lovely pottery canisters, sure, but also animal parts that appeared a little too overtly what they were and Asian vegetables that weren't obvious at all. The market sprawled for blocks—open-sided building after building and canvas tarp after canvas tarp. At most times of the day, it was teeming. During siesta—the couple hours' respite from the midday sun—when I shopped for lunch, the stall owners might be squatting on their haunches eating their dinner and expecting few customers in the 110-degree heat.

I still kept American hours. I hadn't made that transition yet. So I'd shop from noon to two and the vendors would pull themselves alert to serve me—or not. Maybe they'd serve me instead from a seated position.

My search for marketplaces worldwide was more than a quaint attraction to the rancid odors of wilting lettuce and aging papaya. Very simply: open-stand produce and meat markets were part of my heritage.

My father, the second youngest of eleven children, left school and went to work at age ten. Not everything he did in those years before he married my mother at thirty-two made good stories. Much he refused to speak about. But he spent a savored part of his youth elbow deep in bananas and cantaloupes, russet potatoes and pears. (*He* could tell a Bartlett from a Seckel, a ripe melon from one that would never ripen.) His favorite story was about the poison that had run up his vein from a fetid butchered rabbit.

My father knew markets.

My dad had left the market behind him decades before, but his best boyhood friend had not. Uncle Milt was a big-time wholesaler now. He commanded railroad cars full of baby Bibb and scallions and sold them to Baltimore's finest restaurants: the Harvey House, the Eager House, and the Pimlico House. When I was a child, my father drove across town to Uncle Milt's market every Saturday and brought home bushel baskets of beans to string, peas to shell, oranges to squeeze for fresh juice. My father's greatest disappointment was that not one of his three children ate his peaches, apples, or pears.

"I had to give them away," he'd tell his friends about our uneaten fruit years later. Pepsi and Juicy Fruit, Mars Bars and Good Humor ice cream had ruined his kids' taste for the more subtle sweetness of a ripe peach. "But," he'd grin, "Inette loved the green grapes."

The rare trip with my dad to the market was my first foreign travel. I savored the sights, sounds, smells, the commotion—the *life* of it—and its steady coolness on the hottest days. I came by my love of the market honestly.

The Central Market in Saigon was Baltimore's Lexington Market, Broadway Fish Market, and Pratt Street Meat Market rolled into one, then multiplied by Doctor Seuss. I'd walk the mile from my office for the simple pleasure of its organic coolness, where the moist feel of a banana skin would remind me of home.

This particular day I felt hot and bedraggled, and I was doubting the worth of each step I took in the direction of the market. Instead, I straddled my Honda for the short trip, parked it on the sidewalk, and strung my rusty, four-inch-link, five-pound chain through the wheel and around an iron signpost. I locked it tight with a three-pound padlock—but never through the spokes and never with an ordinary bike chain that any Vietnamese kid over six could (and would) shear like butter.

I dragged my sodden body into the heart of the market and picked up a hunk of bread from a man who recognized me and some sliced ham from a woman who did not. I grabbed a bright red apple and thought of my dad. Normally, I'd find a little shade and then settle on a curb to eat in the shadow of this liveliest part of the city. This time, though—the reverse of a cat searching for his spot of sun—I couldn't make myself comfortably cool. "It's *hot*," I muttered aloud. "I've got the bike. I'm going home." It was something I never did.

I drove home, ate, and then stared down at the story I'd been working on. Maimed Vietnamese war veterans were accusing their government of outright neglect. On my portable typewriter, I pecked out the first words. "'I'd rather die than prolong a life like this,' a homeless, legless, South Vietnamese veteran told me." I called it a day.

So it was not until early the next morning when I got to the office that I heard. A rocket had sailed into the middle of the Central Market and exploded just past noon the day before. Random, as they always were, and shot from three miles out in the countryside. Launched toward the city's center without hope of discerning a target. Shot, I imagined, without a trace of specific rancor. Shot only as a warning to a civilian populace that might have grown comfortable under the relative affluence of an American puppet regime. Comfortable, since the last warning.

Only eight dead, only twenty-five wounded—it was midday after all. So, only the man who recognized me behind his stack of hard-crusted breads and the woman who didn't at the sliced-ham table and the other market vendors in their black satin trousers and conical straw hats—peasants, eking out an urban living, feeding families, ignoring the heat, pondering the prices they might extort from a rich American—only they were there to absorb the rocket blast and die. I never had the stomach to go back and find out.

My assignment to cover the Big Red One's (1st Infantry Division) withdrawal from Vietnam and the ceremonies surrounding it was one story Bob Anson did want, but it was already mine. Marsh, the arbiter, handed it off that morning. General Creighton Abrams, the US Army commander for the war, the top military banana in South Vietnam, and his civilian counterpart US Ambassador to Vietnam Ellsworth Bunker would share the podium.

Anson wasn't alone. Most male journalists—here and in Annapolis—were suckers for big-name politicians. I wasn't entirely free of their enthusiasm, but my reasons were less fundamental to my nature, more imitative of the values around me. It was less who I was, more who I was trying to be because someone told me I could not. I doubt I was the only young woman at that pivotal time—or perhaps even now—who struggled with this.

I stood with a couple dozen reporters and photographers under the unremittingly intense sun on the black tarmac for an hour and a half. Bunker and then Abrams spoke. The lines of 1st Infantry troops baked next to us—at attention, in uniform, and in formation.

I wrote:

> After fifty-seven months of combat and 2,714 Vietnam battle deaths, the very first infantry division to enter Vietnam packed up its banners and left. The pullout of the famous World War II fighting unit was largely symbolic. In truth, the majority of the men would simply be reassigned to other units in country.
>
> The Ambassador enunciated the US mission in Vietnam. "We're here to preserve the right of the

Vietnamese people to live under a government of their own choosing."

His words embarrassed me profoundly. I thought, was it still possible to believe this? Or was he callous?

"At the heart of the matter," Ambassador Bunker said from his shaded platform, "is whether we as a nation have the patience and the will to accept the responsibilities of power?"

I recorded these words, but I thought they spoke more accurately to the anti-war movement that had labored long and hard to stop the war. What kind of war was it, I wondered, when the identical words prompted tears in angry opponents? The hearts' imagery was at odds.

I wrote:

As the Division banners were furled and covered for their return to Kansas, "Taps" was sounded and one by one a clear voice enunciated every 1st Infantry Division Vietnam battle by name.

The troops standing at attention turned graver and shed surreptitious tears.

I filed my story that evening, carefully omitting my internal commentary, and Marsh was pleased with it. He'd not yet found reason to fault any story he'd assigned me. It seemed that Phil Evans had taught me well.

Marsh was hanging around the office late that night because Pippa was in Hong Kong at their lavish getaway apartment, on family business. When I wrapped up the file, he scanned it.

"Well done. Are you hungry? Want dinner downstairs?"

"Sure, I'm starving."

He handed my story to the telex operator for immediate transmission via the Saigon censor to New York. Then he picked up his pen, stuck it in his pocket, and we left the office. I walked with him through the dim musty hotel corridor, into the metal latticework elevator, and down to the lobby. It was about 9:00.

"Downstairs" was the Continental Palace Hotel's terrace—the wide, deep terrace where Marsh had interviewed me two months before over a *citron pressé*. But at night—I realized only then that the 1880 hotel terrace felt considerably altered, mellow and magical. Long, white tapers flickered on top of moonlit linen tablecloths. We were surrounded by the invisible darkness of the Saigon night, my bare skin exposed to the humid breezes. It looked like a Hollywood stage set for a 1930s film, conspicuously romantic. I could easily imagine a graying Humphrey Bogart and a young Lauren Bacall playing our parts. I could *see* Graham Greene, Somerset Maugham, and André Malraux sitting right here—exactly as they had in the same dark city. The terrace, which I bounded across in daytime without a second thought, radiated eroticism when the sun was gone.

But this was *Marsh*. So, although I was alert to the circumstances and undeniably aware of the potential—an attractive man, a young woman, a perennial summer sky and wine—I was safe.

Safe was not something I felt at all times in Saigon. It had less to do with a possible rocket attack and more with the ratio of eligible American men to women. I was under siege by other than just gaping children. I was rare and visible, a young American woman among all those semi-available men. *Married* was what I wielded to keep me safe.

"How's Bob?" Marsh sagely asked.

Marsh and Bob had met a few times and Marsh liked him immensely. Most people did; he was easy. "Such a fine mind and a jovial nature masquerading as an Army private," Marsh said at the time.

Bob returned the affection. "Amazingly, he doesn't intimidate me."

Marsh had not stinted on graciousness, and in Vietnam Bob

was starved for simple civility.

"He's not doing so well," I answered Marsh. "Depressed—he hates himself for agreeing to induction. He's living for R&R."

"Where are you two going?"

"Hong Kong in August."

"Stay at our flat. I think you'll like it."

"I wouldn't think of it. We'll stay in a hotel."

"Listen, Pippa and I are leaving Saigon in September; our two years are up. The flat will be empty all of August and I'd like to think of you two enjoying it before we give it up."

"You've twisted my arm. *Thanks.* It sounds fantastic."

"Good. Remind me to give Bob the name of my Hong Kong tailor. He does fine work, and he's cheap."

Marsh was a good man who, although he undoubtedly knew he was attractive, offered himself solely as my supportive mentor. He hinted at nothing else. I was young and probably more vulnerable than I realized, but he never came near to exploiting those vulnerabilities. Despite wine, candlelight, and the stereotypically alluring setting, he mindfully directed our conversation, and *married* was what we both used as shields.

If there would ever be a time when I wouldn't need that particular shield—when I could more *directly* protect myself—I didn't know it at the time.

I was curled up in the outer office early one morning with nothing much coming down the pike. Marsh summoned both Anson and me to his inner chamber.

"I've got a story I'd like you both to take on. That all right with you?" He looked straight at Bob Anson, who did not look at me. "Sure," Bob said, "Why not? What's up?"

"That Dallas billionaire is back in Saigon, his private jet crammed with food supposedly for American prisoners of war.

The North Vietnamese don't even notice him, let alone allow him near our POWs. Is he a nutcase or just an ego the size of Texas? Who knows? You guys find out. This time he brought seventy stateside reporters with him, demanding to tour the North Vietnamese POW camps. Go over and interview him. See what he's up to. He's expecting us. His name is H. Ross Perot."

We crossed the street to the Caravelle—Saigon's finest, Perot's hotel. We had no time for legwork beforehand. Marsh had implied that the man wasn't worth taking seriously.

But we were wrong. Perot, holding court in his hotel room, was absolutely a man used to being taken seriously—kowtowed to, in fact. He was neither generous nor easy with reporters who dared to question him.

"Mr. Perot, do you think the North Vietnamese will permit you to see our American POWs?" I warmed up gently.

"What sort of stupid, hostile question is that?! Of course I'll see them or I wouldn't be here!"

It was an unpleasant hour. I'd never before met a public person as defensive as this short, balding, middle-aged, private man with public interests—and I'd never once since, until the 2016 presidential campaign. I thought Perot wanted it both ways: the freedom to do what he wanted as a private businessman and the attention and influence due a public one. A decade later he announced his candidacy for US president.

"Unemotional," was what I contributed to our joint story, but in fact he was easily roused to anger. To make that point I wrote: "He uses the word 'humanitarian' but seems entirely without sentiment." I called him, "Shrewd, cocky, accustomed to success—and knows how to use his billions to insure it. 'I earned my money,' he spit out. 'Like Horatio Alger.'"

Very simply, Perot did not see why he had to answer our questions, despite summoning *Time* to his suite. He assumed an adversarial relationship. The planeload of junketing reporters were a different story. They were flying free as his guests, so he figured they were in his employ.

Anson and I were unusually polite to this disagreeable man. I suspect we each wondered why there were two of us. Clearly the number exacerbated Perot's paranoia. One on one, he might have felt the advantage and been more amenable to our questions—but then, maybe not.

It wasn't obvious what Marsh was up to, sending two to do one person's job. Was it a punishment to the outspoken Anson? Or a gift to me, the kind of experience in store for a woman in an unwelcoming man's game?

Between 1965 and 1973, a total of 1,742 American reporters were accredited to American news outlets in Vietnam: 232 of them were women. Half of the total were in country for less than a month, something of a *vacation* at war. Most never left Saigon.

In 1971, my second year in Vietnam, there were twenty-eight accredited American women correspondents.

Denby Fawcett, working for the *Honolulu Advertiser*, preceded my tenure by three years. She wrote an essay in the edited book *War Torn*, forty years later: "I never made an effort to be friends with other women reporters in Vietnam. I am not sure why. When I think back now, I am sad, knowing how much we had in common and how we could have supported and comforted one another."

I've mulled the truth of her words. Certainly, we called ourselves feminists, trailblazers in a male world. We were—perhaps by nature—ambitious women, eager to make our own way. But I remember no support groups in Vietnam to bolster our individual efforts and no tête-à-tête over a café au lait.

Sadly, in that place and that time (at a loss to both ourselves personally and to what we now know to be collective empowerment), covering the war in Vietnam seemed to take all of our singular efforts.

I chose to celebrate my twenty-fourth birthday—May 12—by getting out of Saigon for the day. Bob was stuck in the provost marshal's office, six to six. I was getting out of Vietnam entirely—going back to Cambodia. It was a press junket that just happened to coincide with my birthday.

The American military wanted to show off its measurable accomplishment since deposing Prince Sihanouk and installing Lon Nol. Accomplishment had been elusive during the two-week massive American and Vietnamese troop penetration into the pristine Cambodian countryside. The countryside, until then, had been spared the ravages of war. In just a fortnight, it had been systematically violated by marauding ground troops—Americans accompanied paradoxically by Cambodia's traditional enemy, the Vietnamese.

The coup d'état was our ticket to ride—and ride we did, like a herd of elephants across a corn field.

Purportedly, we were after the evasive, substantive Viet Cong Pentagon, what the Americans called COSVN (Central Office for South Vietnam)—situated *somewhere* inside jungle cover just over the Cambodian border, the staging area for all Viet Cong subversion into Vietnam.

Purportedly, we overran Cambodia's idyllic countryside to take some of the pressure off Vietnam. But from day one, we saw that purpose was fiction—jungle warfare did not build pentagons. Only in the American political imaginations did COSVN exist.

So, in the face of the heavy political toll that the Cambodian invasion extracted on American college campuses and beyond, President Nixon wanted to fortify public opinion. He wanted to show off the booty claimed from our incursion onto a sovereign nation's soil. Flying fifty-one men and me—journalists all—to look over the captured Viet Cong arms (some Russian artillery, some Chinese rifles) was one way to get the word out. The word we were expected to deliver was this: The attack was working. The military found exactly what it expected to find—*except* for COSVN.

The press junket began with a surge of testosterone. Fifty-two reporters and photographers clambering onto a 1945 freight plane, a C-130: big steps, considerable jostling, shoving, and bodies pressed against mine. I didn't know any of the men. We crammed onto the floor of the plane. There were no seats, just tiny dirty windows. The men spoke among themselves.

I alone represented *Time* and I was entirely inside my head hoping not to do or say something stupid to expose myself for the novice I was: just twenty-four today, on my first press trip, my first military flight, and my first time ever in a pack of reporters. A girl among men—I assumed they knew what they were doing.

I'd bought spanking new fatigues and combat boots two months before but hadn't had them out of the wrapper until my birthday. Correspondents wore fatigues with the intention of being inconspicuous in the field, blending into the jungle foliage. Mine were crisp still, deep olive (not yet faded) and already huge. The canvas and leather boots were surprisingly comfortable. I'd never had so much toe maneuvering room in any pair of shoes.

Mostly I was ignored, shoved aside without a "pardon me," pressed up against—invisible. There'd been no rudeness. I was just conspicuously unnoticed.

"I'm Peter Arnett." I was awakened to the warm deep voice with an imprint of native New Zealand and I turned just my head because my body was firmly tangled among three sweaty ones. "I don't think we've met. Who're you with?"

Peter Arnett, my God! I couldn't have been a more adoring fan if I were meeting Jerry Garcia. *This was Pulitzer Prize-winning Vietnam correspondent forever—Peter Arnett!* All of it traversed my mind in a second.

"I'm with *Time* . . . Inette Miller."

I yanked my legs free, turned my torso, and faced the dark-skinned, dark-haired, stocky man with a wonderful grin. We shook hands.

I confessed immediately to his warm smile under his floppy boonie hat that I was new, just two months in country, my first military flight. But I let him know too that I'd already been to Cambodia, and when. He listened, nodded, and then asked my opinion of the stuff going down in Cambodia. *Peter Arnett asking my opinion!* I offered it willingly.

"I feel like I'm witnessing a crime," I said. "I saw the eyes of the Cambodian people before any of this happened. I saw the kind of place Cambodia is. I'm very afraid for this country."

He offered me something in return. Instruction on disembarking when we touched down. "Keep your head down and run like a bat out of hell for cover."

I never forgot—and that not-forgetting served me well.

On the ground about thirty-five miles into Cambodia, the pack of correspondents wandered the unbearably hot, dusty edge of jungle. We meandered among a neatly arrayed display of captured artillery and AK-47s of recent Russian lineage. It was like a fifth grade field trip. But this time the teachers wore uniforms and the Koontz Dairy produced advanced weaponry instead of milk.

I looked away from the weapons towards the two dozen Cambodian faces staring at us blankly from the edge of the clearing. Dazed, bewildered faces. Men, women, and children—villagers—expecting nothing, understanding none of this. My heart contracted.

It had been just over a month since I'd strolled the welcoming streets of Phnom Penh. A month and a lifetime—20,000 American and Vietnamese troops tramping Cambodian hearts and innocence—from my stroll in the park, to flattened villages. Five or six weeks since mothers' teenage sons were stripped of their shorts and put into uniform, armed with machine guns, and told to fight for their homeland. Against whom? It wasn't yet clear.

It was not clear to the stunned, confused eyes staring at us—staring at fifty-two uniformed foreign journalists writing notes on narrow pads, snatching photographs of unsmiling eyes, and darting among a supermarket of weaponry. I began to understand the meaning of "quagmire."

We were handed C-rations. Peter and I settled apart from the others under the trees. I pried off the lid and scooped out the peaches from the syrup, the wieners from the beans. I sipped from my canteen filled with boiled water.

"You know, I used to read your stuff coming over the wire in Annapolis. I really admire your writing. That story last year, the American combat company that refused orders to fight—it made me cry."

Peter gulped back his reaction to my tribute. "Thanks. Means a lot from a colleague." Then he said, "I'm leaving for New York in July. I've been here eight years. I was here at the beginning."

He looked off at the piles of artillery shells, the intact grenades, the vacant human faces, and he waved his arms in a gesture of resignation at the Cambodian jungle around us. "And now it's starting all over again. I'd just as soon sit it out this time. This one is yours."

Collectively we snapped enough photographs to satisfy the military press officers and then we were herded without explanation into a massive Chinook helicopter. We entered it through a huge loading ramp in the rear of the chopper. It was stuffy, unwieldy, and very loud. A couple of reporters threw up their C-rations. Amazingly, I did not.

We disembarked deep inside Cambodia at the Neak Loeung ferry crossing on the Mekong River. Reporters around me were scrambling to imagine why we'd been hauled here. I was content under Arnett's tutelage.

Thirty-five feet up river, the pack spotted Vice President Nguyen Cao Ky standing alone. He was handsome, outfitted in a snug black flight suit with white art nouveau embroidery and a purple neck scarf. He stood erect and transparently gloating.

The triumphant hero in repose, the vice president of South Vietnam, swaggered over the sprawl of his nation's troops throughout the Cambodian countryside. Proud to be, finally, the colonialist, the occupying force in the historically despised Cambodia.

With absolutely no prodding, Ky held the press conference he had contrived.

"Vice President Ky, what are you doing here?"

He smiled like a Cheshire cat and said nothing.

"Will you be out of Cambodia by the end of June as Nixon promised?"

"No." Ky had learned well the words of the occupiers. "The Vietnamese Army has no intention of withdrawing from Cambodia when the US Army does. We have to take care of our own interests. We'll be in Cambodia for at least months. We might build an airstrip here in Neak Loeung. *If* we withdraw, the Cambodians can use it."

"Chutzpah," I filed for *Time*. (They translated it: "The height of diplomatic folly.") "The absolute, ultimate chutzpah—the puppet tugging the strings of Washington. Vietnamization gone berserk."

CHAPTER 7

DIGGING IN

MAY 1970

Alone in that whitewashed room with one screen window and one screen door—shuttered against the sun and the rain—we created a private world. The life that Bob and I shared was amazingly domestic, remarkably conventional—considering. Considering Bob was an Army private at the mercy of the US military in Vietnam. Considering I was a young woman doing emphatic things for reasons I didn't yet understand; looking for a thunderous war to silence my self-doubt.

A girl shouldn't, couldn't, isn't!

I worried less that I'd be blown to bits by a land mine than that I'd be found out to be an imposter.

The life Bob and I shared was domestic, like this. Once a week I stripped the set of plain white sheets from our bed and, along with my drip-dry-for-war three dresses and one pantsuit, took them to our tepid shower and scrubbed them hard with a bar of funny-smelling dark soap. Then I carried them in my arms, dripping water the length of our room, to a clothes line by the river's edge to dry. I sat with a book next to the line to safeguard them from theft. (Mrs. An advised it.) They dried in that tropical sun in no time.

Or like this. I boiled water on our hand-me-down from a departing radio correspondent, two-burner (only one worked) hot plate; bottled it; and put it in the three-foot-high refrigerator to chill.

The water from the tap was contaminated, and I was never confident that boiling it would be enough. There were a couple of days when it was not. For forty-eight hours I was doubled over with intestinal pain. I vomited violently without pause.

Domestic, like this. On the mornings I was in Saigon, I'd drive Bob to his day job across town, drop him off, and go to work myself. I'd pick him up around 6:30.

Bob's family shipped us salami, cheese, and brownies. We devoured them in that room. They sent us Monopoly, too, and for a while we were cutthroat. I took the first game, he took the second; me, the third, he, the fourth. Then, our interest waned.

Poppa died in May. We grieved Bob's 95-year-old grandfather in that room. He'd lived much of his life with Bob's family. I'd met him once. The bedridden Irishman demanded to know if I was Irish.

"Russian," Bob told him, because it was somewhat less horrible than telling him "Jewish."

We looked for something to pass the hours and dull Bob's accumulated misgivings. Talk wasn't always enough.

Whatever the outside threat—the creeping smell of sewage, urine, and rotting garbage through our windowless window, or the tumult of rifle shots, motorcycle engines, and high-pitched

Digging In

Vietnamese voices—Bob and I could dance. It was the thing we did best of all. We danced more easily than we shared feelings. In many ways it was *how* we made love, how we shared feelings.

I was walking across the room on a mindless errand to hang up my navy dress and Bob grabbed me firmly, his hand to the small of my back, mine settling lightly on his shoulder, our other two mingled in the air.

"When I woke up this morning, you were on my mind."

I tossed the dress in the vicinity of the hook. We started out together slowly and then whirled apart. We went where the music moved us: slow, fast, faster, slow again. The music moved us around that small concrete room on the fringe of war.

"Yesterday, all my troubles seemed so far away."

We huddled around the Armed Forces Radio broadcast and listened to its boxy sounds from the little plastic radio. I remember just a single station and the modulated voices of American DJs. If I tried, could I have heard Vietnamese voices as well?

"Rock and roll forever will be."

We danced together under the fluorescent light and ceiling fan next to the tiny refrigerator we'd bought at the PX, danced until we fell together onto the big bed. I was the dancing child of dancing parents. I learned the ballroom steps earlier than I learned to ride a bike. I learned them in our knotty pine "club basement" along with my parents' neighbors—four Jewish couples who'd hired a pair of Italian dance instructors to teach them the mambo, cha-cha, and much more, once a week—for years?

But at fifteen, with the Twist, I branched out on my own. I realized I no longer needed a teacher. The music was all I needed to tell me where to step and when. Dance was how I adhered to my mother's mandate. I remained untouched primarily *because* I could dance. I danced my appetites into obedience.

Girls Don't!

Tonight, I welcomed the balm and comfort of Bob's weight against me, welcomed his substance. I guessed that my mother too required a quiet, substantial man to persuade her she was safe from her own pretense.

After dinner and an impromptu dance, we lay together on the diagonal across our huge homemade bed. I lay on my right side, Bob on his left, parallel bodies a foot apart. Bob ran his right hand, his long white fingers, over the mound of my shoulder and down the curving outside edge of my body.

Bob saw with an artist's eye, and the world he saw lay in lines, planes, and especially curves. He had rejoiced in the curves of architectural Florence. Now he celebrated mine. He ran his fingers slowly at deliberate distance.

Later—years later—we could afford, sadly I think, to be more direct. But this was a May evening in Saigon. We were newlyweds, and this was our solemn hiding place from the fireworks outside. We needed soothing—knowing and being known—more than we needed explosions.

"*Slip slidin' away. Slip slidin' away. The nearer your destination, the more you're slip slidin' away.*" Simon and Garfunkel were nearby.

Afterwards, splayed across the balled-up sheets, Bob stroked my arm. "I couldn't do this place without you."

I peeled my eyes open, rolled onto my stomach, and searched Bob's eyes for clues. "You don't have to."

"I mean I'm not sure I can do this, even with you."

Neither of us moved. Neither of us fell asleep, either.

I wasn't much older than five, sprawled on the steps leading to the front porch of our brick row house. It was a Baltimore summer, sticky and hot, but the leaves of the huge maple at the curb shaded me.

Digging In

I sat with my brothers—Harmon, nine, and Buddy, thirteen— each to his own step. I wanted to crawl onto one of the steps next to them, but I knew they wouldn't be pleased. I wanted nothing more than to please my brothers. I thought them strong, adventurous, and fearless. The world was their playground.

Before I'd begun kindergarten that September, the boys had instructed me to ask old Mrs. Loppheimer (she'd been their ordeal before she'd become mine) if at recess I could play "hooky." In all innocence and ignorance I asked. She was irate. I was humiliated.

Now, I was receiving new instructions from the front steps.

"See that little girl," Harmon pointed from the cool porch to a four-year-old skipping down the sidewalk under the trees. "I want you to beat her up." Buddy laughed his support.

"Beat her up? I don't know her. Why?"

"Because I said so."

I knew hesitation would reveal cowardice and weakness.

I tore myself off the step, ran recklessly at that child, and threw the entire force of my five-year-old body on top of her. What I lacked in finesse, I made up in resolve. I kicked, punched, and tackled her to the ground, and I didn't stop until my brothers told me I could.

The girl cried, filthy in her wrinkled pinafore, and ran home. I don't remember consequences—parents talking to parents. But I remember immutably judging myself as the kind of kid who beat up other kids—girls and boys—to get what I wanted.

We didn't have much in that first year of marriage, but we had what we needed. The Honda, the radio, the typewriter, and three polyester dresses—sure. But a couple of beach towels, too. Bob's four uniforms, Army issue and baggy, with underpants and socks to match. My second uniform, hemmed narrow at the hips and ankles, with "US Army" across my left breast.

"*Whose* were these?" I asked when I lifted my second, well-worn, well-tapered pair of fatigues from a heap of used uniforms at an infantry post not far from Saigon. I was out on assignment, I needed a second pair, and they were free.

A Vietnamese seamstress had almost certainly run up the seams on request, snug to accentuate some young GI's swagger. I held them against my torso. When I got them home, I found they conformed to my new body like dream, low on the hips. But I got no answer to "Whose were these?"

"Take what you want. This is the slush pile." Was I walking around in a dead boy's clothes? Were they some grunt's who'd left a leg behind? Beneath my new fatigues I knew there was a story, and I reimagined it every time I wore them.

Down the river in front of our solitary room, the rats were big and sassy. We sat in the evening and watched the orange ball of sunlight set over the filthy water. We sat on a decommissioned, leaking rowboat that never left port. We sat there alone—Bob and me—and watched the garbage float by.

Our neighbors regularly walked to the edge of the river, turned their wastebaskets upside down, and shook them. We watched kids play catch-me in the rice field, forty-five feet away on the other side of the river. We lived at the exact point where the city gave way to the countryside.

At night when we slept, the countryside pressed hard to come inside. The rats made a racket in their futile search for food. The artillery explosions just across the river sent projectiles over our heads and into the heart of Saigon.

Ours was a time outside of time in the room by the edge of the river. We were counting down days exactly like every other GI plopped down in that contradictory and difficult place. We knew exactly how much time we had to kill.

Asked, on May 20, 1970, "How many days until DEROS?"

Bob snapped without hesitation: "Two hundred and eighty one." No calculator was necessary. This was America's first war—ever—served up in one year chunks. Every soldier arrived at Ton Son Nhut airbase on day 365 and left on day zero. DEROS—date of estimated return from overseas. Every American soldier knew precisely how many days were left to his particular nightmare, and the day he became a "double-digit midget." You could wake him in the middle of the night and he'd tell you. You could tap his shoulder in the middle of a firefight. "How *short* are you?" He'd tell you. He knew exactly how many days until his private war ended. The larger war? It went on forever.

It was in late May when my enthusiasm for most things Vietnamese—my excitement at having pulled off getting myself here, landing the job, and being near Bob—dissipated. For the first couple of months I was running on exhilaration. I'd also remained planted in my black-and-white campus mindset: the US had screwed up an idyllic nation. It was a paradise lost. I grieved for the Vietnamese people.

Now I cared a lot less about all that. I felt *personally* burdened by the hardship around me. And that included to no small degree a husband who was trapped by the American military and its madness.

"The sergeant is screwing me over a haircut. My hair touching my collar! No days off for two weeks."

In May, the heat began to wear on me. Until then, the daily military briefing—parodied by the press as the Five o'clock Follies—I had dismissed as ludicrous but inconsequential. Now, though, it infuriated me. I was furious at the blatant lies, enraged that the US constitutional guarantees of a free press and an informed electorate were seemingly dispensable.

At a typical briefing in late May, I listened to this exchange.

"Hey, Colonel, what was the body count from Pleiku yesterday?"

"American losses minimal: two dead, five wounded."

"I was at that firefight, Colonel; the 'losses' were not 'minimal'—they were screaming for their mamas."

"I've answered you, Joe. Another question?"

"Yeah. How come *you* don't count the twenty-five body bags I counted tossed onto the Medevacs?"

"This briefing's over. Good day."

I was angry too that *Time* officially supported this lunacy. That Americans broadly and vehemently approved of what they knew not. That it was my uphill duty to see that they knew, and that they cared.

I was angry that the South Vietnamese were governed by a bunch of corrupt losers; that the South Vietnamese people suckled at the breast of America's military and economic largesse.

The Viet Cong—hell, I still thought them admirable warriors and nationalists. But it became a lot less easy to idealize their disingenuous backsides. They too made deals, intimidating the hell out of the populace they were "protecting."

None of the politics was as simple as it had been at Berkeley—or at Time Inc. headquarters either. But personally, it was wearing me out.

I did not want to have to *think* about the war incessantly or talk about it every minute of every day. There was never a conversation with a colleague—and few with Bob—that did not circle around the war. It was our occupation, sure, our profession—GI and correspondent alike—but it was our preoccupation as well. It blanketed every part of our lives. I yearned for more, or less.

It was only May and I was already sick and tired of it—the war and this grisly, compromised place. But I'd worked too hard to get here to lose enthusiasm this early in the game.

"Everyone," my friend Bill Dowell took me in hand, "comes to Vietnam with this great need to be tolerant, to love everything about it."

Digging In

Over a cup of good espresso at Brodard's, Bill lectured me at the exact moment he knew I needed to hear it.

"Then," he said, "a couple months later, it goes the other way. Everything becomes intolerable and you can't imagine how you're going to make it. Eventually," he promised, "you'll strike a middle ground." He'd been here twice.

"I hope so," I answered skeptically. But like the view from any pit of despondency, it was hard to imagine being anywhere else.

Bob and I read aloud to one another often. That particular night, it was Ken Kesey's *Sometimes a Great Notion*. We read eclectically: *Madame Bovary*, followed by Tom Wolfe's *The Pump House Gang*. We were always in search of a decent book. They were hard to come by in Saigon.

Alone, I silently screened out the radio news and the unhappy world Bob inhabited with one book on the heels of another. Reading John MacDonald's sequential thrillers was a tawdry passion I'd acquired from the buried contents of cast-off USO books: *A Purple Place for Dying, A Deadly Shade of Gold, Pale Gray for Guilt*—hardly classics, but anaesthetizing page turners.

This night, after dinner together, it was Kesey.

Inside the four whitewashed walls, a half dozen pale geckos sucked the concrete looking for bugs. The transistor radio softly hummed Armed Forces Radio music.

"Under the boardwalk, with a blanket for my baby."

The radio news was just background static, white noise behind the words I was reading aloud to Bob. But Bob heard it all. He heard the words "Kent State University." He heard "Four college kids shot dead by the National Guard."

"Jesus," Bob screamed into the torpid air. "They're killing college kids! They're fucking killing our own kids now." He smashed his fists into the table, pushed himself to his feet. He was in tears.

"What are you talking about? What!? *Tell* me."

Between obscenities and sobs, he told me.

I didn't say a word because I couldn't wrap my mind around it. I could not imagine the immensity of the crime. *Maybe* back in suburban America, the murder of the Kent State students by Americans in uniform felt like a discrete and separate violation. Perhaps back home, it felt like a big black anomaly, a wart on the creamy face of the American government.

Here, though, it was part of a progressive melanoma. Here, it was a consequence of what we'd witnessed in Vietnam—now, starting all over again in Cambodia. It was national arrogance transfigured into tyranny. No democracy ours. No safe haven for good thought, good will, or compassion. It was a nation cut off from its heart—a plundering, pillaging madhouse. That's what the blood of college kids, peacefully protesting the American invasion of Cambodia, felt like to us in our sanctuary on the rural fringe of Saigon.

It was against all odds that I did not get the news first over the telex in the *Time* office, or from another reporter. Instead, I heard about the escalating violence in the single place where Bob and I clung to the life and love between us.

We'd heard other slices of the world that we'd left behind via that radio.

Apollo 13 faltered after we'd arrived. We paid it no mind; it felt like another planet. It couldn't compete with the life on this one. But the Kent State kids were *us*. The American military was shooting us.

The matter of complicity haunted Bob. He'd read newspaper accounts of Vietnam veterans being assaulted by anti-war vigilantes when they returned home. Bob said, and he meant every word of it, "If they spit on me when I get off the plane in Oakland, I'll deserve it."

I was a reporter, apart.

I remember when we first started smoking dope. I mean, regularly. Not the occasional toke back in college at parties, when we passed earphones with the joint. Always it'd been more Bob's thing than mine.

But in Saigon, it was different. We bought our dope prepackaged, filtered, and cellophane-wrapped from the corner cigarette vendor—any vendor, any corner. "*Can sa*" was one of the few Vietnamese terms I could pronounce correctly. A prewrapped pack of twenty-four joints cost us thirty-five cents.

But more than the ease of acquisition was the quality. Incredibly potent Thai grass was the standard. They were the succulent unfertilized buds: mind altering, fear obliterating, angst-dousing strong.

I can remember exactly when we began smoking in Saigon, and why. So many good reasons—apathy, deception, betrayal, corruption—but finally just this one, Kent State.

"Don't Bogart that joint, my friend, pass it over to me."

We were seldom together in that white room after that when we weren't either stoned or sleeping. In the way that I now know women take estrogen to even out the moods and flashes, to dull the body's erratic hormones, Bob and I smoked dope. And we were not the exception there; we were the rule.

It was the way: with grunts in distance firebases; warrant officers about to pilot Cobra gunships; correspondents at ease. It was the fine wine of *Time* official parties. The *best* stuff carried the prestige of a choice Bordeaux. Marsh's generation opted for booze, but for the rest of us marijuana was the drug of choice.

It was the way that GIs in Long Binh, far removed from any danger, dealt with the boredom. The way pilots, who dropped napalm, dealt with their consciences. It was the grease of almost all American and European social intercourse. Abstinence was the aberration. Good strong Thai dope smoothed the roar to a hum.

But there was no guarantee our trips would be uniformly soothing, and sometimes they were not. Three weeks after Kent State, a trip to oblivion turned ugly. Bob struck a match, pulled a joint from his pocket, lit it, and passed it to me after dinner. Almost immediately, what I called *reality* slipped off a precipice. The ceiling fan in our room began slicing the fluorescent light above it into distinct outlined chunks. I panicked because I could not force the pieces back into a whole. Life was tearing apart at its darkly outlined seams. Light, shadow, light, dark. Each revolution ended (I feared forever) light—and life.

I wailed my terror at Bob: "Help me! I can't make it stop!" He smoothed my hair, held my arms snug against my sides, hushed me, and told me it would be all right. But, of course, it was not.

The pieces began to weigh heavily in May. The rains set in. They came gradually, at first only briefly in the afternoons, then in the evenings, too. By the end of the month, it felt as if all good intentions were being drowned in inaction.

Bob and I held tight and hid out. We imagined safety in that white room with the lizards on the wall and the radio playing rock and roll. But Jimi Hendrix and Janis Joplin were dead now—and there were four dead kids at Kent State as well.

CHAPTER 8
TAKING RISKS

JUNE 1970

Just after daybreak, Bill Dowell loaded me and my small tote bag onto his powerful Moto Guzzi and we headed for the distant western edge of Saigon where he parked the bike, locked it, and we rendezvoused as planned with Murray Sayle, who'd wrangled himself a lift there.

As the city crowds thinned and the fields opened broad, flat, and green, I saw—sidesaddle from the rear of the motorcycle—water buffalo grazing and farmers bent low over rice paddies. I threw my head back and felt an enormous release from the confines of urban ugliness and filth. The breeze tunneled under my sleeveless shirt and lifted me like I could fly.

Forever, if I were stuck for long inside the sprawl of a city, I'd itch and scratch to get out. I'd get claustrophobic over time in cramped urban places. But it took me years to identify that cause and effect.

Saigon, of course, was the extreme example: bodies against bodies, thick toxic air, and unrelenting noise. The cure was mountains, oceans, rivers, or trees. My body already knew it, but it had taken water buffalo grazing on a green field to remind me.

We convened, the three of us.

"Any second thoughts?" Bill asked the air.

"This escapade's insane," Murray answered.

"Marsh thinks I'm nuts," I echoed. "He refused me an official assignment. Just whatever I bring back."

Bill laughed. "It's a Sunday drive in the country. Let's get started."

We grabbed our individual sacks and reviewed the plan. The trip was Bill's idea. Hitchhike along Route One for the 170 miles to Phnom Penh. Overland, to see what was happening beyond the border in Cambodia.

Marsh had reacted: "Hitchhike in Cambodia?!"

But if the question was: What are the American and Vietnamese troops doing in—or to—Cambodia? the answer could not be found in planes or helicopters. We aimed for closer to the source—challenging the terrain, engaging the people, yielding to serendipity.

We expected the trip to take us one day—no nights—and then a week's stopover in Phnom Penh. Worst possible scenario: if we fell short of Phnom Penh, we'd target a large town along the way and get to safety before nightfall. We were not prepared to tempt the fates that accounted for our missing friends and colleagues—Mike Morrow, Elizabeth Pond, and Richard Dudman—absent one week in rural Cambodia. Their disappearance hung heavily over us.

Bill knew I'd be game. I'd already been to Phnom Penh and he figured me the willing and somewhat experienced companion for his adventure. Murray was recruited for his political acumen, and for his wit. Danger, Bill decided, demanded a sense of humor. Murray Sayle—with the *Sunday Times* of London—was British, jowly, and about forty.

Our trip had been hastily determined, Bill's whim over café au lait and my acquiescence. My "Can we do it?" His "Why not?"

I wore a pair of Vietnamese black satin pajama pants and a cotton shirt nipped in at the waist, both freshly run up by Mrs. An's seamstress. I packed a 35mm Pentax that Marsh had picked up for me in Hong Kong. I carried John MacDonald's *Darker Than Amber* to pass the time between transport, a toothbrush, soap, a hairbrush, one change of underwear, a single change of clothes, eyeliner, and mascara. I suspected from the look of Bill's daypack that he had less.

It was hitchhiking as I'd loved it in Europe, only better. No autostrada or autobahn, no freeway ramps at all—just rural roads, roasted bananas over open fires at roadside stands, and squatting on my haunches while sucking up steaming bowls of noodle soup. There were flies, and the soup spoons were dipped only once in cold water between servings, but I could ignore that. We met generous people and there'd been ample reason for laughter.

First we took a taxi to the provincial limits, and then we caught rides in private civilian vehicles. Later, we bounced high off the bed of an open-back US Army truck. It barreled, pedal to floor, nearly hitting but just missing any number of tiny Hondas puttering down the narrow roadway next to us.

We were screaming over the noise of the truck engine into the face of a redheaded GI from New Jersey. Murray thrust an obscure history book he'd been reading into the boy's hand.

"Read this!" He pointed to a place where the Chinese dictator Chiang Kai-shek had refused America's offer to "Take Indochina!"

"No, thank you," Chiang Kai-shek had demurred. "These people wouldn't mix well with mine." We three had laughed at his wisdom; the story was instructive.

But the young private first class read the passage to himself and he stared up vacantly. He didn't get it, and he surely didn't know that he'd been expected to laugh. Murray took back his book, transparently disgusted.

I looked at Murray and I thought: It's easier to be British over here—detached and cynical about the American war. It's more complicated to be an American.

The boy looked up at me and rallied. "I've only got thirty days left. I'm *short*."

I smiled brightly: "Wonderful."

A kind word was all he needed. He was off. "I liked the Vietnamese when I got here. I wanted to come, wanted to save them from Communism. Now I hate them. They're out to get us."

Over the rumbling engine and the sound of wind in the truck bed, the redheaded PFC shouted his stories into my ear. The people he'd come to defend had stolen his camera, jacked up the prices the minute they set eyes on his GI butt, and sold him down the river for a buck.

"I just want out of here. I want to go home."

I listened to the dejected nineteen-year-old. We were five years apart. We shared a generation, but educationally and socially we were strangers. I wondered: Was it easier back home to stomach a war where only our undereducated and poorly nourished were maimed, defeated, or killed? Did we discount their bewilderment because they hadn't sufficient words to express it or the economic clout to make themselves heard? I heard the redheaded boy and I grieved for him.

Willingly, Bill, Murray, and I climbed into any passing vehicle whose driver consented to fit three more bodies inside or out. It wasn't necessary to screen for psychopaths. Ironically, this was safer than hitchhiking in America. Every ride offered, we accepted.

Twice though, we hesitated—room for just one. Then we agreed to separate.

"Meet you at—" we shouted and climbed onto separate Hondas, later into individual US Army jeeps.

The GIs in my jeep stared hard at me. I was somewhat tired of amiable prattle, so I slunk back into silence in the rear seat. I had turned down the privilege of a front-row seat next to the driver. But the driver wasn't so easily discouraged. He leered over his shoulder, "I couldn't *believe* it. I saw you standing there and man, I couldn't believe you were for real."

I smiled mildly, feigning humility.

"Cambodia?" he asked. "Do you have a pistol?"

"Nah, I don't carry—"

"Are you crazy? What if you get stopped by the VC?"

I was glad to be out of the jeep, reunited with Bill and Murray. I repeated the warnings.

Despite his placid demeanor, Bill had his own demons, and he'd burned the midnight oil figuring out a system to foster our release if captured. To that end, he forbade our wearing fatigues. His system involved assurances that we were noncombatants, journalists (*bao chi*)—neutral. All true enough.

He speculated. The toughest part would be the first couple hours of captivity. If we made it past those, he said, we'd have it made. It wasn't in the Viet Cong interest to kill correspondents.

I heard Bill out. Silently, I rebutted. Tell that to an ignorant foot soldier with a rifle to your head and no common language.

The trick, according to Bill, lay in being calm and docile and getting past the low-level grunt who couldn't distinguish the political liability inherent in killing an American or British journalist. The trick was to get passed up the ranks to headquarters, where they knew the political value of a captured reporter, returned.

Murray scoffed at Bill. "Poppycock. Reasoning with the unreasonable."

I humored Bill with silence, but his words were much too theoretical for my taste. At twenty-four, I knew better than to believe I had the vaguest notion how I'd respond to a gun held against my temple, or to capture.

Bill's Vietnamese language was all we had between us. It was not terrific, but he'd been dating a Vietnamese woman for six months so we granted him the honors. Not one of us spoke Cambodian. Brashly, we didn't think it mattered.

Route One ran seventy miles from Saigon to the border. It was a narrow, one-and-a-half lane paved road without a center line. It cut through rice paddies, grazing land, rich green grasses. The main road passed dozens of village turn-offs—smaller dirt paths. We stayed on the straight and narrow.

It was only one o'clock in the afternoon when we reached the border crossing into Cambodia. The sky was blue, the sun intense overhead. There wasn't a single cloud and almost no shade. We carried our bags to the tiny shed that passed for the official Vietnamese-Cambodian customs office in that remote outpost and Bill knocked on the dirty window set into a rusty door. He turned his dazzling smile and his rudimentary Vietnamese on the young customs officer. The officer had roused himself from a sunken armchair and answered Bill's Vietnamese in French.

"No crossing without proper papers," he insisted.

"Of course, monsieur," Bill said and gathered up our passports.

"These are not right."

Bill collected our Vietnamese press passes and handed them to the man who stood to the middle of his chest. Bill, well over six feet; the officer, about five feet two. Bill never stopped smiling; the man never began. He frowned and shook his head resolutely. "No!"

Bill offered the expected bribe that every Vietnamese civil service transaction required, 1,000 piastres per bureaucrat. You couldn't *leave* Vietnam without greasing palms. It was a process that made me uncomfortable and I was grateful for Bill's dexterity. But this time, it made no difference. The answer remained implacably, "No."

It seemed we were not to pass without the express written permission of General Do Cao Tri, commander of the Vietnamese invasion forces in Cambodia. We had no idea if acquiring that permission was a reasonable possibility or a pipedream. Disheartened, we agreed to head back to the road and stick out our thumbs. We needed a ride to Tay Ninh, fifteen kilometers north.

"Since when aren't passports transit between countries?" Murray griped.

I echoed his frustration. "A letter from General Tri?!"

"Bureaucrats will be bureaucrats." Bill tried to pacify the troops.

General Do Cao Tri waited out the late afternoon rain under a temporary shelter in the military complex at Tay Ninh. He was as jubilant as the crossing guard had been dour. He was delighted to speak with us—in English to boot.

"I like being a hero," he chuckled good-naturedly, describing his post as liberator of Cambodia. "I'm in no hurry to leave Cambodia. But of course," he moved fast to cover his rear, "that will be decided in Saigon."

The husky, round-faced Tri called the Viet Cong "completely disorganized." They were far too weak, he said, to stage a counterattack on the Cambodian territory that ARVN now occupied.

"I wish they *would* ambush us," General Tri goaded between leisurely inhalations off his cherry pipe. He was confident his troops would hold firm.

He admitted a downside: the intransigent Vietnamese refugees still living in Cambodian border territory. "Don't talk to me about them," he implored. "They are my headache. They tell me, 'We won't move unless you kill us.'"

"Tri described his recalcitrant countrymen's refusal to return to Vietnam as though their threat was an entirely possible solution," I wrote later for *Time*.

The general was more than willing to write a letter for each of us—rather, to sign one. He'd ordered his adjutant to type it up. His letter granted us full access to Cambodia—anywhere, anytime. He wanted us to see what he had accomplished. He was proud that it now lay within Vietnamese authority to grant entrance to Cambodia.

We hit the road again at around five o'clock.

At 7:00, we were just seven kilometers from an unknown speck on the map: Go Dau Ha, South Vietnam. We'd been defeated by impending nightfall, and heading, we hoped, back to Saigon for an early start the next morning. But we were nowhere near it, nor near much of anywhere else either.

What had begun as a free-flying venture into the bucolic Vietnamese countryside was hardening in the pit of my stomach into dread. The morning's confidence had evaporated. There were few ironclad givens in the Republic of Vietnam, but one of them was this: No matter what part of the countryside the American military claimed to have *pacified*—pulled under its protective belt—none of their claims amounted to squat after the sun had set. After dark, every road between towns, cities, and villages belonged to the enemy. After eight o'clock, roads were said to be *closed*. Sometimes barbed wire was stretched the width of a roadway to prevent passage or to remind the ignorant of the obvious. Bill, Murray, and I never planned to be out after dark—let alone on foot.

Taking Risks

Our backup plan—to settle into a large town by nightfall—was looking pretty pathetic. The combination of the inflexible border guard, our retraced steps to Tay Ninh, and the opportunity to interview the proud General Tri to get our papers stamped had eaten away at our plan, and our time.

Desperate for a ride, we'd foolishly hopped onto one of the few trucks leaving Tay Ninh at that time of day and headed southeast, without asking how far the driver was going. He was headed only to where we now sat, the dirt cut-off to the soldier's village home—seven miles north of Go Dau Ha. Nowhere. A beautiful nowhere, to be sure.

We sat by the edge of the narrow road on the grass. Over the hill from us, the red ball of sun was about to plunge invisibly behind the vivid green hillock. A young shepherd was calling in his cows for the night. The boy, who paid us no mind, counted the calves and smacked a stick against his thigh directing them home. Feeding time was over. Truly, it was a scene, fanciful and idyllic.

With a tent, a sleeping bag, and a couple of good friends, it'd be the perfect spot to camp for the night. Except we had only the friends—and this perfectly beautiful spot sat in the middle of someone else's war.

"*Seven Klicks from Go Dau Ha*," Murray ruminated. "It's a fantastic title for a novel."

"Perfect," I agreed. I welcomed any fantasy that promised to tranquilize my abdominal spasm. We tripped off on the wonderfully distracting fiction of would-be novelists. Murray had discharged his responsibilities; he had Bill and me chortling—belly-loosening hiccups of laughter.

But it was short-lived. A multiple crack of rifle fire just over the hill broke the moment. We snapped to attention, and silence.

Bill took charge. "Stay low, stay quiet, and cover that white shirt with this." He handed me some dark fabric thing he'd pulled from his bag.

The sky was streaked red and orange. I focused hard on the imagined novel. It was in film production in my head now.

And then, from *another*, undoubtedly fictional, world: I thought what I was looking at was an apparition—as unlikely as a phantom oasis in an arid desert. What I saw and disbelieved was a small blue pickup truck with a Korean driver and passenger.

I could distinctly identify Koreans because they were our warring allies, and because I saw them daily headquartered behind Bob's office in Saigon.

The mirage of a blue truck stopped in front of us. Two civilians—blissfully ignorant of curfews—were headed for Saigon. We jumped in the back, flattened our stomachs to the truck's bed, and huddled against the night and the now drizzling rain. Monsoon rains came up that quickly

The ride was perfect, fast. "We're going to make it," Murray whispered against the darkness. I could feel my spirits rise—almost soar—with the miles passing underneath those little Toyota tires. I echoed, "We're going to make it!" There were occasional shots in the near distance; we'd flatten an impossible inch or two more, and stop whispering. But we were ebullient.

Our luck ended abruptly. The little blue apparition stopped dead. No sputters, no warnings—it stopped. We were at the edge of a cluster of thatch huts, only questionably a village. The men hunkered under the hood looking for a problem or a solution—either would have marked progress. I stood to the side and watched. Their multilingual incantations accomplished nothing.

It was 7:30, and a dozen people from this hamlet with no known name had gathered around us. By 7:40, their circle had grown thicker and tightened around the truck. It was an utterly silent band, only five feet distant and about nine feet deep in all directions and still growing—a village, indeed.

Bill forced a smile. I nodded solemnly to the expressionless faces. Murray and the Koreans kept their backs turned on the growing crowd. It was closing in on full dark. My entire torso, shoulder to pelvis, stiffened. Silently, I asked myself, What *now*?

No sooner had that thought crossed my mind than the crowd around us split like a knife in a pie, a thin wedge opened in the circle, and into the opening swaggered another kind of apparition: a huge, beautiful, blond hunk of southern MP.

"Kin Ah help you, Ma'am?"

"Can you?!"

The MP was en route to Cu Chi when he'd spotted the crowd and braked. Headed home to headquarters for the 25th Infantry Division, the American unit shouldering the yeomen's share of the Cambodian operation. We went home with him.

The Korean civilians chose to stay (against all insistence) with their stalled truck. The quick ride to headquarters in the open jeep was a breeze—two men with machine guns, and us.

We gobbled down pepperoni pizza and listened to mediocre American rock and roll at the officers' club in Cu Chi that night. I slept under homemade quilts next to stuffed teddy bears in a Red Cross Donut Dolly's bedroom on base. She was gone a few days, serving up baked confections and board games to "our boys in Saigon." These were the women who had cheered our troops and buoyed morale since World War II. Inside her frilly bedroom, I scoffed: Another kind of woman, altogether. Within the contradictions of my callow youth, *sisterhood* still lay dormant. But I slept in her bed like a log.

Across the national border in Cambodia the rides along Route One were fewer and farther apart. But the wait between transports was charged and titillating. In some ways, the land was exactly as pastoral as it had been in Vietnam except that this was a work in progress—and the progression was toward destruction.

It was one hundred miles from the border at Tay Ninh

northwest to Phnom Penh. The towns we passed—Chi Phu, Prasaut, Svay Rieng—were familiar to me, the names of recent battles. The smoke was still fresh, thin columns of soft, white mist rising from the ashes, the smells of burning thatch. The thatch smelled innocent, like a dry wood fire anywhere.

The smell of burning humans was more sinister, and utterly unlike anything I'd ever breathed. My stomach heaved close to my throat. I didn't pay attention to Bill or Murray. I was caught up in my own horror. I sat down on the rubble when my knees got wobbly. I drifted off by myself when my eyes started to sting. We silently respected one another's private responses to the smells and the revelation of ruin.

The path of desecration that we followed from point A to point B—like daily accounts in a newspaper—was our side's breadcrumbs: the American and South Vietnamese military trail. The Liberation Front armies had lived clandestinely in this part of Cambodia for years. They had burrowed into forests, under hillsides, and into the hearts of the indigenous people. They were virtually invisible still.

"Guerilla warfare didn't leave monuments," I later wrote. "Americans, on the other hand, had torn up South Vietnam as much with the construction of military compounds to house, feed, and entertain our troops as with the war. Now our military marked its high-tech passage through Cambodia and left sharply delineated calling cards."

Chi Phu, particularly, etched a line of scar tissue on my central nervous system. The village was a hollow shell. One wall was left standing to a single house, and that one was riddled with bullet holes. A girl around six years old rummaged through the ruins. The rest of the citizens were dispersed, or dead. I followed her at a distance, watched her peck and paw through the ashes. For what? I only imagined. A doll . . . a pet . . . a favorite blanket?

I moved through the town, hiding behind my camera and

snapping photographs—the dazed reflections of a shell-shocked child. I was a professional observer, but I didn't yet know how a seasoned professional was expected to react. Were there protocols for responding to annihilation?

I will not be a girl!

In every exact detail, life here had been brazenly interrupted. Scraps of human habitation: four chair legs severed from their seat; a woolen blanket shredded and dunked in mud; a ceramic bowl cracked in two; a book of poetry torn from its jacket, but otherwise intact—Cambodian words arranged in stanzas. Lovers, mothers, teachers, and artists: lives—lived with ambition, jealousy, compassion, or generosity—ended. A village, a home, a leg. Remnants all. It felt surreal. I wanted out of there *now*.

Not one of us—Bill, Murray, or I—spoke a word to the others in Chi Phu. We circled the excrement of warfare and then wandered back onto Route One when we were done. Wordlessly, we agreed to walk the straight roadway for a distance, to walk off the images plastered inside our eyelids. Minutes later, the village was behind us and the countryside looked miraculously intact. A farmer pulled his hoe down a crooked row. His wife pulled vegetables from the bottom of a soggy swamp.

The rides were sporadic on this second day. Our exuberance had ebbed. We'd been slower and more introspective all morning. There were few four-wheel vehicles heading to Phnom Penh. Hondas were common, and we took short lifts on them.

In each town, we would ask about the security of the road ahead. Every time without exception, we were told that the bridge ahead of us was blown and that the road was impassible. In fact, I counted sixteen blown bridges between the border and Phnom Penh. Alternate routes took us onto muddy river beds and through tiny hamlet bypasses.

Our first sight of a military convoy along the road was a

Vietnamese Army expedition. We were sprawled on the edge of the hard-packed dirt road outside of Prasaut nibbling a lunch we'd brought with us from Cu Chi. I was reading my John MacDonald. The lead jeep in the convoy was driven by an American sergeant and carried the senior American advisors to the Vietnamese unit, a colonel and a major.

We jumped to our feet, waved vigorously at the balding colonel and his overweight chauffeur. We were, after all, Western civilians in the middle of warring Cambodia—not an easy sight to miss or pass up. But they did. They whipped by us, did a quick double-take, and neatly averted their eyes, pinpointed ahead at the empty road. They didn't so much as lift an arm to wave.

"Assholes," Bill uncharacteristically seethed.

"Fucking full-bird colonel asshole," Murray clarified.

The convoy of jeeps, trucks, and armored vehicles flew past. But at the tail end of the line, a Vietnamese private pulled his jeep out of formation to the edge of the road. He shouted something we didn't understand, but from his exuberant gestures we figured it was along the lines of "Hurry up!"

He crammed us between and on top of his four comrades, and he rushed to catch up with the procession that had moved on ahead. The South Vietnamese military—to their great and lasting human credit and to their ultimate logistical failure—were not sticklers for military order.

We had gone a dozen or so kilometers and knew we were fast approaching the site where new fighting had been reported. We flew past clustered huts, isolated pagodas, and the occasional mom-and-pop commercial enterprise scattered across rice paddies. As we ticked off kilometers, my shoulder muscles tightened. I twisted my neck to loosen them. I looked around warily from the open jeep for signs, sounds, or clues as to what we were heading into. I was both thrilled to be finally moving ahead and at the same time vigorously resisting. I pressed both feet firmly on the floorboard in front of me, flattening an illusory brake and halting our progress into the war.

As though responding to my imaginary brake, the entire twenty-plus vehicle convoy screeched to a sudden and unexpected halt. I was fearful and curious and addressed my fears best—always—by taking action, *any* action. I hadn't yet harnessed, at that age, the power of doing nothing in the face of fear.

So I hopped over the lap of an ARVN private, cleared the side of the jeep, and began barreling questions: "Where are we? What's up? Who's calling the shots?"

The American colonel spotted me and then saw Bill and Murray. He turned beet red and tore over to his Vietnamese counterpart with the apparent order to "Get rid of them!"

One of the genuine ironies of this war was unfolding. The colonel was officially an *advisor* to this Vietnamese military unit and, much to his fury, he could order us nowhere. He was forced to convey his deep displeasure through the Vietnamese colonel.

But the sweet Vietnamese colonel had little stomach for antagonizing anyone. He said to Murray, ostensibly the most senior among us. "It is most dangerous one mile ahead; best you go back now." Murray pulled out his letter from the colonel's boss General Tri authorizing us to be exactly where we were. The colonel was duly impressed. We stayed.

Still, the reason for stopping eighty men just a mile shy of the fighting was elusive. The soldiers milling around us were as much in the dark as we were. We didn't have long to wait for an answer. The American colonel wanted to take snapshots. He'd pulled eighty soldiers over to the side of the road in a conspicuously dangerous spot so he could take pictures of an exceptionally lovely Buddhist pagoda.

"Here." He cocked his Instamatic and passed it into the hands of his sergeant chauffer. "Me and the colonel," he ordered. And the two colonels, Vietnamese and balding American, stood erect and not touching, framed by the pagoda and grinning for the camera. Then it was the major's turn: same spot, same pose.

I was blown away by the audacity. But the young soldiers—and Murray—were laughing hard. Photographic buddy-buddy, then back to their separate but somewhat less than equal battle stations. This was how it was done.

The war was all around us but the fighting was elusive. Either it had already rolled over the towns we passed through and we'd record the puzzled faces and limp words of the survivors—or it was still hovering ominously on the horizon.

We left the convoy at Svay Rieng.

From Svay Rieng to our planned destination, Phnom Penh, Bill negotiated a ride in a Peugeot. The owner of the car sold seats to passengers for the equivalent of a dollar. He asked us for five times that amount. Bill had compromised at $3 apiece. "We take up more space."

Eager to make a goodly profit, the man sold seats in his very small station wagon to twenty-five people. Granted, two were infants, a good number children, and three of the men sat on the roof; nevertheless, it was a stretch. Squeezing an inhalation or exhalation took up more than my allotted space. The very old man who shared the front seat with me, Murray, Bill, and the driver teetered on the edge of passing out.

There were other inconveniences: the Cambodian Army's every two-kilometer road checks. It seemed that each young Cambodian male with a set of fatigues and nothing much to do that afternoon put a stick across the road and declared it a checkpoint. Because we were foreigners, crossing the checkpoints became an ordeal. At each stop, one or two soldiers would try their best to make out the words on our inscrutable passports. This was *not* the place to show a Vietnamese general's letter of permission.

Meanwhile, their comrade would rifle through the bags we handed out over the old man's head. Murray kept up a steady stream of deprecating checkpoint humor, secure that no one else among us spoke English. I had neither the room nor the inclination to laugh. I felt guilty for impeding the progress of the other passengers, but they were uniformly patient and remarkably kind to us.

For that reason, I was stunned when we were unceremoniously dumped out of the car in midafternoon. We were way short of Phnom Penh. The driver left the three of us and our bags by the side of Route One with a few peremptory gestures and *no* attempted explanation in any combination of languages we shared—neither French nor Vietnamese. The car turned into a nameless place, a rural cut-off from the main road, unmarked on our map. He took a sharp left into a car-width path through the rice paddies.

We stood dazed and abandoned and kissed our $3 each—and any chance of reaching Phnom Penh by nightfall—goodbye.

"What *now*?" I asked aloud this time. None of us had an answer.

We watched two Cambodian men and two women walk toward us along the edge of the road. They had big smiles, like almost every Cambodian we'd encountered so far. Our welcome had been uniformly warm. This time, the greetings were in French, Vietnamese, and even a bit of English.

"Good day. *Bonjour*."

"Hello," I tried English.

"You are American? Where are you going?"

"Phnom Penh, but our driver left us here. Turned down that road."

"There is a reason."

"A reason?"

"It is Liberation Front-held territory; you would have been harmed." This was said without expression or judgment. There was no way of guessing the politics of our conversant.

"Oh."

"Last week, three Americans, two men and one woman—like you—were taken from this place."

My heart tightened. Journalists Mike, Elizabeth, and Richard missing for a week and unaccounted for in Cambodia. My God, where were they now? Dead? Alive? Within shouting distance of us?

The rice paddies on either side looked less ordinary than they had a minute before. I wanted nothing more than to cry. But that was never a real option. I looked over at Bill and Murray. They looked unflappable. Did I?

A half hour passed. We began to make out the bare outlines of something moving up the narrow path through the field, where all things, animate and inanimate, seemed to vanish forever. In the dead flat distance, the motion through the paddy took on the shape of a car, then gradually became recognizably *our* car, and finally materialized fully at our feet.

The passenger door flew open. The old man pried himself from the front seat and we were invited to climb back inside. We squeezed in as directed. Not a single word was offered, or requested, about the detour.

Navigating the road itself became increasingly arduous. Land mines were sprinkled along the dirt and rock roadway like dandelions in a suburban yard—with that predictability and inconsistency. The mines were camouflaged poorly to look like fallen tree branches or with what, at first glance, seemed to be a piece of cardboard litter. But tucked under the limbs, leaves, or cartons was enough explosive to leave serious questions about the size and shape of the vehicle we'd been riding in when we passed over it.

I'd suck up my breath and hold it long after our driver had crept around the explosives.

Twenty-five years later, I would still hold breath, squint eyes, and harden my hold on the steering wheel when I couldn't avoid hitting a piece of cardboard or a tree branch on an American freeway.

The road was just a couple of feet wider than our jeep to begin with, and the recurring obstructions were unfailingly placed so as to force us within a hair's breadth of natural barriers: a three-foot-deep drainage ditch in one place; a wall of enormous trees in another. The choices were invariably grim and relentless.

I remember the last pontoon bridge between the border and Phnom Penh because, remarkably, it was still standing. But positioned on top of the only intact bridge we'd encountered along Route One in Cambodia was an enormous Shell Oil truck. Routed to deliver gasoline even in warring Cambodia, it was hopelessly stuck. The cumulative wisdom of the two dozen drivers backed up behind the truck and in front of us hadn't yet figured a way to dislodge the behemoth.

The alternative was the mud road that had been built up into the river. Impetuously, we pulled around the line of parked vehicles onto the river road—and got irrevocably stuck ourselves. I got out and watched in amazement as our spinning tires dug riverbeds of their own in the mud and water.

Working as one, we twenty-five passengers (less infants and children in arms) put a hand or two against the Peugeot and pushed that car into the river. I slogged with the others through thigh-high muck. The river was shallow, torpid, and thick. I struggled (shoeless now) to stay on my feet on the slippery river bottom as I shoved at the semi-floating station wagon. It was like searching for traction in a landslide. Again and again, I slipped and fell. I was drenched, disgustingly muddy, crusted to my chest,

Girls Don't!

exhausted, and sweating from the exertion. My reserves were dwindling. It was a day seemingly without end, an adventure without redemption.

Was it only last night that we'd huddled on the darkened road outside of Go Dau Ha? Just this morning when we poked through the ruins at heart-numbing Chi Phu? This very afternoon—agonizing over our missing friends down a road through the paddies?

Phnom Penh had become the carrot at the end of a consistently shifting stick. The Phnom Penh I remembered was resplendent, unaffected, and gentle. Did it still exist? Had it ever? Was this countryside of blown bridges, flattened hamlets, ravaged families, and hidden land mines the same nation I'd cherished? Was it even of the same universe?

Our last geographical challenge was the Neak Loeung ferry crossing over the Mekong River. Neak Loeung, where Vice President Ky had boasted to the press corps the previous month of the Vietnamese military's intended entrenchment. The ferry was the sole means to cross the wide brown river. But when we reached the shore, the ferry was "temporarily" and inexplicably "out of service."

It was late afternoon, and I was far less willing to find Murray amusing when he looked across the river at the stalled ferry and said, "It makes the *African Queen* look like the *Queen Mary*." I was pretty sullen.

But we waited just an hour. A suddenly, enigmatically recommissioned ferry carried us to the other shore, and the Peugeot took us that last stretch into Phnom Penh. The elegant city was hidden by nightfall.

I declined the invitation to join Murray and Bill in the Hotel Le Royal bar where they regaled our colleagues (who'd taken commercial jets from Saigon to Phnom Penh) with an account of our trip.

"You don't know what you're missing," I heard Murray gloat to the tableful. I headed up for a hot bath, a quiet room-service dinner, and the silence of my own thoughts. I'd reached the bottom of my emotional reserves, and I couldn't scrape up enough stamina to be one of the boys over a couple of beers in the courtyard bar.

The bath felt sufficiently hot and totally indulgent; my muscles slacked for the first time in . . . was it just *two* days? Within seconds, the huge porcelain tub looked like the muddy Mekong. I barely summoned the energy necessary to climb out, empty the water, and start over again. My thoughts tonight ran only toward muscle ache, hunger, and exhaustion—my physical needs. The more ethereal ones—victims and victories, bruised hearts and scarred souls—would have to wait.

Phnom Penh was every bit as beautiful and decent as I remembered her three months ago. She was a little hotter, perhaps, but blooming still with brilliantly colored flora and shaded with massive branching trees. It was a small town still, not yet a city, and its people were open and genuine.

Only *now*, there was a black market, armed boys in uniform on every corner, and the beginning of a displaced refugee population crowding the streets. The word "Royal"—as in, Royal Cambodian Post Office—had been blacked out on every bank and government sign. It was a new, more oppressive government trying to obliterate the memory of the former kinder one. I thought about all of this for the week I was there and I resolved none of it.

Phnom Penh surprised me most with its remoteness from the unfolding events in the countryside. The city surprised and heartened me with its refusal to change. But the destination had never, in fact, been the point of our trip—only the tangible reassurance at the end of it.

We had set out to trek the slow, treacherous ground route, to see and feel the land, its people, and what they each looked like at this exact moment in history when war was transforming them. We had set out with no specific goal in mind, unless happenstance is goal enough. We had asked, "What are the American and Vietnamese troops doing in—and to—Cambodia?" We had gotten our answers.

Murray stayed on. But I flew home with Bill in my first-ever "Loach" (LOH—Light Observation Helicopter). It was a tiny glass bubble with a tail, from which I could see forever: see the narrow dirt roads we'd walked; feel the remembered sun baking my parched dark hair and my dry tan cheeks.

I looked down now from a tantalizingly safe distance over this nation so newly at war, at a Cambodia born again in the imaginations of presidents and generals. And, I realized, me too—born again into mega-macho journalism. I was collecting my chits and proving I belonged beside my colleagues—or next to my brothers.

Only I'd just begun to doubt whether that was enough.

CHAPTER 9

FACING DEMONS

JULY 1970

So far, twenty-three journalists had been captured in Cambodia, three killed. Most often it was the photographers who put their cameras and bodies in harm's way. A few of the photojournalists were legendarily fearless: Sean Flynn, Tim Page, and Dana Stone.

We reporters would laugh and call them out: "Weird nutcases." We'd accuse them of courting death. But we'd say it with the deepest admiration, even awe. They set the standard for the rest of us, defined the outer edge of courage. Esteem—by the rules of this game—went to the guy who jumped fastest into the conflagration, with pure gut instinct and no second thoughts.

Sometimes those heroes emerged from the inferno, sometimes they did not. When they did, they often had the goods—incredible photographs of events I could only struggle to put into words.

By the time I was five years old, I was afraid of a remarkable assortment of things: massive and puny dogs, flying and crawling insects, lightning. I was afraid, too, that burglars would climb up the walls of my house, open my window, and slide inside my bedroom. I was filled with unspecified fears, and I secretly sucked my thumb until I was almost ten—to the shame of my parents.

My mother and father dealt with my fears in very different ways.

Bugs terrified me. It had nothing to do with stings, bites, or pain, all reasonable worries. Glowing green-and-black houseflies were monstrous, erratic. That was enough.

On an unexceptional August afternoon, hot and muggy, my mother handed me a black rubber fly swatter with a foot-long wire handle and locked me outside the kitchen door onto our back porch just above the garbage cans.

"If a fly comes near you, kill it." She gave me her best advice and sent me to war. My mother—who loved me always—believed then and forever that fear was something you overcame, conquered, or, at the very least, denied. "You can't give in to it," she told me.

She listened to my terror, my screams, and witnessed my tears with just a screen door between us for more than an hour, while I dodged a host of monster flies drawn to our garbage. She kept her back turned on my fingers clawing at the thin screen door and she prepared dinner.

"Don't break the door," she said once.

Just before my dad came home, she relented and let me inside. I hadn't squashed a single fly. The gore would have been intolerable.

My father dealt with my fears in another way.

During summer thunderstorms, I hid. I crawled under my bed, box springs pressed into my back. My father found me there one night and peeled me out gently from the underside of the mattress. He held me tight against his huge shoulders, in his massive arms, and whispered.

With very few words, he cradled me and convinced me to let him open the window.

"I'll stay with you."

It was never so much the words my father spoke that made things better; it was the touches. "You're affectionate," my mom repeated as a mantra, "like your daddy."

"Look!" my dad said, kneeling next to the open window. "Look!" He held my just bathed body in cotton pajamas up against his chest, pressed to him and facing out. "Watch how beautiful it looks when the lightning shows it off. Look how bright . . ."

Slowly, I relaxed. Half a lifetime later, I still walk through a thunderstorm with awe and excitement.

I was the child of both my parents. I could hide my fears with the best of them. And years later, I could comfort Bob's as well.

Bob was a Spec 4 now, a Specialist Fourth Class. The promotion came with the territory. Any enlisted man who spent five months in country and hadn't yet killed an officer was automatically promoted. There'd been a minor ceremony that involved a photographer recording Bob's sergeant standing to one side of him pinning the new stripe on his shoulder, and his colonel, on the other side, shaking his hand.

When we'd get stoned, Bob and I would stare at that photograph and descend into fits of laughter. The snapshot was duly somber—and ludicrous.

What the promotion meant most of all was $70 more a month in pocket and $30 more a month mailed to his wife *back home*—an automatic deduction for any married man. If felt like a lot of money. The "home" part was going into an after-Vietnam savings account in Baltimore. The in-pocket part we put aside for Hong Kong next month. More and more, the promise of Hong Kong was keeping us sane.

Girls Don't!

"My colonel wants to see you," Bob dropped into the silence at dinner one night.

"Me? I'm not one of his soldiers. Give him my number at *Time*."

Bob did no such thing. A few days later he was called to the colonel's office again.

"Spec 4. Your wife knows I want to see her?"

"No, Sir! She's in the field this week."

"When she's back, I want her here!"

"Yessir!"

Together that night in the room, Bob repeated, "The colonel wants to see you."

"Who gives a damn? I'm a correspondent. If he's got a story, he can call my office. I've got no other business with him."

For me, it was clear principle. I was here as a reporter, not as a military dependent. Bob's superior officer had no claim on me.

But it was more than that. I'd always been knee-jerk in the face of authority. My brother once said, "Tell Inette where she *has* to go—and watch her go 180 degrees in the opposite direction." If the sign says "Do not enter" I will scale the fence. Tell me what a girl can't do—well . . .

But, of course, the colonel had a very clear claim on my husband. There was a third summons, another refusal. Then this: "Soldier. Tell your wife if she doesn't appear at 1300 hours tomorrow, you will suffer the consequences."

I wore my most serious and sedate navy blue sheath with the white stitching and appeared all smiles before Colonel Peterson.

"It's nice to meet you, Colonel. I understand you wanted to speak with me."

The colonel was no fool, and there was little chance he would be charmed by the wife of a drafted Spec 4. He cut to the chase.

"*Mrs.*—if anything from this office appears in *Time* magazine, your husband will be knee-deep in mud, humping the boonies. Do you understand?"

"Of course I understand. Colonel, it's been a pleasure."

To myself, I choked. What an arrogant bastard. He actually thinks *Time* cares about the Saigon provost marshal's office!

Colonel Peterson was not an anomaly. There were any number of jealous officers who gave Bob a rougher than necessary time because his wife was in Vietnam, and theirs—despite rank—were not. Unfailingly, Bob would get the longest work shifts, the bulk of twenty-four hour alerts, and very few days off. I felt responsible.

Always, Bob did what he was asked to do. But it cost him. The pettiness—the tiny minds and hearts that controlled his every move—exhausted and demoralized him. We were (had they not noticed?) fighting and losing a war. Yet there was time for this nonsense.

Line them up: lieutenants, captains, majors, and colonels. Staff sergeants, even. "Anybody," Bob said, "can tell me what to do." Still another new sergeant had ordered, "Get your hair cut!" This, just a day after he'd been to the barber. When told that fact, the new sergeant took a ruler to Bob's head and measured the longest hair from crown to neck. "It's five-inches soldier, regulation is three. Get a haircut!"

But for Bob, the Army was a familiar tableau. He'd been long bullied by a patriarchal tormentor who predictably acted from an absence of reason.

At the first dinner I was served in Bob's home in San Jose, I was charmed by his handsome father, who focused the force of his dark blue eyes, long black eyelashes, and glittering smile on his son's girlfriend—as he'd no doubt done during World War II when he wooed and won the lovely, classy, Irish American nurse.

They served abalone in honor of my introduction to the family.

The dinner was delightful, and I thought then that the disconcerting family stories I'd heard from Bob in Italy were a distortion—heavily colored by a twenty-year-old breaking free. But I was wrong. By the second dinner, reality replaced company behavior. I saw the man Bob lived with.

Bob was a boy whose family sat around the maple kitchen table in silence. Only one person spoke—his father. And his father spoke like this.

"Whatsa' matter—you don't like broccoli?!"

"Don't want any," the night's chosen child mumbled somewhere below audible.

No one could predict who'd be targeted for the evening attack. Bob's raging father (angrier with every glass of wine) would strike like lightning.

"You don't know what's good for you! Take some!"

There was no refusing. Only one child in five refused, and he was locked into that refusal for life. But it was not Bob. Bob was the oldest son, the second child, and he could only comply and hope in his heart that the compliance would lead to a note of gratitude or kindness.

I, for one, could not, after the abalone, swallow food at their dinner table.

So, for Bob, "No salad? You need more!" meant he filled his plate and ate every unwanted forkful. His father ladled rage and lettuce onto his son's mashed potatoes.

"I was taught to clean my plate," was the first family thing Bob told me. It was different in my home, where each child had a dinner prepared to his particular taste and cut into bite-sized pieces—until we went to college.

Around Bob's family table there was insufficiency—seven mouths to feed on a postman's salary. But most essentially, there wasn't enough of their mother.

"My mother loves kids," Bob said simply. "She's on our side."

There were five of them, and every one of them was a gift from God to warm his mother's cool, dim life. Then there was his father.

She punished him each year with a new baby, newly loved. He punished her with his silence and his parsimonious heart. He never raged at his wife; he poured that onto her children. The kids were the rag dolls between them. The lines were drawn.

Because there was no trace of insubordination in Bob—his pre-Army bohemian clothing, long hair, and shaggy beard had less to do with defiance than with self-expression—the US Army had its perfect grunt. Except for this one thing. Bob was a very intelligent man who detested idiocy and loathed pettiness. He didn't mind authority so much as he resented stupidity.

I watched Bob being worn down by the Army and I summoned everything in my power to reverse the effects. I was Bob's best audience.

I saw him challenged by a redneck lieutenant's sarcasm. "Hey, *city boy* . . . do you know where that thing comes from?" They were staring at a gigantic beehive encrusted with the honey of a thousand worker bees.

Bob snapped, "From the biggest bee you've ever set eyes on. *Sir!*"

I loved his wit, laughed easily at his word play, and told him so.

He answered, "Yeah, right."

He'd dismiss my compliment and refuse to say "thank you" because that might mean he actually believed it. If he believed it, then he'd have to judge himself insufficiently humble.

If it had always been an uphill climb to affirm him, now, under the weight of his acquiescence to the military, it was a vertical climb up a glacier. I never stopped trying to love Bob into happiness.

Sometimes, doing everything within my power required

breaking a couple rules—or simply ignoring a few of the military's unremitting regulations.

Anticipating our R&R the first week in August, Bob asked his mother to send him a stack of real clothes: his blue jeans and sports shirts, blazer and khakis, Converse high tops and Weejuns. They'd arrived, and I for one could find no reason to let them sit in the box until Hong Kong.

"Take off your fatigues, put on a pair of jeans, and let's go out to dinner."

"Uh, there's the small matter of the US Army."

Soldiers in Vietnam were strictly forbidden to wear civilian clothes.

"Who will know?"

"Any patrolling MP. Anyone who knows me."

"But they don't eat where we eat."

"I can't."

"Okay, just put on the jeans and that red Izod. Let me see how you look."

He was transformed. Color! There were roses in his cheeks, a sparkle in his eyes. In sum, he looked human. I wrapped my arms around his shoulders, gazed into his face from about four inches away, and then went all Scarlett O'Hara.

"Why, Bobby, I do believe you are the handsomest man I've ever set eyes on. Would you consider accompanying me to dinner?"

He went. Wooed less by my words, I am certain, than by his own image in the mirror. Six months of endless olive drab and jungle boots. In sport shirt, jeans, and tennis shoes, he looked like the college kid he'd so recently been.

But he was pretty paranoid. He kept studying faces on the street and in the restaurant for traces of recognition. "Oh, shit, is that Drucker?" The first night out was not relaxing.

But when that one went without a hitch, we tried it again,

and again. It became a part of our routine. As soon as Bob got off work, he'd crawl out of his fatigues and into his civvies, and we'd paint the town, or just cool out inside the room.

In civilian clothes for a few hours each week, Bob could behave like any other American citizen in Saigon. Without the uniform, the US military did not recognize its own. Without their recognizing him, Bob could think of himself as something other than a Spec 4.

The rare American soldier on a motorcycle, usually a passenger, was required to wear a helmet. Without one, he'd be stopped by an MP routinely and hauled off to the brig. Nobody *but* American soldiers wore helmets. There was little need. The traffic bottleneck typically crept along at five miles an hour. A GI on a motorcycle with that huge fiberglass helmet looked like an alien from some planetary war zone. The helmets were unbearably sweaty in 110 degrees. Bob hated his, but he wore it to and from work. Now, though, when he was out of uniform, he wore no helmet.

So we bent the rules. Let me count the ways. I was a *wife* in Vietnam, where military dependents were strictly forbidden. Bob slept, without authorization, in the home of a Vietnamese family; he was *required* to be in his BEQ (Bachelor Enlisted Men's Quarters). Bob eschewed the mandated uniform for blue jeans and tennis shoes. He drove a motorcycle without the required helmet.

For me, ignoring the rules was exhilarating. For Bob, who wasn't nourished on defiance, it was simply a way to breathe. In any case, there was no turning back.

On Bob's rare Saturday off, we ranged further and further. We rented an old wooden Chinese junk and floated blissfully down the Saigon River past the ancient shanties that hung precariously and picturesquely over the river's edge. We might have been tourists in any peaceful Third World country; we were that removed. Along that river, there wasn't a trace of American impact or aesthetic, yet we were barely out of eyesight of central Saigon. Just a hill separated us.

The junk's captain set his conical straw hat on my head to protect me from the sun. I thanked him, then moved it over to Bob. He was sure to burn without the protective Army cap. I snapped a picture of Bob in the too-small peasant hat. We were a couple of kids playing at sightseeing on a summer day in Saigon.

On another Saturday we took the ancient, semi-ailing Honda on its first distance trek about twenty miles out of Saigon—south on a narrow provincial roadway—so Bob could see something of the countryside.

We ate, squatting over rice and vegetables at a roadside café. I was smug that my American calves could balance me in a mealtime squat, exactly like the Vietnamese who were born to it. We stopped in a beautiful village with palm trees, exquisite gardens, and thatched houses and then wandered among the surprised villagers with our arms wrapped around each other's waists. We sat on the grass and watched the water buffalo graze.

"I hope the Honda makes it back to Saigon," Bob worried. He needn't have. The engine strained and coughed and the bike moved very slowly under our combined weight on the open road. But we made it back just fine.

One Saturday night, we put our head into the lion's mouth. With my press pass, the equivalent credentials of a major, I suggested that we go—Bob and me—to an officers' club for dinner and music.

"Are you nuts?"

"Nah, I'm allowed to bring a guest. You're in civvies. Who'll know?"

We went, ate enormous T-bone steaks cooked medium

rare, foil-wrapped baked potatoes with sour cream, salad with Thousand Island dressing, and three-layered devil's food cake. We emptied a bottle of California red wine, tapped our toes to jazz, and came home.

Sure, I was trying to nurture my husband's sanity, but I was also behaving true to form and having great fun doing it.

"Never again," Bob said, after that night. For him, it had been a mistake. It was not sport to frolic at the mouth of the beast.

Still in uniform after work one night, Bob—on a lark—suggested that we *both* go to his BEQ for dinner.

"They've all heard about you, they may as well see you."

"Are you sure?"

"Yeah—it'll be a trip."

I wore my bright red polyester pantsuit with the gold buttons. I was the only spot of red in the sea of olive drab. Three hundred enlisted men, privates to sergeant majors, waiting in line with plastic trays or sitting elbow to elbow along eight-by-two-foot tables.

Rows and rows of them without break under fluorescent lights and over linoleum floors—very young to very old, dressed in fatigues and hunched over trays of baked chicken, instant mashed potatoes, overcooked carrots, Wonder bread, and chocolate pudding. There was also milk.

Bob and I went to the end of the long line and there was a momentary stunned silence, then a roar of words. Every single one of the three-hundred faces turned toward mine and smiled broadly. They were just plain *happy* to see me, to see something familiar, to remember what America—home—still promised them.

I smiled back at them with all my heart, just a trifle embarrassed, and waved a little Queen Elizabeth royal wave. I saw the full flush of American generosity in these men's faces. It was a lovely evening.

"Please, after you."

The men passed me up the line and made way for Bob to follow. Not one of them could live with himself, it seemed, if he filled his tray before I filled mine.

"Thank you," I stammered. "Thank *you*. No, that's all right, I'll wait. *Thank* you."

"Please, Ma'am, after you."

The most complicated choice of the evening, after milk or coffee, was where to sit. Men all over the room were hailing Bob.

"Hey, man, there's room over here."

"Bob! Bring her to your own unit!"

The senior sergeant major settled it by insisting we do him the honor, and I was saddened by the need to choose a single table—the ranking enlisted man's at that. But during dinner and after, dozens of men, one by one, came over and exchanged a few words. They seemed compelled to make contact.

"Can you believe that passes for food?"

"Not home cooked," I laughed.

"I hope your dinner's not too cold."

"It's just fine," I smiled.

"Forgive our staring at you."

"I appreciate your kindness."

"It means a lot, you eating here with us tonight."

"The pleasure is mine."

Or to Bob: "Hey, Buddy, bring her back. Don't be selfish!"

And: "Bro, that's one fine woman."

Bob was flying high after our meal, proud of himself and proud of me. For one evening at least, he remembered how good it felt to be together in Vietnam.

Less than a week later, we went to my colleague's Saturday night dinner party. Bob had the day off, so we'd accepted the invitation. I don't think either of us looked forward to it. This one was at the home of a radio correspondent and his wife, who freelanced for *Brides* magazine. I mused. After the first Vietnamese wedding story, what on earth did she write? There were four other couples—all but us, male reporters and their wives.

Now, of course, I realize the wives of correspondents in Saigon had it pretty rough. There were almost no avenues to establish their own identities. They were in the shadow of powerhouse men driven by demanding jobs, obsessed with the war, and seldom home. There was little social life for these women, there were so few of them.

But at the time, I simply did not want to be mistaken for them. Uniformly, they joined the nearest thing to a country club, the Cercle Sportif. They played tennis, sunbathed, hired Vietnamese cooks and maids. They occupied very little firmament in their husband's world.

For me, there was nothing but confusion at these rare couples' dinner parties. For Bob, there was no place at all. Clearly, Bob was not one of them; he was a *draftee*, for God's sake. He wasn't even a ranking officer, and thus perhaps a potential news source.

Dinner conversation that night veered toward Cambodia. It was esoteric, and you would have had to have been to that country. Bob and the women had not.

"How long do you give Lon Nol?" someone asked over salad.

"Without US troops, less than the rainy season," another answered.

We left the downtown, fifth floor elevator apartment around 11:00 and headed home. The Vietnamese cook had done an extraordinary job with dinner. The spring rolls in particular floated off the plate. The flan dissolved on my tongue. I was satiated.

The streets were busy but not daytime packed. Bob drove. I sat sidesaddle behind, one arm loosely around his waist. We stopped, then started again at a dozen traffic lights heading up Tran Hung Dao. Neither of us attempted conversation over the traffic noise, so I heard them distinctly—sudden shots at very close range.

I heard their loud crack over the Honda's engine. Bob jerked the bike to a stop with the hand brake and his feet, burning shoe leather on the asphalt. He shoved me hard to the ground, plunged down full length on top of me, and pulled the bike on top of us both.

From that position on our backs, we both saw the tracer bullet etch its fluorescent path where our heads had been seconds before. We intuited the trail that the unmarked bullets followed.

We stayed in the middle of the boulevard exactly like that for some time. My heart rate was off the charts. I was sweating and my adrenaline was lighting the way out of there. I wanted to run. Bob stayed protectively on top of me and held me in place. His gut instinct had been to take care of me; my gut instinct was to trust him. We waited for the next burst of gunfire, but it didn't come.

Tentatively, he pushed the bike off of us; we sat up and breathed. Bob lifted his legs off mine and released me. We looked around, saw only a Vietnamese policeman armed and at the ready on the corner, and the beginning of traffic making its way around us.

I shouted to the policeman: "What happened? Who was it? Were we the target?" He smiled and shrugged; told us to get home before curfew. I was shaking hard and leaned into Bob's back when we climbed onto the Honda, not sure if the sniper had targeted us or we'd serendipitously stumbled into the path of someone else's trouble.

Even after we were in bed, holding our bodies together, I was scared. But with Bob, I didn't have to pretend I was not.

"Wild bunch" photojournalists Sean Flynn and Dana Stone were captured in Cambodia, then killed. Tim Page had taken shrapnel in his head in May, and surgeons excised a large chunk of his brain at Walter Reed. The losses among us were mounting. Thankfully, Mike Morrow, Elizabeth Pond, and Richard Dudman were released from Khmer Rouge captivity after forty grueling days.

Fearlessness remained the primary measure of a successful war correspondent. But I had begun to doubt if accepting that standard—if being one of the boys—was asking enough of myself.

The game looked increasingly empty; the results, perhaps inadequate. The search for physical risk as the preeminent measure of success led rather inconsistently to either incisive reporting or good storytelling. Those at the cutting edge of risk were neither the deepest thinkers nor the most compassionate humans. They were not necessarily the men most capable of weighing the social, economic, political, or military costs in front of their eyes.

I began to suspect I might have something more to offer *because* I was woman. *New York Times* correspondent Gloria Emerson had written—and later taken awards for—her deeply compassionate series on the Saigon streetboys: children who eked out a hardscrabble life by their considerable wits. Because of her work, the kids I stepped around—avoided daily for the rawness of their demeanor—became real to me and to Gloria's readers, too. They became somebody's children.

Why, in all these years, had no other reporter thought that story worth telling?

I hoarded my own first-person accounts, kept them from *Time*, and sent them to Phil in Annapolis. When I'd once shared my *Evening Capital* clips with a British colleague, he'd sneered at their intimacy and candor.

The story I sent Phil about hitchhiking in Cambodia was

very different from the one I gave Marsh. "With the approach of nightfall, my fears intensified. In the dark, snipers had free rein. A pitch-black bedroom without the blessed nightlight, I knew, had been the source of many childhood nightmares."

"Why would you write *that*?" my colleague ridiculed. I was unable to answer.

Bill Dowell, equally unenthusiastic, tried to explain the reaction. "When you put yourself into the story, it becomes less important."

CHAPTER 10

DRIVING RAINS

AUGUST 1970

The military's intent was neither sinister nor punitive. It was simply bureaucratic. But Hong Kong did not happen.

No doubt, Vietnam was unique in the annals of American wars in more important ways, but from the perspective of the typical draftee, the only two that mattered were: a *measurable* exit date (or DEROS) and R&R (rest and relaxation). In the thick of jungle warfare, every soldier was yanked out of his or her war for a single week, after which he was plopped back into the exact unit he'd vacated. He could choose to spend that week in Honolulu, Sydney, Bangkok, Taipei, Manila, Singapore, Tokyo, or Hong Kong.

Only three Air Force seats were allotted to Bob's battalion for August R&R in Hong Kong, and there were four applicants. Three men had been in country longer than Bob—one by a couple weeks, one by days. It was that simple. Our bags were already packed when we got the news: "R&R not approved. Permission denied."

I was crushed. Bob was inconsolable. There could be no measuring how much we'd lived for the time away from Vietnam. Hong Kong was the magic mountain. If we could get to it, then maybe we'd make it through the rest.

Bob turned taciturn and insisted we now put off R&R as long as we could stand it. "So the time left afterwards won't seem so long." He filed a request for November. Marsh's lavish Hong Kong apartment would be long gone.

We were just halfway through the obstacle course: six months behind us, six months ahead.

But even more wearing than the "Permission denied" were the continuous, interminable rains. Rainy season would be over in November. In August, we were in the thick of it.

Never in my life—before or after—have I known rains like those of August, September, and October in Vietnam. The skies opened; the torrent smashed down on our heads. There was no strolling through it, no dashing from place to place between showers, no feeling secure in raingear. It was diluvial. It had the force of the angry hand of the gods. What more appropriate place for them to serve up their displeasure than in Vietnam and Cambodia?

So instead of Hong Kong, we got monsoons.

On a Friday night, Bob and I got caught in one of those storms. We'd finished dinner and tried waiting it out in the small café for a half-hour, then an hour, then an hour and a half. "Two more espressos, please."

But it got late and there was no hint of letup, so we set out. We stepped out the door and into fist-sized drops. Less *drops* than columns of water, narrowly spaced and not so much *falling* from the sky as being pitched by the strong right arm of one of the greats. Don Drysdale or Tom Seaver come to mind.

Stupidly, we'd left our trench coats at Mrs. An's. But at some point we agreed, "It's just water," and turned our faces into the pitch. We mounted the Honda, the engine started up, and we drifted blindly through the pillars of water. By the time we'd gone a mile—still twelve American city blocks from home—we were drenched and, even in the unremitting heat, chilled.

Drenched doesn't do it justice either—too surface. We'd been pummeled so that our internal organs felt the thrust.

We turned the corner from a neighborhood street onto one of Saigon's wide, east-west boulevards. It was a thoroughfare that in any Western nation would count as a six-lane highway, with a center strip of parkland. Typically in Saigon that space had no lanes at all—neck to neck bicycles, motorcycles, and pedicabs—with cars and trucks thrown into the mix. Nothing was as contained or patterned as lanes, lines, sidewalks, or parkland.

Now the boulevard had become a thigh-high river flooded with rainwater and traffic. Hundreds of motorcycle drivers, headed in every direction, were trying to ride it out. We tried, too. We gurgled through water that covered the engine completely; we were making waves. We counted on inertia. How long could a moving motorcycle continue to move under water? We dared not stop; it'd be impossible to start up again.

Garbage floated past us, and possessions no longer possessed: Coke bottles, hats, eyeglasses. Bob took one hand off the handlebars, pulled his glasses from his nose, stuck them in his shirt pocket, and buttoned the pocket down.

Three blocks along the boulevard, the Honda failed. It choked, sputtered, and died. All around us, motorcycles were giving up the ghost. One by one they sputtered out a circle of current into the river and stopped. It was no longer so much a river with its small flotilla of outboard and inboard vessels; now it looked more like a scene out of *The Cat in the Hat*.

Bob was cursing, spitting out the rain, and *pushing* the bike through deepening, hip-high water. It was no easy chore. I was thankfully wearing pants, not a dress. I pushed myself alongside Bob but I was laughing—hard. I couldn't stop. Eventually I had to hang onto the Honda as well because the current and the uncontrolled hilarity threatened to suck me under. It was treacherous and at the same time absolutely ridiculous.

"Let me get a grip."

The streets were filled with Vietnamese men in silk pajamas or business clothes and women in *ao dai* and conical straw hats pushing dead motorcycles through resistant, deep water and maintaining better traffic patterns than I'd ever seen in Saigon. Everyone kept to the right of the center strip, off the sidewalks, and in lines. Hundreds pushed east; hundreds pushed west. We were part of a Seuss-like army connected by handholds to our de-motorized vehicles, slugging purposefully through the floating garbage on the lifeblood artery of this enormous city. Not a single soul expressed anger or frustration, and I was the only one laughing.

This, after less than two hours of rain.

There was no fighting the rainy season. There was no fighting *during* the rainy season either. Our lives in Saigon slowed measurably: slogging through the deluge, waiting out one storm or another, sitting in my bedroom for more hours than I'd ever had to—reading and listening to the pounding on the tin roof. It all felt like a giant metaphor for the winding down of the war.

Combat had virtually frozen in place. Neither side saw to its advantage heading into the mud for engagement. The only war casualties now were from land mines planted months or years before, and jeep accidents.

Driving Rains

The rain on asphalt streets in Saigon was nothing compared to the rain in the rice paddies, or in the jungle. In Saigon, within hours after a storm the rain had disappeared. It drained away. But the mud that covered the countryside was there for the duration. It was soft and deep. Even truck-tread combat boots or VC sandals wouldn't know when they hit bottom. Attempting to wage a war in fields of deep, unremitting sludge was agonizingly slow. Finally, the grinding crawl hardened in place. When the monsoons settled in for real, both sides gave up the effort.

"Hey, the war's ended and nobody knows it," Bob laughed. It felt true.

But within the silence, the brooding, and the absence of reported combat, there hovered a bottomless sense of foreboding among GIs and journalists alike. There flourished a suspicion that the enemy was holding back until the decreasing American troop strength hit its low point. Then, the other shoe would drop.

So the monsoon season was not a palpable, gentle, slowing down—a meditation and an invitation to peace. Rather, it was slow, like dangling from the swinging cage at the top of a Ferris wheel while the lower ones were unloaded. Slow, like paralysis in eight lanes of rush-hour traffic on the Washington Beltway. Slow, like a Saturday morning synagogue service when you arrive at 9:00 and feel your stomach rumble with hunger as it passes noon with no end in sight. Slow, like a drive across the country with two small kids. "Are we there yet?"

The killing war was dead. There was no pulse at all.

Bob went to an opium den. It seemed to be the thing to do. I wasn't invited, and I wouldn't have gone if I had been. It was a GI extracurricular activity. He went with his buddies to Cholon, the Chinese sector of Saigon. The opium den looked, Bob said afterwards, "exactly like you'd expect."

An ancient Chinese man with a wispy white beard and a very large brass water pipe supervised. Bob paid $10 MPC up front. It bought him an hour on the pipe. There were filthy foam pads around the floor, one per customer, and only one shared pipe. The room was a hovel.

"As dimly lit as a Bedouin's tent," Bob said. It was only slightly sheltered from the city's traffic noise and not at all from the sound of monsoon rain against the roof. But with his first suck off the magic hookah, all noise faded. The edges peeled off the sights, sounds, rain, and war. The path to opium illumination was entirely interior.

"It was veeerry relaxing," he intoned after.

Each man sucked in the magic and crawled off to his own place. Only men, maybe a half-dozen before Bob and his friends arrived, splayed around the edges of the room.

"Not like grass," he said. "No energy rush, no giggles, no sugar craving. No stream-of-consciousness insights—just reeeal peaceful."

Did I approve? Hell, no. Did Bob care? I think not. Was I afraid he'd suck up things that antibiotics couldn't touch? Sure. Was I terrified that he'd be addicted to the peace inside the pipe for life? Oh, yeah.

Early on in our relationship, I accepted my assigned role. I was the uptight, rigid one—afraid of experimenting with drugs or sex. Bob, on the other hand, was the open, curious one (if *deliberate*). It was what we agreed to, and I didn't challenge those assumptions for a very long time. Now, I see the irony. Who took the risks? Who was the impulsive one? Who was emotionally accessible? I also see the tyranny of assumptions.

There was so much that was tawdry about Saigon during the American occupation. It felt like poison fed through a hookah into the Vietnamese nation.

Prostitution was among the worst of the evils.

There was a desperation and madness about the adolescent-acting journalists who settled wives and kids in Singapore and then screwed street girls newly off the bus from the countryside. The girls were fourteen or fifteen, skinny, flat-chested; their luxuriant hair teased into beehives to look American; wearing miniskirts that barely covered their narrow hips instead of *ao dai*. *Street girls*, who were the sole support of a half-dozen kid sisters in the countryside—a place where they could never, ever return.

Like candid snapshots, a stream of reporters' faces passes mine now—small-minded, vulgar chauvinists. Men who were my colleagues; there's little point in singling them out. They ranged from thirty to fifty-five; there was no age limit on the zest for the chase.

There was never any way for me to excise the offensive parts of the conversations that circled around me; they were woven into the texture of the discourse. Braggadocio was part of the background noise.

"Shiiit, did you see that piece of ass I had last night?"

"Hell, Jack, that was no ass. It was an ironing board."

"Flat? Your whore couldn't fill a training bra."

But imperfect bodies did not deter them. I couldn't hope to silence them, and I couldn't avoid hearing them either.

I was a married woman and an American journalist. My struggles were ludicrously simple: just family and cultural expectations that were a poor fit. But the street girls had none of my advantages; they were denuded of power, self-respect, and choice. They were uneducated peasant girls who'd come to the city to support a family because there was little work in the fields strafed by war. The family offered up its extra mouth to the city—offered her a chance to improve their luck.

She paid a few piastres and climbed on a bus filled with farmers, chickens, and huge bags of rice strapped to the roof. She

Girls Don't!

stepped down at the Saigon bus station, a fourteen-year-old child, alone and confused.

I wrote for Marsh:

> At the bus depot, several old Vietnamese ladies lay in wait. One approaches the girl. She promises her a good job in a good home, and the child follows gratefully. The story is as old as the profession: The girl is imprisoned and raped. Ashamed, she can never return to her family. Almost every prostitute tells the same story.

GIs and foreign civilians lined up outside the bed-sized cubicles off Tu Do Street, waiting their endless turns to drop their pants and assault a child.

The girl was required to spread her young legs to whomever handed her the requisite $2. She passed the cash on to her pimp. He hailed the passing soldiers: "My sister is a virgin. You want to fuck her?" He ushered them inside. She was recompensed with a stream of heroin to dull the pain and to keep her compliant.

I walked Tu Do Street with my Vietnamese interpreter looking for girls who would talk. It took some doing. They'd look around fearfully to make sure their pimp was nowhere in sight and that there were no customers. They were shocked at my Western woman's interest; shy at first, but eventually pleased and relieved to talk.

I listened to five girls tell me their stories. It was a little past noon on a lazy midweek day when business was slow. They absolutely refused to let me pay them for their time. The girls were sleepy, druggy, and oh so terribly young. One would tell her story and the others would nod vigorously or giggle nervously. Then another would pick up the narrative.

She was a whore for life, each one told me. There was no return trip from that. "The girls live in fear that their families will find out the truth about their city job," I wrote. "They are at the mercy of pushers and pimps."

They could never again see the family they came here to save. They stepped off the bus with hope, but they were drowned in their shame. They wrote lies to their mothers and sent money to their fathers. They gave birth to children who were doubly despised: transparently half-American, half-whore. "Estimates place the number of prostitutes in Vietnam between 200,000 and 400,000," I wrote. "On the average, each prostitute had one illegitimate child, almost all by a foreign father."

I thought I broke ground with the story, just a small step in the right direction. I don't believe it occurred to my colleagues to look into the hearts and lives of the girls they hired for sex.

The GIs I forgave. They frequented the whores in ignorance, and in need. They'd rush to Tu Do Street on payday with a half-dozen buddies to get laid. They were kids themselves.

The journalists were harder for me to absolve. We were the tellers of the tale. We were the ones entrusted with the job to witness and speak the truth. It was our responsibility to tell the story of this exploited people and the defeat of their way of life.

In the middle of August, I jumped at the chance to get out of Saigon. My excuse was an assignment to Da Nang. Of course, Da Nang would be no less rainy, but it was a place I'd never been. The entire Saigon bureau was divvying up a story we'd proposed to New York. It was a rainy season story, to be sure—real stories were in short supply. We had to be creative. It was a story that could have been written six months before, or six months after. No one was fooled.

We were to examine the refugee phenomenon: the massive influx of population from country to city (farmers forced off of ancestral lands by American bombing raids) and the urban realities that resulted. I was assigned the Da Nang leg of the story.

To get to Da Nang—or any other place in Vietnam—I took a pedicab to Ton Son Nhut, flashed my press card at the military dispatcher, and asked if anybody was heading my way. I couldn't afford to be choosy about what I flew. Sometimes, I lucked out with a direct flight. Sometimes I grabbed whatever was heading in the general direction I was going and then hopscotched onto another plane or chopper from there.

Da Nang was an uncomplicated destination, the second largest city in the Republic of South Vietnam. There was always air traffic carrying mail, munitions, and whatever constituted daily military necessity. I was scheduled to fly again on an old World War II C-130, the war horse of Vietnam. They were hot and uncomfortable; it was like riding in a stifling tank. There would be no windows worthy of the name, just fold-out canvas slings for seats and deafening noise.

Seated in the airport waiting for the plane to refuel, I looked up from my book and saw a remarkably familiar face.

"Joey?"

"Inette!"

And then, in unison: "What are *you* doing here?!"

Joey had been my friend and mentor, a senior to my freshman, at the University of Wisconsin. *The Daily Cardinal*—where we'd worked together—was an independent, student-run college newspaper with a strong lineage of left-of-center reporting. It was a proud paper, with a defiantly outspoken staff.

Joey told me he'd come to Vietnam for just a month—as a freelance photographer—then back to Madison. We reminisced about the Dow Chemical riot, spring 1965. Dow—the manufacturer of the thick chemical gel that burned leaves off of living forests and skin off babies. Dow—the manufacturer of the napalm used *here*!

Five years before, a couple hundred students gathered outside a campus building where Dow held job interviews for its future employees. We chanted: "Dow off campus!" And then they tear-gassed us. It was my initiation into college life: the canister exploding, the smoke, the scorched eyes, and the subsequent chaos.

We laughed now, Joey and me, nostalgic during the fifteen minutes we had together before boarding planes in opposite directions. We slapped backs and hooted at the shared anti-war memories. We had *marched, sat in, slept in*—our opposition took every possible physical position.

Then, in the here and now, we swapped a quick hug, stepped out into the driving rain, and ran onto our separate planes heading into the heartland of Vietnam.

Already, at only twenty-four, I yearned for my simpler past: friends of my age who thought as I thought, believed what I believed, and didn't waste energy challenging each other's assumptions because we were too busy challenging the university's and the US government's.

Joey—and our brief shared reminiscence—was wreaking havoc with my conscience. I was feeling the first wave of defensiveness about my role in this war. In Wisconsin, and later at Berkeley, there had been no room for compromise. You were with us or you were against us.

Here, I worked for *Time*, and *wanted* to work for them. Here, I worked for a Republican bureau chief, an ardent supporter of the war—and I admired him. Here, I wrote stories that were so thoroughly rewritten in New York that only a few direct quotations remained of my intentions. I envied Joey his camera: a photograph was a photograph. Words, on the other hand, invited multiple interpretations and rewrites.

Here, my morality got tangled with my career and personal ambitions. Joey and the Dow Chemical riot were reminders of a time without confusion or compromise.

Girls Don't!

Da Nang turned out to be more than just a break in the monotony. It was actually a bit of an indulgence. I stayed at the Marine Corps Press Center on the edge of the South China Sea. The Press Center was infamous among journalists for how diligently the Marines catered to the needs of an erratic and demanding press corps. I'd heard that they served up the best: steaks, movies, pleasure boat at-dock, chauffeurs as needed, and girls. The stories were true.

Idiosyncratically, the building looked like a 1950s motel set right against the ocean. I had a clean room of my own, meals at the Press Center restaurant, Coca Cola at the bar, and I saw *2001: A Space Odyssey* in the theater for the third time. It was the first English-language movie I'd seen in Vietnam.

The Press Center was empty. Just a couple of correspondents were in residence. One, a forty-year-old American, had camped out at the Marine center well past the two-week limit on hospitality. I never saw him without bourbon in hand clanking ice, visibly working only on his next drink. The war was stuck in the mud. Da Nang, as the jumping-off point to the northern battlefields, was temporarily beside the point.

Come December, when the fields dried out, the dozen rooms would be booked tight; the party would be in full swing. My colleague, if he found his way back then, would not have to drink alone.

I wrote:

> The entire concept of cities is a new one in South Vietnam. Under the French, Da Nang was 25,000 people and a well-planned town with electricity and utilities serving the entire population.
>
> In the last five years, Da Nang has grown like a tumor. In 1965 there were 100,000 citizens in town. This year, there are 400,000; it grows still. When the countryside was bombed—no longer secure to work in the fields—villagers

Driving Rains

had the choice of starving or resettling in the urban centers which held the promise of both safety and jobs.

I was imagining the unimaginable. Tiny Annapolis, penned in by the Severn River and other natural barriers to growth, crammed over just a few years with the overflowing homeless from the nation's capital—literally filling every sidewalk, city park, and parking lot with shanties. It was like that in Da Nang.

Half the residents of Da Nang were squatters on public land. Alongside every city street on what at one time were sidewalks, I walked past both shanties and elaborate constructions. Whole neighborhoods grew up on vacant lots. Uniformly, they lacked electricity, toilets, running water, and garbage collection. The city was filthy; garbage was heaped on every corner.

The paradox: Da Nang had the potential to be a very lovely place. It was surrounded by green tree-covered hills and pure white beaches—a bay, a river, and oceanfront. But because so much of the surrounding land was now military reservation, the 400,000 were contained in an extremely limited space.

"The greatest urban need in Da Nang is clean drinking water," I wrote after I interviewed American economists and urban planners. "USAID [United States Agency for International Development] allocated funds for a two-million-gallon water purification plant with a pipeline to encircle the city. The pipeline was supposed to reach Da Nang last month, but somewhere along the route the pipe itself was diverted. It simply disappeared. Da Nang officials are 'searching for the pipe.'"

Sewers, too, were nonexistent; sidewalks made do as toilets. The city was punctuated with potholes, and when it rained hard, as it did now, rainwater and sewage were trapped together and flooded. I swatted mosquitoes everywhere. I took weekly malaria-inoculating pills, but the Vietnamese did not

The city lacked telephone service almost entirely. It lacked, too, its own newspaper. It was impossible to communicate health education, or much else either.

American bureaucrats loved to blame the long-gone French bureaucrats for retaining a strong central government in Saigon. I wrote: "'The French left the Vietnamese in a lurch, with no experience in local government,'" said Harry Fowler, a sincere but weary and impotent American and senior advisor to the mayor of Da Nang." Fowler also blamed the French division of labor. "'One person drives the fire engine. One person buys the gas for it. But neither would consider putting gas into the engine.'" Of course, it was easier to blame an absent villain than to take responsibility for a solution.

Even within the generalized malaise, torpor, and sludge of Vietnamese cities during the rainy season, the suffering in Da Nang was flagrant. Very simply, it stank. Da Nang was a gentle town bloated by hundreds of thousands of farmers who had no idea that city life didn't have to be like this.

Five days later, I returned to Saigon—this time in a posh, cozy VIP jet with passenger seating for just six. There were five of us: four full-bird colonels and me. The spiffy gentlemen were delightful company, eager to learn where I'd been and what I'd seen of the war. I was glad to tell them. I omitted just a single detail—that I was married to a draftee who was in their service.

They were returning from an inspection tour, and because the war had all but stopped, their inspection had been pretty routine. They were in high spirits.

"There isn't a cloud," one of the middle-aged officers said. "What say we bypass Saigon and fly straight for the Delta?"

The others quickly assented, so he turned to me.

"Are you in a hurry to get back home?" he asked. "Or are you up for a little joyride with four men old enough to be your father?"

"I *like* my father," I laughed. "I'm in no hurry."

Driving Rains

We flew the entire length of the South Vietnamese coastline. The views were spectacular. The whole northern edge was lined with magnificent beaches and a thousand lush islands. The dark green mountains of the Central Highlands were to our right; the blue-green ocean to our left; then, straight ahead of us as we flew south lay the flat, bright green Mekong River basin, the Delta. It was splendid. In the face of man's obscene behavior, it had been easy to be blinded to nature's insistent beauty. But at this privileged viewing, it would be an obscenity to be unaware.

Out of the plane at Ton Son Nhut, I waved down a pedicab, climbed in, and arranged my belongings around me in the open front seat that was large enough for two. My seat was propelled forward by a driver on a bicycle behind me. Typically, drivers were thin, wiry, and taut from exertion, with sun-dried skin, deeply lined. Most drivers looked older than they were. Before we'd moved an inch, I initiated price negotiations in a combination of street English and pidgin French. It involved several layers of intricate bargaining.

"How much?" I asked innocently.

"2,000 P," he answered with just a hope and prayer of anticipated success.

"Beaucoup!" I acted disgusted. "I give 50 P."

"No!" he returned my disgust. "Tee tee! 1,000 P."

At which point I grabbed my bag and began to climb out. He waved at me to stay put.

Ton Son Nhut airport was the worst place in the city to catch a pedicab because foreigners flying into Saigon for the first time—ordinarily with no idea of the prevailing price structure—overpaid by twenty times. The pedicab drivers who served the airport were accustomed to foreigners who were rich and stupid. I was not rich—and my momma hadn't raised me to be stupid—so I bargained hard and paid a very fair 200 piastres.

We set out for the four-mile trip to my home; we'd gone just a matter of blocks when I felt an enormous tug at my left arm. A passing motorcyclist had leaned into my seat and briskly grabbed one of the handles to my overnight bag; the other handle was looped over my left arm. The motorcyclist accelerated. I quickly sized up the situation and yanked back. It was a tug of war set in the midst of midday traffic. Other vehicles sped up around us, weaving in and out in the Saigon manner, missing us by inches. The thief accelerated again. My pedicab driver, with a serene look of the Buddha, decelerated. He was barely pedaling. He looked as though he hadn't noticed that his pedicab was tethered to a passing, rapidly accelerating Honda. He looked as if it were just another day in the park. He looked, as I saw out of the corner of my eye, as though he didn't see his passenger lunging over the front end of his pedicab, teetering close to falling nose first into the traffic and refusing to relinquish her half of the overnight bag to this scum of a kid on a motorcycle—didn't hear her screaming for him to speed up, either.

In the matter of loyalties, it was no contest. I was the foreigner who'd bargained him down to the going rate; the kid was Vietnamese. It passed through my mind: maybe they were a team. Maybe they intended to split the booty.

I hung on. The two of us weaved in tandem through the impossibly impacted Saigon streets. But nothing on the face of this earth would have convinced me at that moment to let go. My arm stretched and ached, my hand was being rubbed to blisters. Still I held.

Then the handle snapped—the piece I was holding—and the kid disappeared into traffic, clutching my bag. I held the disembodied brown leather handle in my left hand. I gestured angrily to the pedicab driver to keep on going and he picked up speed. I gathered my wits and realized that my purse, with everything of value to the thieving kid on the Honda—passport, cash—was hanging off my right shoulder intact. Then, I actually smiled.

The kid had made off with my dirty underwear, a pair of Vietnamese silk pajama pants, and some almost-emptied makeup. I smiled again and pictured him peeling open his hard-won treasure.

When I got home from Da Nang, I wrote an answer to my mother-in-law's last letter. She had asked, "Isn't Bob lonely with you away so much? Wouldn't he rather you stay in Saigon?" I wasn't impervious to my mother-in-law's expectation of a dependable wife for her son. I loved Bob's mother. I was vulnerable to her implicit criticism, that wives belonged with their husbands; I could recite that one in my sleep. Living it would be a whole other story.

I wrote her, "Bob is happy to see me get away. Sure, I travel for work, but I travel too because I'm curious. Getting away from here makes me easier to live with."

It had been just six months since I'd worked as the education reporter for the *Evening Capital*, with a circulation under 20,000. Now, for five days, I'd been elevated to *acting* Saigon bureau chief for *Time* magazine!

Marsh asked me to sit in for him. Literally. Sit behind his big desk in his plushy office. Marsh and Pippa were in Hong Kong, closing up their apartment. He was scheduled to leave for his next assignment, Jerusalem, in just a few weeks. I dreaded his departure.

A combination of obligations and vacations kept our shrinking American staff from filling in for Marsh and he turned to me. It was just five days, but it was enormous fun.

I was responsible for supervising a Vietnamese office staff of eight: Nga, Luong, Co, Dang, Luu, Long, Le Minh, and Pham Xuan An. They'd ask questions, I'd answer them; I'd ask questions, they'd answer me enthusiastically. There was a deep pool of experience and wisdom in that office.

Deeper than we knew at the time. After the war ended—to the shock of every *Time* staffer who'd worked alongside the indispensable An—he revealed himself to have been the most powerful North Vietnamese spy in South Vietnam. He actually chose the Saigon targets for the infamous 1968 Tet Offensive—and *then* successfully spun the Tet reportage (what could easily have been perceived as a failed attack) into a convincing worldview of a crushing Communist victory. For his service, then-Brigadier General Pham Xuan An was named a Hero of the People's Armed Forces—and simultaneously vested in Time Inc.'s retirement plan.

In my brief tenure, I handled correspondent and photographer problems from the field by phone and by telex. Bob Anson needed to borrow piastres to get out of Saigon and back to Cambodia. It was late at night, so Bob and I loaned him what we had at home—the equivalent of twenty dollars.

"I'll pay you when I get back."

A freelance photographer wanted to send pictures to New York in the *Time* official courier packet but not for *Time* use. Would that be okay? It would not. A staff correspondent wanted to get a message to his wife in Singapore before he took off; could we relay it? Of course. Like that.

We filed the week's stories. We responded to New York's queries. Not one person challenged my right to make decisions; they just wanted someone to make them. The staff continued to do what it was most used to doing, and the office sailed through my fleeting period of responsibility. I could have gotten very used to Marsh's chair.

But the cream on the berries was Marsh's apartment. Bob and I inherited it for the duration, and it was a pretty fair replacement for the lost week in Hong Kong. Marsh's place was around the corner from the office, smack in the center of town on the topmost

Driving Rains

floor of one of the taller buildings in Saigon. It had a huge sun porch off the kitchen, furnished with a large bamboo dining table where we ate and matching lounge chairs where we read or sunbathed overlooking the city—all of it, seven stories above the daily annoyances and irritants.

A maid arrived each morning and cleaned up after us; Marsh instructed that we were to make no beds and wash no dishes. He had a *television* that we'd barely turned on and air conditioning that we never turned off. There was wonderful, expensive food in the refrigerator—caviar, brie, grapes—that Marsh insisted we finish off, and a varied collection of magazines and books—the *Atlantic Monthly*, Kafka—scattered across the tables. He had floral sheets and a good mattress. (The mattress at Mrs. An's had become increasingly like pudding, soft and lumpy.) There were no bugs, lizards, or rats—not a single sign of Saigon as we knew it.

We could watch the sun rise *and* set over Saigon from that porch, and we did. It was dazzling. From Saturday evening, when Bob got off work, until Monday morning, we never set foot outside the apartment. We ate what we found in the refrigerator whenever we pleased—totally abandoning official mealtimes. We danced to the Frank Sinatra collection, *real* slow.

"Come here," my husband summoned me with a nod of his head.

"My pleasure." I floated into his arms.

We held one another with concentration and focus. There were no distractions—nothing and no one to blame, complain, or feel guilty about. The mud, the military, the regulations, the streetboys, the drugs—the war itself—could not touch us from Saturday evening until Monday morning.

My husband, in that place, was mellow, relaxed, and darling. He savored my triumphs, exulted that I was Marsh's replacement.

I felt more intact than I had in months. Perhaps for the first time, being both bureau chief *and* wife felt like two halves of a seamless whole.

But when Bob shut the apartment door behind him on Monday morning to grab a taxi to the provost marshal's office and I stayed behind to pull together our few belongings, we both heard—from opposite sides of Marsh's front door—the mournful echo of the other's deepest sigh.

And I felt those sounds reverberate from that ephemeral pocket of solitude and peace to the very edge of the grisly war.

CHAPTER 11

TESTING LOYALTIES

SEPTEMBER & OCTOBER 1970

Bob Anson was the only staff member missing from Marsh's going-away party. His nighttime visit to borrow 18,000 piastres from Bob and me—while I was filling in for Marsh—was the last time any of us had seen him. He flew into Cambodia, spent a few days in Phnom Penh, grabbed a rental Ford, and headed for Skoun in late afternoon. He drove directly into the surprised but willing arms of the North Vietnamese. He was taken prisoner. More than that, we did not know.

The *Time* bureau moved into high gear like nothing I'd ever seen before in my life. Marsh spent every waking hour pulling the innumerable legal and diplomatic strings available to the powerful publishing empire to locate Anson and to set him free. So far, Time Inc. clout had not found him. New York was breathing down Marsh's neck, but they needn't have; Marsh felt humanly and personally responsible. There was a pall over the office: Marsh was about to leave; Anson was missing. Only Jim Willwerth, the Vietnamese staff, and I would be left behind.

I spent hours at the office, shoulder to shoulder and heart to heart with Diane Anson, Bob's wife. She'd flown up from Singapore where she lived with their two small children. She was frightened and predictably overwhelmed. There were no right words. I was simply a woman with another woman, a wife with another wife. The unofficial office policy was banter. We told jokes at Anson's expense. Bureau chief and colleagues encouraged the bravura and Diane acquiesced.

"What chance do the North Vietnamese stand against your husband's arrogance? Shiiit, Diane," Willwerth said. "If his steak isn't medium rare, he'll walk out of there."

Like that. Diane forced a smile. Days passed. She left for Phnom Penh to be part of the search and then went back to Singapore where the kids needed her. Weeks passed. Still, there was nothing.

I'd close my eyes at night and try to place Bob Anson somewhere I'd been. I remembered how quickly safety and tranquility turned to terror. I'd visualize Bob's wild blond curls, his irreverent smile, his husky build—and his absolute confidence. Just two years older than me. I would not allow myself to imagine him dead.

Now, Marsh was leaving, too.

It took an exquisite office dinner party on a floating Vietnamese restaurant in the Saigon River to distract us from our incessant preoccupation with Bob; to console ourselves over Marsh's departure; to welcome Jonathan Larsen, his replacement. There was an extra wrinkle to the new bureau chief: Larsen's father had been vice chairman of Time Inc. Murray Gart, *Time* chief of correspondents, had flown in from New York for the coronation of the successor. Marsh set up interviews for Murray, Jon, and himself with South Vietnam's President Nguyen Van Thieu, with US Ambassador to Vietnam Ellsworth Bunker, and with the American military top gun, General Creighton Abrams—all before the dinner party. In that way, the nobility from *Time* met their domestic, diplomatic, and military counterparts. It was way out of my league, but I watched and listened; their preparations entertained me.

For months, I'd grieved Marsh's impending departure for Israel. Marsh had been singularly responsible for opening every door in Saigon to me. He trusted me; he enjoyed me; he kept me amply supplied with work and income. He was from a different generation, with an entirely opposite political mindset—but he was my friend, and I was going to miss him sorely. Whoever replaced him could not possibly relate to me in the same way. He would not have listened to my innocence, stared into my ignorance, and watched me grow.

At my request, Marsh wrote a letter of recommendation for my future files. He said in part, "I have assigned her to some very demanding and intricate stories involving both Vietnam and Cambodia. She has been professional in every way. I recommend her unhesitatingly as a good reporter with much promise and a worthy personal representative."

In truth, I was exceedingly uncertain of my standing without Marsh.

The party was a great success. We indulged in a dozen different courses of Vietnamese delicacies: crab and corn chowder, rice wrapped in palm leaf baskets, roasted bananas soaked in rum. Marsh asked the Vietnamese staff to choose the restaurant and arrange the menu. They'd taken the task to heart. At dinner, they sat clustered, according to unspoken rank, around Marsh and Pippa—at the far end of the table from where Murray Gart held court. Bob and I were at the end with the newcomers, Jon Larsen and his wife Wendy. We were hitting it off remarkably well. Next to me was the delightful John Saar, *Life* magazine's only Asia correspondent; he worked out of our office when in Saigon. Next to him, Dick Swanson, a *Life* photographer with his wife Germaine.

It never occurred to me that a *Time* bureau chief could come in a package that looked nothing like Marsh. But Jon (and Wendy) did. Jon was shockingly similar in appearance and manner to my brother Harmon: dark, handsome, authoritative, and only thirty. Wendy was his blonde, smart, genteel match.

Bob and I discovered in them two people who felt more like a couple we'd choose for friends than we thought possible in Saigon—let alone in the *Time* bureau. That they spoke our language was immediately evident. Wendy had her own job lined up. She was teaching English literature at the University of Saigon. Jon made rock and roll allusions. He wasn't an overt Republican. His independence and energy had not been sapped by his loyalty to the institution.

Wendy's dead-on first question: "Is it harder to be a female correspondent over here?"

"It's different," I hedged. "Very different."

She raised her eyebrows in acknowledgement of what I'd said, and had not said, refusing to press the point over dinner.

"Are there many draftees who hate the war as much as you do?" Jon asked Bob, when he got a scent of his politics.

"Sure," Bob answered. "The war is full of ignorant kids whose simple idealism—Jesus on our side, godless Communists on the other—doesn't last the first month. We are an army of the defeated, the demoralized, and the stoned."

Jon and Wendy listened raptly, soaking it up, and, as it turned out, *memorizing* Bob's quote.

The party was glittering. We all had too much to drink.

The excellent French Beaujolais ran from seemingly bottomless vats. Bottles were emptied and replaced; glasses were miraculously refilled. The conversation flowed, the social lines between Vietnamese and American staffer, between the chief of correspondents and the girl reporter who found a job over here by the grace of Marsh, melted away. For this *one* night there was no mention of our colleague—a prisoner of the North Vietnamese—or his grieving wife. No mention either of the endless monsoon rains or the waiting-for-the-other-shoe-to-drop war. For this one night, I did not fret over my husband's self-esteem or my place in the universe of men and women. Tonight, it was just a beautiful farewell party for my much cherished Marsh Clark and a warm and gracious welcome for a couple of kindred spirits.

But, of course, all of that lasted for just one night.

When Mrs. An's daughter, Nhung, said to me, "You're afraid of everything," I thought she'd seen through me. But she had, in fact, only noticed my reaction to rats, lizards—creepy crawly things.

Nhung was like a younger sister, the one I'd dreamed in adolescence would take the pressure off me. *She*—the imagined younger sister—would skirmish with our mother over clothes in Loehmann's dressing room, leaving me free to do other, more compelling, things.

Among Mrs. An's children, only Nhung spoke English, so it was natural that we'd find each other. At nineteen, she was the oldest child at home. Lively, twenty-year-old Mai was at school in Switzerland. Beautiful, indolent Phuong was fifteen; studious Hong, twelve; Truc, seven, was the only son.

I would have spent many more evenings alone—Bob only intermittently there—if not for Nhung. Sometimes she was her mother's mouthpiece. She'd invite me next door for fresh pineapple soaked in rum. Mrs. An would teach me how to peel and slice the pineapple, and I'd sit with the family for an hour in the evening. Either Nhung translated or we'd all speak French. Even little Truc made fun of my mispronunciation. "*Non, Madame Inette, ce n'est pas le* leevrah, *c'est le livre.*"

But mostly Nhung knocked on my door and asked me on her own behalf to go for a walk. We'd wind down dirt paths into parts of our neighborhood I probably would not have ventured into alone, at night. She'd tell me stories about her country, her family, and her own heart. We'd stop at a café; I'd buy us something to drink. Our talks, like our walks, wandered into astonishingly unpredictable places with little expectation where they'd end up.

When we passed a bakery one evening, Nhung babbled about what seemed domestic trivia. "We use butter in our cakes and they taste heavy and rich. American cakes, on the other hand," she taunted, "taste like air." And I knew—because I knew Nhung—she was talking about something other than cake. She was figuring out the places where our dominant culture was blind to the obvious, and where we cut corners.

Later on that same night, she veered off the side roads and headed straight onto the boulevard. "My grandmother prays at that pagoda every morning. She prays for our ancestors. I'm taught Buddhism by my grandmother and Catholicism by the nuns at school. But I think neither one answers the needs of young people—the questions of war."

In America, Nhung would have passed physically for fourteen. She stood five feet tall, was as slight as a prepubescent, and had thick, shining black hair halfway down her back. She had a wonderful gap-toothed smile. With me, she grinned freely and spoke her mind. It was a mind, I found, bursting with ideas—complex and naïve in equal mix. To the world, she was shy.

"I've never met a shy American," she said. "I don't think one

Testing Loyalties

exists."

I told her that Bob's younger sister was the shyest person I knew. She refused to believe it.

"If I get married," she told me on one of our walks, "I hope I'm like you and Bob—not very rich, but very happy." Those words were aberrant. Usually, she swore she'd never marry. In Vietnam, that was a simple acceptance of reality: so many dead soldiers, so many waiting brides. Nhung had never had a boyfriend.

Nhung's dreams, like mine, took her across the ocean and away from family. On the one hand, she was thoughtful and mature. "I want to be a doctor. I want to do something for the poor people in my country." On the other, inexperienced. She was shocked that I wasn't pregnant in my first year of marriage. She couldn't imagine that American women might choose not to have babies.

Through Nhung's eyes and words, her family became three-dimensional to me. She confided that the tall, beautiful aunt who lived in her father and grandmother's sector of their home was her father's mistress, not her aunt at all. Nhung told me this with considerable equanimity—and just the slightest embarrassment for my Western sensibilities.

"Widowed grandmothers expect to live with their eldest sons," she said, and hers did. A genuine aunt, her father's favorite sister, lived with them as well. "Because widows never remarry."

Her mother lived with the children in the main section of the house. That, Nhung told me, had been the arrangement since Truc was born, seven years before. After four daughters, her father had a son.

Nhung called her slim, easygoing father "a dreamer. He plays cards, visits friends, and smokes opium."

Her mother, she didn't need to tell me, was the go-getter—ambitious for her children and very good with money. Mrs. An was an astute businesswoman.

Nhung described herself as "deep, thoughtful, and spiritual." I agreed. Although she loved her family and sorely missed sharing a bed with Mai since she'd left for college, she saw herself as "different." She didn't share what she called her mother's "materialism." In some ways, this delicate Vietnamese girl was a mirror of my own uneasy spirit, although mine was housed in a sturdy American body.

The family was relatively wealthy, though the wealth was largely hidden away for the children's education. They lived rather austerely. "For years, my family owned an ice factory." Nhung pointed to the spot in front of their home diagonally from where we stood at the edge of the river. "Electric refrigerators finished off the ice business. But my mother knew what she needed to do."

Mrs. An built two small apartment buildings where the factory had stood, rented that space to Koreans, and made money. Nhung's father never worked again.

Because I was a married woman, infinitely more respectable than a mere girl, Mrs. An allowed Nhung to wander freely with me. She entrusted her single daughter to my care. We went to old French movies with multiple—Vietnamese, Chinese, and English—subtitles. We zipped around the city on my Honda, or on hers. We searched through college catalogues for an American university suitable to Nhung's pre-med ambitions.

On a whim, I proposed a trip with Nhung to Nha Trang, one of the most spectacular beaches in Vietnam. Nhung, who'd never ventured more than twenty miles from Saigon and who had never been inside an airplane, restrained her impulse to scream "Yes!" Of course, she had to run the idea past her mother. But Nhung's eyes sparkled.

Mrs. An immediately approved her daughter's adventure. I had my own hurdle to cross. Because Nhung was not an American citizen—was in fact *only* a citizen of the country we were "saving from Communism"—she would require a special travel permit to ride on a US military plane, to stay in a military hotel, or even to cross the threshold of any American-occupied building.

To me, it was one of the bitter ironies of the war. A Vietnamese citizen needed *me* to travel within her own country. But that was the fact. In a country where our friends and foes were physically indistinguishable from one another, we claimed that need for security reasons. But the humiliation inherent in any redneck in an American uniform refusing a South Vietnamese citizen entry to a building within her own nation stuck in my craw. The only Vietnamese who passed muster at the gate had agreed to work there, polishing boots and ironing shirts for the GIs.

I had learned the hard (and embarrassing) way that I could not take Nhung into an officers' club for lunch as my guest. I could have taken *any* other civilian—with European features. I begged Nhung's forgiveness when we were abruptly turned away. But she hadn't been surprised. "Americans pay to keep President Thieu in power. He cares only for his own pockets, not his people."

Marsh approved the paperwork for Nhung's travel permit in his last days. She'd pass as my interpreter.

But before we took off for Nha Trang, the bureau erupted in euphoria. Exactly three weeks after he'd driven his rental Ford to Skoun and been captured—just a few days after Marsh's party— the North Vietnamese released Bob Anson.

It took the war's end before any of us discovered that our own staffer—Pham Xuan An—had been the influential lynchpin in Anson's release. The powerful North Vietnamese spy, covertly embedded in our office, had secretly vouched for Anson's anti-war credentials.

Of the twenty-six newsmen who had disappeared in the first six months of the Cambodian War, only eight had reappeared.

Minutes after his release, Anson was pressed by colleagues in Phnom Penh into an impromptu news conference, where—utterly consistent with his pre-capture positions—he spoke out.

"I never considered the people of Vietnam or Cambodia or Laos to be my enemy. They knew that I believed in peace, so they treated me like a friend. Some of the soldiers got to be brothers. I've made friends with soldiers on both sides. I just don't want to see my friends dead."

Anson returned to the Saigon bureau for just two days. There wasn't much opportunity for personal closure. He was there, and then he was gone again to Diane and the kids. I found that I was shy with him in light of his incredible ordeal. In brief: he sat in the office, wrote and filed the story of his capture, thanked Marsh and Murray for their efforts on his behalf, greeted Jon, whom he'd known in California—and then went off to pack up his family in Singapore.

The story he wrote for our employer never saw the light of day. It was revised in substantial ways and deeply cut "for reasons other than space." *Time* in New York had written him off. In the parlance of the military and Time Inc., he had "gone over to the other side."

I should have expected it. Anson himself had explained Time Inc. and its intrigues to me last March in Bangkok. Instead, I was shocked and disgusted. A *first-person* account—where was there room for debate?

In a single impulsive moment, Anson quit. But a few days later, with Diane's prodding, he *re-upped*. I understood: *Time* reached more American readers than any other publication; it was a source of incomparable influence; that influence was a tough drug to give up.

Before capture, Anson had been handed his next assignment: a plum job in the Beirut bureau. He was on the fast track. Now he was about to be punished—forced to prove his loyalty. Beirut went to someone else. He disappeared into the New York bureau of *Time*—assigned to cover anti-war protests. It was a trenchant reminder just how narrow was the acceptable deviation from the magazine's adherence to Cold War chauvinism.

Nevertheless, I was strengthened by Anson's integrity. What I hadn't been able to put into words for him, I put into personal resolve. I would live my remaining months in Vietnam from principle.

Marsh left for Jerusalem; Murray, for a stop in Bangkok and then home to New York. Nhung and I took off for the beach. She spent half the flight hunched over a sick-bag, vomiting. The American food we ate at the airport had been a bad idea. "My first hamburger!" she had enthused, bluffing her way past the nausea. I doubted there would ever be a second.

She remained determined to see it all, do it all. She was unceasingly grateful. She was a willing partner, with a fresh set of eyes through which to see the world. She was a child in her enthusiasms, a grown-up in her sensitivity to politics and human nature.

Sterile American office buildings she called "beautiful!" The views from a cranky old World War II plane were "miraculous."

I awakened the first morning to see Nhung kneeling next to her bed—in prayer, I assumed. I'd assumed wrong. She was making her bed as she'd done every morning of her life, kneeling quietly on the floor to tuck in the corners.

Still in the depths of the rainy season, our three days in Nha Trang delivered just ten hours, total, of sunshine. But the hours had clustered in late morning and early afternoon, so we had our beach time. In the heart of monsoon season, I managed to get the first terrible sunburn of my life. It would be years before sunscreen was invented. Suntan lotions were expected to enhance a tan, not blunt it. That we Millers tanned well was the family vanity. But I had not factored in the tropics. I hurt for days, and a week later I peeled.

Nhung did not own a bathing suit and would not have worn one if it were offered. She waded in her black satin pajama pants and shirt. Paradoxically, the married chaperone wore a bikini; the impressionable girl covered herself shoulder to ankle. There was ample irony. Because she was with me, I could take greater liberties than I would without her. Because I was with her, her whole world opened up.

While we baked on the beach, four Air Force officers struck up conversation. The men were proper gentlemen: sweet, and each rather handsome in an all-American, WASP sort of way. On a whim, one asked us to join them on their boat for the day. The others echoed approval. Nhung and I looked at one another, grinned, and shrugged, "Why not?" It was hot; the boat would be cooler. They promised a picnic lunch. It was the maiden voyage of their handcrafted boat and the men wanted this final decorative touch: women on board.

Nha Trang was beautiful by any measure—no need to handicap it for the war. The small city was surrounded on three sides by round, lush mountains. We were floating on the third side, on the bluest, clearest ocean I'd seen since Mykonos, Greece. It was dotted with islands.

We cruised along the coastline and ate the lunch they'd packed: peanut butter and jelly sandwiches, potato chips, Oreos, beer, Cokes. What had once been familiar comfort food now tasted exotic and delicious. Nhung skipped the beer; she chewed long and swallowed hard on the peanut butter.

I dove off the boat without waiting the mandated half-hour after eating. I stroked hard and fast, long laps parallel to the shoreline. I'd been a swimmer forever, spent every summer of my life on Atlantic beaches. I had no trepidation about water. The water was as warm as the Gulf Stream off the Carolina coast, and although it felt cool to my skin, it took no getting used to. I could see almost to the bottom. One of the airmen gave me his hand and hoisted me back into the boat.

Nhung didn't know how to swim, but I realized that, alone, she'd been holding her own with the young men. Her English, which she judged inferior to her French, was more than adequate. Her confidence was soaring.

"No, no!" she was laughing, "I am not impressed with the superiority of male '*know-how*.'" She pronounced the last two words for the first time—formally and stiff. "But I do approve of your boat." The men were rightfully proud of it, a remarkable accomplishment of know-how and make-do.

We cruised only within the strict and narrow limits of authorized exploration, but none of us minded. We played on the water until the rains hit, then made a run for shore and said our quick goodbyes. "No," I lied, "we already have plans for dinner." There was no sense pushing it.

Nhung had never before spent an entire afternoon with an American man (other than Bob). With the added information, she was revising her views. Still no shy Americans, but not every man was a barbarian either.

That respite from the city and the rainy season's oppression was brief. Saigon was essentially unchanged—in any but a couple of starkly significant ways.

Quickly, it had become clear to me, Jon Larsen did not have the same priorities that Marsh had.

He was warm, gracious, and socially inclusive. Bob and I had dinners with Jon and Wendy on their terrific rooftop terrace and shared superb conversation. But it was the rainy season: there was little enough work to go around; Jon was new in country and he wanted to experience it. He had, as he saw it—and I understood—to prove himself a war correspondent. Being bureau chief could have been a more than adequate excuse to stay in Saigon and administer the office from behind the big desk. But Jon didn't see it that way. He was young, a *Time* veteran but a Vietnam novice.

So the priorities went like this. First, Jon picked the stories he wanted for himself—and he wanted a lot. Then, he assigned to the sole salaried staffer, Willwerth, most of the rest. There was little left over for me. Unlike Marsh, Jon didn't feel any obligation to keep me in rent money. I was paid for the days I was on assignment, and the assignments in September and October were few and far between.

If I were going to work for Jon, it became crystal clear, I would have to hustle. I'd have to send myself into the field and hope for irresistible stories that Jon couldn't refuse. I'd also have to wait out both the rainy season and Jon's rookie enthusiasm. None of it felt like good news.

The news in Bob's office turned sour about the same time. In very different ways, we were each forced to begin again.

Bob's actual office space was quite charming. He sat alone inside a twelve-by-ten-foot alcove surrounded on three sides by bowed bay windows. They were old and creaky windows, hard to lift and almost impossible to shut again, but they let in a flood of afternoon light and looked out over a lively garden. Vivid yellow trumpet blossoms and bright red hibiscus filled a yard protected by a white stone wall.

The villa that housed the 90th Provost Marshal's office of the 716th Military Police Detachment was white stucco with an orange tile roof, architecturally compatible still with its origin as a private French residence.

Under a large spinning ceiling fan, Bob typed letters for each of the officers. He didn't type very fast and he wasn't particularly

Testing Loyalties

motivated to build up his speed, but he plodded at the direction of his superiors. He peeled off a letter, handed it in, saw it returned for changes, retyped it, and handed it back. There were other clerks like Bob, lesser clerks, who typed up arrest reports, and they were spread over the big central room.

Then there were the sergeants—stacked up hierarchically to a single sergeant major. And around the perimeter of the large room, hidden in private offices behind solid doors, were the colonel, major, captain, and lieutenant—in rooms of decreasing size and amenities.

Bob had one particular friend, also a college graduate. Eddie was a clerk, a Spec 4 about to make sergeant. He was from Minnesota; he'd arrived four months after Bob. Eddie was a conscientious worker, a docile man, and I think he saw Bob as the unconventional one—he appreciated Bob's cutting repartee.

So when Bob hung the four colorful cartoons over his desk one afternoon, carefully mounting them between two windows in his alcove so the pictures wouldn't be harmed by rain or scotch tape, Eddie laughed, jabbed Bob, and encouraged the mildly defiant decor.

It was not unusual for clerks to decorate their desks with family photos, high school mascots, reminders of home. Bob hadn't thought twice about how he'd decorate his office.

Years later, when we argued about what constituted tasteful furnishing, he accused me—who then favored English antiques—of creating an "old lady's parlor." I accused him—and his propensity for magazine-clipping art and plank-and-board bookcases—of "adolescence." So it was completely in character that Bob personalized his office space with colorful, full-page, satirical cartoons from *Rolling Stone*.

I remember the pictorials in only the most general sense now. Each full page featured a particular American patriotic icon, slightly altered to make a clear and provocative statement of opposition to the American war in Vietnam. The Statue of Liberty, I remember, had a Hitler mustache and a swastika on her sleeve. Mt. Rushmore's presidential faces wore jungle camouflage combat helmets. The images were wordlessly powerful, visually haunting—and very, very funny.

Bob put them up exactly the way he'd put on a red wool vest with a work shirt and blue jeans—to customize his world and make it fit a little more comfortably. He was not looking for a fight, and he was the most surprised of all when he got one.

"Bob," the lieutenant said, "the major doesn't like your pictures. He asked me to tell you to take them down."

"Screw the major." Bob laughed at a man he knew was delivering a message without any heart in it. "Tell him I don't like that picture of his ugly wife either." They both laughed.

"Spec 4," the *captain* said two days later, and cleared his throat. "Uh, it might be a good idea to take down those pictures."

"Yessir!" Bob snapped. But he looked at the cartoons, grinned to himself, and thought, "Even these assholes can't be serious."

But they were. The *major* was unwilling to risk a face-to-face refusal, so he took another route and wrote, "You are ordered by your superior officer to remove those unpatriotic, anti-war posters from your office wall by tomorrow morning or face an Article 15 disciplinary hearing."

There can be no explanation really for why, at this point, Bob decided to sink in his heels and stiffen his spine—unless we see the past nine months as cumulative: "Yessir!" to ethical and intellectual midgets; guilt accruing with every American bombing run and every dead Vietnamese civilian. My husband labored less under the demands of an office job than the moral weight of "having leant my body to this bullshit war." This was the man who had wanted to be a monk. But this time, he refused to suffer in silence.

The *Rolling Stone* cartoons would speak the words he hadn't been able to speak when he'd been drafted: "Hell, no, I won't go!" The major was quite right. Bob's refusal to remove them was an act of insubordination.

Whichever direction Bob turned, he suffered. He either ignored the fury of his conscience (and those slick cartoons had become emblematic of his ailing conscience) or he went up against every protocol of his upbringing and rebelled.

Bob wrote this response to the major's order: "I did not relinquish my First Amendment right to free speech when I joined the US Army. I defend that right under the Constitution of the United States of America. The free expression of my ideas in no way hinders the exercise of my duties to the US Army."

All hell broke loose.

Bob was charged with insubordination under an Article 15 judicial act. He would be brought before a panel of military judges. A military attorney would be appointed to defend him. The major did not wait for the disciplinary hearing. He stormed into Bob's office and ripped down the offending cartoons. Bob was livid.

The charges carried a possible prison sentence. "A prison within a prison," Bob said. It was an altogether new take on the sarcastic GI response to military authority inside Vietnam. "What're they going to do to me? Send me to 'Nam?"

I went with Bob to the adjutant general's office for the first meeting with his attorney—a Jewish Harvard Law School grad, building experience before he landed at some big Boston law firm. He listened with compassion. He nodded at the appropriate places. I had no doubt he could fix this for Bob. But I was wrong.

When Bob said, "First Amendment," the lawyer cut him off and shook his head. "This is a military court, Bob; the rules are different. You are not protected by the usual constitutional guarantees. There's absolutely no way you can win this."

Bob sank in his chair, defeated but not contrite. I charged in. "What if you go to the mat on this? What if you challenge the military rules in light of the constitutional guarantees?"

The young lawyer looked more and more like the enemy—he would not help.

Bob went to that hearing without a trace of anger. He was determined to be honest and strong, and he was both. He argued that the cartoons were an innocent lift to his sagging morale; that in his private office no one else had to look at them; that he was still an American citizen with the right to free speech.

He was found guilty, by unanimous vote. But because this was war, and even in Saigon there were more important derelictions than Bob's, the judges didn't choose to send him to prison. Instead, they busted him the two ranks he'd routinely climbed in Vietnam. No longer a Specialist 4, no longer a Private First Class, Bob was a flat-out private. He was returned to the rank he held when he'd entered Basic Training the year before.

Bob arrived in Vietnam a private, and he left as one. It took some doing, and it was the one thing about that war that he was genuinely proud of.

Bob's older sister, reflecting his family consensus, wrote, "Didn't Bob think it'd be better to get through the war by making no waves? Didn't Bob think it would have been smarter to follow Army rules and make no trouble?"

Bob didn't answer, but I did. I asked her: Who the hell did she think she was—sitting pretty in suburban California—to second-guess Bob? I wrote, "If you were capable of recognizing backbone, you'd be proud of your principled brother. I sure as hell am."

My mother-in-law answered. She said that although she understood my defense of Bob, I needed to know that I had hurt his sister's feelings. I wrote his sister a letter of apology, but it took her years to forgive me.

Back in early June, Bob had applied for an extension to his service time in Vietnam; he'd asked for two more months of war. This, I know, needs some explanation. Any draftee—at the time of his induction—was obligated to twenty-four months of service. Two of those were spent in Basic Training, three more months in obligatory Advanced Infantry Training. Afterwards, the draftee was routinely shipped to Vietnam, with a twelve-month commitment to the war. At the end of that year, the typical draftee had seven months left to serve at a stateside Army base.

But the Army offered its Vietnam veterans another choice, because reassigning hundreds of thousands of soldiers to little-needed, overcrowded stateside bases was inefficient even by US military standards. Each soldier could, alternatively, opt to extend his duty in Vietnam by just two months (or whatever remained of his twenty-four) until he had only five months left to complete his military stint. *Then*, the remaining five-month obligation would be dropped and the soldier would be discharged from the Army at the exact moment he returned to Oakland from Vietnam.

It looked, at first take, like a harder choice than it was for most soldiers. Vietnam was, to be sure, the place to leave behind. But if the military was oppressively petty and exasperating inside a war zone—where many regulations were by necessity relaxed—how much greater the torture of stateside bureaucracy *after* Vietnam? There were stories of mythological proportion: Vietnam veterans going berserk under the gratuitous demands of stateside military spit and polish. As a result, Vietnam draftees overwhelmingly opted for the extension and the *early out*.

For Bob, last June, there had been a protracted period of indecision during which I kept silent. Four months ago, when that decision was made, I loved my job, suffered no doubts, and was more than eager to lengthen my stint as a war correspondent. For Bob, it was the Army here or the Army there; the Army for nineteen months or the Army for twenty-four. He filed his application in early June and put the whole thing out of his mind.

Now—after four months of monsoon rain, a rejected R&R in Hong Kong, and the uncertainty of my job; *now*—two days after Bob had been tried, found guilty, and busted—he got notice that his two-month extension of service in Vietnam had been approved.

On October 19, we'd had 106 days until DEROS, just three-and-a-half months left in country. On October 20, we were back up to 165 days, almost six months left. Bob was full of futile second thoughts.

April 4, 1971 was our new DEROS. I anguished, trying to imagine how we might fill those days. I hoped for just a shred of truth in Bill Dowell's promise that after the early enthusiastic months in Vietnam and the subsequent grueling ones, we'd be rewarded with an acceptable middle ground.

I had never been very good at middle ground.

CHAPTER 12

COMING UP FOR BREATH

NOVEMBER 1970

I flew into Hong Kong on a wide-body Pan Am plane and arrived mid-morning. The landing in Hong Kong took a feat of aeronautical precision. I'd flown from Saigon to the tiny island entirely over ocean and then, with nothing more than a "Please fasten your seatbelts" in four or five languages, we were pointed straight down the steep side of a jagged green mountain with absolutely no flat spot or airport in sight. Within seconds, we touched ground. An airport (and a magnificent city) had materialized from impossibility.

Bob arrived just minutes later on an Air Force jet.

I will admit, up front, to the shimmering dissonance between the extraordinary deprivations of Vietnam and *this*—the indulgent week in Hong Kong. The American military imagined a policy to ameliorate the "stresses" of war. Were they successful? Was jungle to family in Honolulu (or to bargirls in Bangkok) for a single week, and then back to jungle, anything short of insane?

For Bob and for me, it worked. I remind myself that this guerilla war was being fought on more than one front. My job (and Bob's) took me into the *official* Vietnam War; my youth took me into another—the war within. That one, the girl from Baltimore figuring out what was denied her, and what she alone could refuse.

There were several chartered buses waiting to transport a plane-load of rowdy grunts to one of a dozen US military-approved hotels. I'd agreed to ride the bus to the Hilton. The bus ride was a zoo. It was like payday on Tu Do Street or maybe a junior high school lunchroom—not at all what I had in mind for our time in Hong Kong. I was ready to grab Bob's hand and bolt the minute we arrived, but he patted my shoulder and counseled patience.

"Take it easy, girl."

We'd picked the Hilton because it was at the upper end of the list—the most expensive of the tourist hotels the military had contracted with, and then discounted. We'd chosen it because we doubted another GI would. But twenty-six men on Bob's flight had flagged the Hilton, and when we hit the lobby it became quite clear that the soldier-customers—still in travel-mandated fatigues—were handled differently than the other more respectable customers. All GIs were warehoused on floor three, segregated from the other guests.

In truth, I couldn't blame the Hilton. Many of these men were raw and raunchy. There was a distinct "live for today, because tomorrow . . . " quality about the party. Who could blame them? Freed from the jungle for one week, then returned to the mud without hope or prayer of another reprieve.

Nevertheless, the prospect of a week in Hong Kong housed inside a fraternity party revolted me.

I straightened my back and walked to the front desk alone, putting the greatest possible distance between me and the olive green line of men queuing up to register. I explained that *I'd made a reservation for my husband and me* and, "Didn't they have something *quiet* with a nice view on one of the upper floors?" They were delighted to accommodate.

While the hotel processed the embarrassingly loud collection of American soldiers, Bob and I followed our luggage to a room on the sixteenth floor. "How'd you manage to pull that off?" he asked as he tucked me under a snug arm when we stepped into the elevator.

"Just a trick of the trade."

"What trade was that? It didn't look like reporting when you grinned into the eyes of that poor old desk clerk."

"Millers," I said. "The way Millers do things."

The room was perfect, quiet above the city sounds, with a staggering view of the Hong Kong harbor. A single enormous window filled an entire wall with streaming sunlight and unimpeded vistas of little white ferry boats crossing water that was as clear and blue as the sky it mirrored.

Bob was out of his fatigues faster than the bellman could wrap his fist around our five-dollar bill. We were eager to get out of doors, to see the city, but there were matters closer to home to attend to first. There was nothing deliberate about our touches that first morning in Hong Kong. It was about ridding ourselves of the gritty residue of the past ten months and purging our souls of the nasty imprint of a troubled place.

This, I genuinely believed, was where our marriage would begin—in the way young people mark successive beginnings and dismiss history. This would be our honeymoon.

It was wordless sex that morning in Hong Kong—anger purged, frustration vented—exactly what we each needed.

"*That's* better," he said after.

Lying next to Bob on ironed sheets, less satisfied than unburdened, with the sun touching my air conditioning-cooled arm, I tickled the little patch of hair in the middle of his chest and then rubbed the back of my hand across the stubble on his cheek.

I could not have been happier. Everything until then had been warm up; everything after, like an inverted pyramid, would build from the serenity streaming to my nerve endings next to this wonderful boy. I could not have imagined then, nor would it have benefited me if I had, that everything we wished to rid ourselves of had already marked the direction of our lives. It was already a part of who we were and who we would forever be.

I could make them out on the pier in the New York harbor, standing pretty much alone at the end of the wooden dock and at the beginning of the water. My mother was waving a white plastic rain bonnet as the USS Aurelia *edged slowly offshore and into the harbor. My father was standing stock still beside her, not waving at all.*

It was September, 1966; I was barely twenty. My thumb had been long since tucked into my pocket; my braces, gone. I'd been two years away at Wisconsin, but still, I was their little girl. I shivered at the enormity of my decision: a full year away from them, a toe stretched into the cold Atlantic Ocean and beyond. I shivered, too, with excitement.

"Wisconsin isn't far enough?" my father asked when I told him I was spending my junior year in Italy. He picked his fights carefully

now. He knew that this one, he would not win.

I guessed that my father was dealing with his own toe in the water—sending his baby girl, his hardened teenage daughter, across the sea. He'd launched his sons with a sense of accomplishment, but his daughter was a more confusing proposition: a girl who might go anywhere—and bring home, what?

I saw the plastic rain bonnet aloft; Daddy at my mother's side growing dimmer. What had he said to me before he left me on the deck of that ship—my first transatlantic crossing?

He said, "Don't bring home an Italian."

Four months later, New Year's Day 1967, on a different ship crossing the Mediterranean from Haifa to Genoa (Christmas in the Holy Land was part of the school's itinerary) I recognized Bob. I recognized him less in the kiss he'd summoned the courage to take after much deliberation than in his holding my hand. Until then, we'd been buffered by crowds of students, distracted from one another by the throng.

Bob, of course, was not Italian, but his grandparents were, his neighbors were, and he was *Catholic. To my Dad, it would amount to the same thing.*

Bob led me, arm around my waist, off the ship's dance floor and onto the deck. Then, he bent me backwards like Arthur Murray dipping Kathryn in the tango and he kissed me.

"I felt like Hamlet," he told me afterwards, "pacing the deck trying to decide whether or not to kiss you." I kissed him back, warm and close and just a little bit titillated.

Bob was entirely unlike the boy who'd mesmerized me for my first months in Florence and then disappeared into Paris: that exciting, handsome, dangerous boy who wrote sullen poetry and drank too much—not a person I'd ever marry. But then, not marrying was never a serious option.

Bob kissed me that night, yet if the Mediterranean hadn't rocked me into submission—seasick to overflowing—I might not have hesitated long enough to hold his hand and really notice him.

He knelt by my narrow ship's berth—my sickbed—for days, and held my hand. It was not yet love, but he was fast becoming my friend.

Later, I saw the violent vomiting and subsequent exhaustion as how I'd made way for my new friend. In that enforced pause in my usual frenzy, I allowed Bob to quietly enter my life. And, of course, the only way Bob could enter a place was quietly, and after considerable hesitation.

Rarely did we mention Vietnam during those seven days in Hong Kong, and when we did, as if by silent consensus, we referred to it only as "the other place." After those first four or five months in Vietnam, when we'd eagerly snatched whatever novelty was thrown in our faces, we had closed up shop to inviting new sensations. Better to refuse to see, hear, smell, and feel than to take deep breaths of life and drown in them. In Hong Kong, we were free again to reclaim what we'd given up for lost.

Colors were sharply outlined and heightened: water, a pulsating blue; little girls' confirmation dresses, blindingly white. Smells mingled flora, sea water, and Peking duck, with a fleeting hint of Fabergé. Sounds were living music: orchestral, vocal, lilting Chinese pronunciation and British inflection. Taste. We denied ourselves nothing we could wrap our appetites around.

But it was what we could feel that was miraculous. We were free to feel joy.

We arrived in Hong Kong with $2,000 spending money—a fortune—and we spent every cent of it. Until Hong Kong, Bob had assumed he was most at ease in jeans and a blue cotton work shirt. He'd owned just one suit in his lifetime, bought for high school graduation and long since outgrown. There'd been no other occasion in his life when a navy blazer would not do nicely.

But Marsh's tailor and I worked hard to change his mind. Custom-tailored clothing for a song was an essential piece of the

Hong Kong experience as translated by Marsh. Men got fitted for suits; women bought cultured pearls; everyone bought cameras. We already had the camera.

The tailor's shop and Bob's new clothing were a game to us. He could not actually imagine where he'd ever wear the clothing he bought. But I insisted that it would increase his "options." In fact, I was already fine-tuning the direction of Bob's options. The son of a civil servant, he'd pictured himself a school teacher. I thought he could do better. With his keen mind, I saw him as an academic. I saw finely tailored suits and sports jackets as how he'd look the part.

The first floor of the multi-storied tailor shop was filled with rolls of English woolens—tweeds, herringbones, pinstripes, solids. Upstairs were the fitting rooms, the button assortment, the rolls of satin linings—and the men with cloth tape measures hanging around their necks.

We'd come prepared with carefully clipped fashion spreads and advertisements from back issues of *Esquire*. Bob was salivating over a Harris Tweed sport jacket with leather buttons, elbow patches, and pocket flaps. It was, we agreed, very professorial—potentially Bob.

Mr. Lee was short, around fifty, and impeccable. "This gray pinstripe you can wear three seasons. The navy is for winter," he instructed. "*That* fabric is very formal; this one you can wear for business." And, "The Swiss military use the brown one for their winter uniform."

Bob didn't pretend to know more than he knew, didn't pretend to understand what constituted a *formal* occasion and what was merely a *business* one. A couple of times during the fittings, Bob balked. "Jesus, where am I going to wear this stuff—teaching high school kids? Or plan number two, graduate school? Then it'll take four more years until I need a suit."

"You never know, Bob."

"Yeah, *right*—my options," he laughed.

Mr. Lee gladly filled in the blanks. He took Bob's education to heart.

On the first visit, we matched our magazine clips and our mental images with the rolls of fabric. They took Bob's measurements. On the second fitting they pinned the puzzle pieces together on Bob; chose the buttons, the lining, and the cut of the lapel. On the final fitting, all the pieces came together perfectly. We were like kids at Halloween playing dress-up. Successively, Bob was amazed, humbled, and delighted at the attention to detail, the attention to him, and the awesome feeling inside a tailored-to-specification suit.

Days later, he picked up his purchases: a gray, worsted-wool, double-breasted suit; a brown herringbone one; the Harris Tweed sports jacket (with a pair of Swiss Army-fabric pants); and a cream-colored, summer-weight, linen sport jacket. All of it—fittings, fabric, tailoring—came to $200.

"*Vestis virum facit.*" He smiled at his image in the Harris Tweed, and at his memory of four years of Jesuit-enforced Latin. "Clothes make the man."

It was my turn. I wanted only one thing, but I really wanted it. I wanted a string of Mikimoto cultured pearls. I seldom wore earrings, never bracelets, and no gold chains—just my plain gold wedding band. I never wanted an engagement ring. Jewelry was not my thing. But a single strand of seven-millimeter, twenty-two-inch-long luminescent pearls were forever. My mother—with drawers full of diamonds and costume jewelry—never much cared for them herself.

Marsh told me what and where. Hong Kong was a duty-free port and sold pearls at a fraction of the market price. The shop was elegant. A beautiful Chinese saleswoman took us to a private niche and pulled out a dozen rows of strung pearls on black velvet.

"May I?" she gestured toward my bare neck. When I nodded, she draped me in black silk and then, one by one, hung the delicate strands around me. The saleswoman—who wore a pearl choker clasped around her own neck—examined me carefully with each strand, and only then was I able to look at myself in the mirror.

She alone answered for me.

"No," she studied my face. "Too small."

The next one she dismissed in her crisp British inflection, "Not long enough." And then, finally, "Ah. What do you think?"

I looked at myself in the mirror. I thought I looked like a queen. I looked at Bob; he nodded. It seemed he thought so, too.

"These are our very best," the saleswoman said.

I needed no prodding. "I'll take them." I'd forgotten to ask; they cost $120.

We loaded our arms with our extravagance—tailored clothing, Mikimoto pearls, and some family gifts—and handed them off to be packaged and shipped home free of charge, at the tiny Hong Kong PX, established for that very purpose.

But, of course, we hadn't come to Hong Kong to shop so much as to indulge our fantasies. The fact that the Hilton turned down our bed and put Swiss chocolates on our pillows at night seemed more than a person might wish for in this lifetime. The fact that Bob and I filled out little paper menus each night, hung them on our door handle, and awakened to eggs Benedict, fresh papaya juice, and steaming coffee; that we slipped on thick, fresh, terry cloth bathrobes and ate looking over the Hong Kong skyline through our wall of windows pushed the limits of imagined indulgence.

We ate filet mignon at a place called the San Francisco Steak House for the nostalgia; lunch at an English pub for the kidney pie; lobster Cantonese at a neighborhood bistro. We ate at every Marsh-recommended place and discovered some of our own. We consumed three big meals every day.

We grabbed buses to distant edges of the island and walked remote beaches without another soul in sight. Every single day, we walked. We waded through ancient neighborhoods and winding paths. Central Hong Kong was dense. It made Manhattan look like a village.

Undoubtedly, there was poverty, but this was no Chinatown. The city was a thriving, modern metropolis and it was exactly what I now needed. For a single week, Hong Kong wreathed me in a sophistication, exhilaration, and anonymity that obliterated any thought of Vietnam.

We saved the best for last. Gaddi's was billed as one of the finest restaurants in the *world*. It sat inside the Peninsula Hotel, the hundred-year-old jewel of Hong Kong. There were steep marble entry steps to the hotel and European opulence—gilt, antiques, and real art. Even allowing for our total lack of experience in what might be factored into the truly world class, Gaddi's distinction was not lost on us.

The restaurant, on an upper floor of the hotel, was expansive: fabric wall coverings, a domed ceiling with airy crystal and filigree chandeliers, and fifteen ample square tables spread over the spacious room. The colors were deep and warm; no table was within ten feet of another.

Around each table there were four plush, substantial brocade armchairs. Two disappeared when Bob and I were seated. Just slightly off-center sat a small hardwood dance floor and a five-piece ensemble.

Now, when I think of that glorious last evening in Hong Kong—two twenty-four-year-old kids who'd been living with cold water and sweltering heat in Saigon; two kids dressed in their Vietnam best, Bob's old navy blazer, frayed button-down shirt, college rep tie, and my polyester navy sheath with sandals—I could cringe with embarrassment.

Surely, no one at Gaddi's looked anything like us. Surely, the other customers were custom-tailored, bejeweled, and internationally elegant—maybe even recognizable. But at that time there was absolutely nothing like embarrassment, only the many-layered graciousness of the staff and my love of Bob.

Every table had five waiters. When they were needed, they were there; when they were not, they were invisible against the satin wall near the kitchen. If there was something else that our waiters would have preferred to do with their lives—perform open-heart surgery or paint daring church frescoes—we were not given a clue. There was neither obsequiousness nor overbearing good will.

In sum, Bob and I were free to focus entirely on one another, and we did. The meal took us three hours to order and consume. We ate slowly, with appropriate space for the conversation to flower. We began with history, Bob's college major and his passion: European versus Asian, how Hong Kong blended each.

"The British were a different kind of colonist than the French," Bob expounded in the judicious manner he adapted when he talked ideas. "The British left less culture—fewer libraries, schools, and gardens—but better manners."

"Are you talking about servility?" I challenged him.

"No, not that. It's gentility." He held forth until the appetizer arrived, then turned to the meal.

The food was exquisite. I remember the melon and prosciutto mostly because three different men served it: the melon man, the prosciutto man, the fork-and-plate man. We chose appetizer, soup, salad, meat, dessert; plus cocktails, wine, liqueur, and espresso—and we finished every morsel. Much of the food was entirely new to us.

Each course barely intruded on our shifting conversation. The soup was a cold, fragrant seafood bisque. The entrées arrived

Girls Don't!

much later, after a pause we barely noticed because we were so caught up in the velocity of our words, now weighing Sartre against Camus; I smile now remembering our youth and the *times*. Both of us were steeped in college philosophy. Bob's leaned more toward the Catholics: St. Augustine, St. Thomas Aquinas.

My entrée was veal simmered in wine with morels, baby new potatoes carved into tiny baskets, and the first I'd ever seen vegetables julienne.

Between bites, we'd pick up wherever we'd left off.

"What're you feeling?" I asked, trying to read Bob's inscrutable face.

"Like I want to take up residence at this table." I laughed.

"I've got a terrific buzz," he said, "How about you?"

"Me, too, just one big goofy grin. But I want *more* from you. Tell me your dreams. What is it that you want from life?"

"Omigod . . . *my life*. You first," he said.

"Okay. But it's nothing you don't know, nothing we haven't hashed a dozen times." I sucked in my breath and looked out the dark window over the blazing harbor lights.

"First, I want surprise, adventure. I *don't* want to know where I'll be next year—or the year after that—or what I'll be doing there, either!"

I forced myself to slow the rush of my intentions. "Second, I don't want to ever own a house; property would tie me down."

"Third," and now I looked up into Bob's pale blue eyes and felt a tug in my chest . . . *more is the pity*. "I don't want children. But, of course, I know that you do."

"Whew," was all Bob said for a very long time. He'd heard it all before, perhaps less succinctly. I knew I could spout more words to silence his silence, but this time I didn't want to.

Finally, he said, "All that without a taking a breath. I'm afraid to ask if there's a fourth." I knew that, less than my words, it was my absolute certainty that staggered and intimidated him.

"Yeah," I said in an effort to lighten the load. "There's more. I want to go straight back to the hotel after this meal and make love until breakfast arrives in the morning."

"Check, please!" We both laughed.

"So, it's your turn," I said. "Tell me something I don't know."

There was a deep, slow silence, and then he unpeeled his words hesitantly.

"I don't know what I want to be when I grow up. I'm pretty sure I don't *want* to grow up." He sighed and looked past me out the window.

"But," it seemed he was dragging the words from a place he thought best left sheltered, "I'm thinking I need to take the Graduate Record Exam next month so I can at least consider graduate school. The GI Bill would pay for it."

"Wonderful!"

"But would you follow me to graduate school?"

"Sure." I didn't flinch. "Every city has a newspaper. I could do that."

"But you don't want to settle down, right?"

"No, I don't."

"I can't picture it—you, a grad student wife?"

"No, *me* a reporter; *you*, a grad student."

"But there'd be expectations—being married, a couple; nothing like here. There'd be sacrifices."

"Like what?"

"Like following a husband, taking any job where I land, stuck there for four years. I don't think that would make you very happy."

The turn of the conversation was beginning to scare the hell out of me. Bob clearly hated what he was forcing himself to say. He poured each of us another glass of wine, not waiting for the ever-attentive waiter.

Girls Don't!

I picked up my glass and drifted. I refused to think about the incongruities. How does marriage mesh with ambition? How would any of it work after Vietnam? I could not be a war correspondent married to a soldier in perpetuity.

"Why do I have to make sacrifices?" is what I finally answered. I still believed we were like empty boxes, freely choosing how to fill our lives. I still thought we were unmarked by what we'd been through together and what we carried of our families. I thought all *options* lay entirely in our hands. Bob knew better.

"This is getting *way* too heavy," Bob said with a gentle chuckle. "See why I don't want to grow up?"

Dessert. Bob and I were both suckers for chocolate, so there wasn't much likelihood we'd reach for the more subtle delicacies that involved fruit, nuts, or honey. The waiter directed us to the chocolate torte, and we consented. Like the Sistine Chapel, the Mayan pyramids, and the tombs of King Tutankhamun, that chocolate torte remains one of the mysteries of my life—cake, cream, light and dark chocolates, elusive to this day.

Any remaining briars of our earlier conversation were firmly buried and forgotten in the chocolate. Between bites, Bob and I couldn't take our sense-starved eyes off one another. Before espresso, Bob asked me to dance. The orchestra played music that I suspect our parents had danced to in the Forties when they'd conceived us. We held tight to one another, moved across the silken floor. I was transported by the music, the food, the wine, the room, and the dance steps with the only partner whose moves I entirely understood.

In a blur over Bob's shoulder, I got a glimpse of benediction: the approving smiles of older, more worldly eyes watching us dance. I remember thinking for one brief self-conscious moment: we were that transparently in love.

CHAPTER 13

FINDING MIDDLE GROUND

DECEMBER 1970

At the bottom of one of my letters, Bob wrote this to his mother.

Dear Mom,

As you can imagine, with the return to eating in Vietnam my stomach is in total confusion. It speaks for the rest of me. I suppose that when we get home, we'll talk as much about this one week in Hong Kong as the other sixty in Saigon. Certainly, we will talk about it with more enthusiasm.

Peace,
Bob

Girls Don't!

He spoke for both of us.

But the breath we'd taken in Hong Kong held us for a good while after we returned to Saigon. We could move more easily about Saigon's thick, polluted air because our lungs were still full of R&R.

As the year drew to a close, the singularity and discordance of my Vietnam experience was on full display. It ranged from rebellious humor to unmitigated tragedy. It was that kind of month.

But maybe, it was just that kind of war.

Long before Hong Kong, we'd become accustomed to a nightly ritual. Lights out, heads on the pillow was the summons to neighborhood rats who made an incursion under our sidedoor, through our bathroom, and smack into our bedroom. They landed noisily in the wastepaper basket where they churned up crumpled papers. I'd climb into bed at night with a shoe in hand. When I heard the wicker basket crackle, I'd pitch a sandal directly at the trash can and jolt it just enough to scare the rodent out of its comfort zone. It ran out, exactly the way it came in.

Just a harmless nighttime ritual. "Good night, Bobby." "Good night, Poo." Lights out and a shoe sailing the length of the room to a direct hit—then the sound of scurrying rodent feet. We barely lost a moment's sleep.

But two weeks after our return from Hong Kong, there was a new wrinkle. A particular rat born inside our room knew no other home. Either he had no idea there was a way out or no desire to find one. He was onto and into everything: the top of the refrigerator, the table where we ate our meals. He gnawed a hole in a Lipton dry soup mix and then stashed it and bits of our chocolate chip cookies inside my suitcase amidst the clean linen.

I was increasingly sickened by the sight of his remains. I'd flick on the light at night and send him into hiding. But he crept out the moment the light went off again. Bob slept soundly, but I wasn't getting much sleep.

I removed every bit of food from the room except what was inside the refrigerator. The rat endured, searching. We nailed patches over holes, searched out every imaginable hiding place. He remained.

I devised a trap. I filled a cookie tin with what I imagined were rat goodies—cheese and cake. Bob made a wooden prop to hold the top ajar. He set the contraption in a corner. The plan was to jump from bed into the darkness and slam the top down on our captive.

We turned out the light and waited. Barely breathing, I hung over the side of the bed and listened.

Absolutely *nothing* happened. The rat, outsmarting our cumulative intellect, never came near the tin.

The next day, I declared war. "Buy rat poison."

After work, Bob reported, "The PX doesn't have any." He handed me a spring-loaded rattrap. "Here."

Neither of us was thrilled at the prospect of flattening the young rat's body under a spring-loaded wire, but I was willing. Bob wanted only to curtail my obsession.

We got onto the Honda, drove to the USO, and bought a 35-cent hotdog to fit in the trap.

"How about I put mustard on it?" Bob laughed. "If the rat doesn't want it, I can eat it for lunch."

We set the trap inside the wastebasket, turned out the lights, and went for a walk. When we got back, the trap and the hotdog were untouched—the latter looking increasingly like Bob's lunch.

It was getting late. We got in bed and turned off the lights; Bob dropped off to sleep immediately. In the seductive silence, I too fell asleep. I was jolted awake by the unmistakable sound of a spring-loaded trap crushing a living being. Inexplicably, I began to cry. Bob, who had slept soundly through the wire snap, awakened to my bewildering sobs.

He carried the trash can, at arm's length with only a glimpse inside, to the edge of the river, where he turned it upside down over the water and dropped the contents—trap, rat, and hotdog—into the sluggish current. We had our sanctuary to ourselves.

After Hong Kong, we discovered the movies. Discovered that, together, we could go into MACV—the Vietnam Pentagon—and watch current American films with the generals and colonels who ran the war. It was a combination of my being a reporter and Bob being military that got us through the doors and into the intimate little theater that was usually only half-full, and free.

We saw just a few films there, but two were life-altering, memorable experiences: *Patton* and *M*A*S*H*.

Patton: while intimidatingly surrounded by the generals who had their commanding fingers on the buttons of the Vietnam War. *Patton*: watching the antics of a despotic, World War II general while seated among the gray-haired, perfectly turned-out eminences who emulated him, who saw his arrogance as prerogative. Bob and I were alive to the irony and to the miracle of our being there.

M*A*S*H was a trip of a whole other kind. Seeing *M*A*S*H* at MACV was like being stoned in Vietnam—a supremely radical act. Perhaps our most political act in Vietnam was laughing our fool heads off at *M*A*S*H* while sitting nearly hip to hip with the generals—laughing particularly hard at the parts that were met with stony silence by this peculiar audience.

Our greatest revenge and our most profound healing came from grabbing each other's arms and laughing until our sides ached and the tears rolled down our faces onto the plush upholstered seats in the air-conditioned theater at the Military Area

Command, Vietnam. Laughing all alone in an audience of forty in the Republic of Vietnam.

In the film, generals and colonels were the corrupt buffoons. Draftees and enlisted men were the irreverent but ethical heroes. There was little doubt who occupied the moral high ground.

"God damn Army, god damn Army," a sergeant-actor seethes in frustration at the dead center of the movie. And the last words we heard as the credits rolled was the reprise: "God damn Army."

Bob and I looked furtively into each other's eyes in that darkened theater, grinned to split our cheeks, and then swallowed our words. Bob signaled thumbs-up in his lap—no one was sitting to our immediate right or left. Presumably, you could not be court-martialed for laughing your heart out at a movie—but you sure as hell would be if you said out loud, "God damn Army." It was pretty tempting.

We were well out of the rainy season. Already, I couldn't remember a day with clouds or moisture. It was hot and sunny, day in and day out.

We were fast approaching Christmas, but you'd have been hard-pressed to prove it by me. No pine, spruce, or cedar in Saigon. In this part-Catholic, part-Buddhist country, there was a confusion of symbolism. We'd stacked the gifts from Bob's family on top of our little refrigerator. We decorated the refrigerator with the cards we'd received and with any whimsy we took a fancy to, like red-fringed firecrackers, gilded candles, and garish tinsel.

In the weeks before Christmas, Bob spent every lunch hour and evening bent over his high school algebra books, studying. It had been five years since his last math class. The GRE—the graduate school admissions test, his passport to a PhD in American history—was scheduled between Christmas and New Year's at MACV. He was less worried about the verbal part: there was no

Girls Don't!

real way to prepare for that one, and he was pretty darned verbal anyway.

It felt more than a little weird sitting around our room night after night. Me—stuck here with no *Time* assignment outside of Saigon. Now, too, no radio music, no grass, and no conversation, because Bob was hunched over our dinner table doing algebra problems.

On Christmas Day, though, Bob and I did what every other American soldier did in every recent American war, conflict, or military intervention: we took the tour bus to Long Binh to watch the Bob Hope Christmas Show. We had press passes that put us right up front.

The press pass conferred on us the privilege to question the cast afterwards. But only one of the twenty-five correspondents at that press conference asked Hope anything, and that question was, "Is this your last Vietnam show?"

Poor Bob Hope. He had paraded the same stale jokes, pretty girls, and macho sports heroes that he'd trundled around military bases since World War II. The girls worked fine—Lola Falana shook her feathers in a semi-erotic dance and the boys ate it up. Vintage Bob Hope: bring some salivating PFC on stage to ogle the dancer's breasts. In this case, she was African American, and so the soldier Hope hauled from the second row was as well.

"Hey, soldier," Hope said, drawing his words out slowly and looking conspiratorially at the audience. "What do you think of this girl here?"

"Uh," the skinny boy from Arkansas said. "I think she's real nice, Sir."

"Nice, huh?" Hope swung his golf club at the air. "Is that the best you've been offered, Lola?"

"Well," Falana shrugged her breasts into the kid's face.

"Private, would you like to kiss Lola?" Hope asked.

"Yessir, I would."

There was the inevitable lunge, the awkward kiss, and the roar of audience approval.

Nothing terribly new, but classic. It was a formula that still worked. Baseball personality Johnny Bench, too—he was the straight man to Hope's punches.

But standing up there alone without Lola or Johnny as props, Bob Hope was an embarrassment, a genuine disaster. The jokes that had worked for twenty-five years in front of gung ho warriors fell flat here. Jokes that might even have worked in a less cynical part of this war were met with hisses and taunts. The tried and true: plug in the names of the current president, the current commanders, Nixon and Abrams and Zumwalt—the keys that were supposed to churn enlisted men's envy and laughter—elicited jeers instead. I was writhing in my seat.

In truth, these 23,000 boys *wanted* to laugh, wanted more than anything else to laugh. It was, as the kid behind me said, "Bob fucking Hope, for God's sake!" But it fell flat. Flat, because innocent, gung ho patriotism didn't play here anymore. Didn't play to our demoralized, disenchanted Army, Navy, or Marine Corps. Nixon was irrevocably withdrawing troops without a single shred of evidence that our mission had been accomplished. Our nation was headed for its first acknowledged military defeat, and these boys knew it first.

So irreverent enlisted men's jokes aimed at puncturing official pomposity were gratuitous. With frightening regularity, American PFCs were fragging their lieutenants—slipping grenades under the offending officer's cot and blowing him to smithereens. Our own officers had become the only identifiable enemy.

Poor Bob Hope. In Long Binh, 23,000 men did not laugh, sometimes booed, and most often moaned at the political *wrongness* of it all—at Hope's absolute incomprehension. None of us could even scrape up the enthusiasm to pretend.

Girls Don't!

Bob was driving the Honda to work one morning, shortly after Christmas. I was hanging on sidesaddle behind him. Typically, it took us twenty-five minutes to get to Bob's office. There, he'd climb off, I'd swing my leg over the gas tank, slide forward, and drive downtown to my office. I was working for Jon on a series of small stories that kept me busy. None were very exciting and most could be accomplished by telephone. All of them kept me within Saigon city limits.

I suspected that Jon, only six years my senior, felt some proprietary traditional male interest in keeping me safe for Bob (as he'd expect Bob to do for Wendy), and that possibility made me extremely uneasy. I was chafing mightily under his well-meant, brotherly protection. I had not confronted him.

So, that morning while Bob and I were passing sluggishly through Saigon traffic, I was leaning against his back and thinking about work—about today's story, my contribution to a larger *Time* piece about Asian leaders who consulted astrologers and soothsayers before making national decisions. I'd already done the research, and I was grappling with my lead sentence as we made our way through the unremarkably thick morning traffic and fumes.

Like a metaphor for the war itself—where Americans tried to convince a guerilla army dressed in pajamas and truck-tire sandals that bigger was better, and where six-foot Americans lorded over five-foot Vietnamese men—in Saigon traffic, the ubiquitous Hondas were just so many flies to the massive, green American army trucks.

Among the motorcycles, pedicabs, and small taxis there had settled a complicated give and take. It was a puzzle that took some learning. But with the huge American army vehicles, it was all horn and brass. From the fly-eye view on my Honda, it was infuriating. I wasn't the only one who got mad.

Finding Middle Ground

On that late December morning, Bob and I were in our single-cup-of-coffee morning fog. We were moving along and not asking much of the larger world. But at that very moment, an enormous two-ton, open-back truck came bearing down on us *much* too fast—making its way where no way was possible. At that truck's insistence on getting where it was going ahead of every smaller vehicle on the road, the young GI driver and his companions smashed into the back of a tiny Honda. The truck driver backed up just a trace, turned the wheel, gunned his big engine, and fled.

Although I suspect the Army would *still* deny it, what these boys had done was the unspoken code of US Army behavior. If you were American military involved in a car wreck in Saigon, you were advised not to stop. It was deemed advisable to return to base and report the accident. But as it turned out, no one much worried about filing the report, either.

What the two-ton truck and its young driver left in its wake was a boy around twelve years old bleeding from his head and going into shock in the middle of the roadway. Without a pause, Bob yelled, "Take care of the bikes."

He hopped off and ran to help the kid. I pulled our bike to the sidewalk and set it down. Then I went back and pulled the boy's bike out of traffic. Bob carefully lifted the boy from the street and carried him to the sidewalk. He plopped himself down on the filthy curb next to the child, pulled off his fatigue shirt, and covered the boy. In only his olive green t-shirt, Bob kept the child still, put his handkerchief against the wound, and persistently asked for someone to please find a doctor. I sat next to Bob and watched his ministrations.

This was the quintessential Bob. I'd been with him when he had, without a second thought, jumped into a street fight in San Francisco, interceding on the side of the underdog. When Bob's ethical standards met his adrenaline rush, he was unstoppable.

Afterwards, he would be drained and shaking, but I found his call to action a lovely paradox in this peaceful, nonconfrontational man.

The twelve-year-old had a sweet, round, fleshy face. He was dressed for school in navy blue cotton slacks and a crisp white short-sleeve shirt. His book bag was still strapped to the back of his bike. The boy was in pain, moaning and writhing under Bob's touch. There was blood from the back of his cracked skull gushing over the ironed white shirt.

"This kid needs help," Bob said to me. "Stay here with him. The hospital's not far. I'll get someone and come back."

"Okay. But hurry."

Bob stood up, reached to pull up our Honda, and was instantly immobilized. We'd been perched on the sidewalk, concentrating our attention on the child, and had not seen the impenetrably dense wall of people who'd gathered, pressing toward us.

We spoke no meaningful Vietnamese and the people around us appeared to speak no English. But the crowd's intent was obvious enough, and it was exceedingly malevolent. There was no way in hell they'd let Bob get his hands on the Honda, and they pushed hard against him to restrain him.

Bob looked stunned; it didn't occur to him to push back. He wanted only to make them understand his intentions, and he was anguished over his thwarted mission. "I'm getting a doctor for the boy," he tried futilely in English. "I'll be back."

The street story had been whispered, shouted, and disseminated. It was clear enough: an American soldier had hit this kid. Now, that American—transmuted into Bob—was leaving the bleeding child. It was an act of everyday unprincipled American behavior.

I'd never in my life stood in the center of such outrage, let alone allied with its target. And although Bob didn't appear to consider being afraid, I was afraid enough for both of us. It was the incredible noise of hatred. The shouting in Bob's face, the features distended

Finding Middle Ground

by fury, the threatening physical crush of a hundred human beings against us. So many of them; the two of us. How could we make ourselves understood in the face of their rage? In the face of *years* of accumulated slights and indignities—our *allies* indeed.

Bob looked to the writhing boy at his feet, gestured to the blood, signaled a symbolic Red Cross, and explained in words and gestures his intentions. But the more he gestured, the more the crowd roared its venom. I think it was only my presence—an American, yes, but a *woman*—that stayed the mob, held back the inevitable explosion.

Then out of nowhere, or from just about anywhere, a well-dressed Vietnamese man appeared speaking firmly and unrelentingly, pushing his way through the mob toward us. The people made way for him. He seemed accustomed to being granted his way, and it soon became apparent that he understood what had happened here. Either he'd witnessed some of it or had come later and heard Bob's entreaties. He spoke to us in impeccable English.

"Did you run into this child?"

"No, a US Army truck hit him," Bob said. "I stopped to help."

"I am sorry," he said to Bob. "We are not accustomed to Americans who help. You must understand that many children have been killed this way."

"I do understand," Bob said.

The man turned back to the crowd and spoke. The mob shrieked its disapproval. They didn't buy it. They wanted an eye for an eye.

The man turned back to Bob.

"Listen to me. You need to leave immediately. I will talk to these people. You must walk slowly through them. Look at no one. When you reach the clearing, get onto your Honda and drive away. These people are very angry. They do not want you to leave. But I will talk to them and if you do as I say you can go safely."

"What about the boy?" Bob asked.

"We take care of our children. Now go." He picked up Bob's fatigue shirt from the child and handed it back to him.

"Thank you," Bob said.

"Thanks to you," the man answered.

With our heads down and our faces averted from the other faces as though in shame, with people leaning menacingly into us and looking always as if they might spit on us or strike us, we did as we were told. We left under the protection of the well-dressed, well-spoken Vietnamese man's umbrella of words.

It felt like forever, walking that bike from the boy's side to the perimeter of the mob. The boy's soft moans and intermittent wails punctuated our footsteps. I held my breath and prayed that the spell of the man's words would hold and protect us, but I never really expected they would.

Bob drove carefully and deliberately towards work; we didn't exchange a word. We moved slowly, still under the spell of the powerful man's last audible words, afraid to break the incantation, feeling a peculiar shame.

There had been no way at all to bridge the cataclysmic gap of understanding. We each felt impotent and confused. When we got to Bob's office, we climbed off the bike and began to tremble. Bob's eyes were brimming; I cried quietly against his chest. We held each other in a vain attempt to find equilibrium. But we understood, in a brand new way, something that the Vietnamese people had long understood. That in this place at this time, there was really no hope at all, for any of us.

In an abrupt late-December contradiction—one that spoke to the tangle of my emotions on any given day in Vietnam—New Year's Eve was another take on the war entirely.

The Flower People of Saigon
Invite you to see,
The Light at the End of the Tunnel
ACT IV
New Year's Eve, 1970
9:30 p.m.
47 Phan Thanh Gian

A full twenty-six names at the bottom of the invitation shared blame or claimed credit for the irreverent wit, including our own Jon Larsen and the "Ghost of Christmas Past," the honorable antiwar US Senator J. W. Fulbright. This was clearly the New Year's party of the year. It was held in an enormous and elegant French villa with gardens sprawled over several acres.

Three hundred of Saigon's movers and shakers of every conceivable nationality were dressed to kill. *Dressed*, in Saigon, where formal typically meant you'd bathed that day. But this party was an exception to every rule I'd come to expect in Saigon. Maybe it took the likes of Larsen, with his impeccable *Time* corporate connections, to help pull it together: diplomats, journalists, Vietnamese politicians, artists, musicians—faces I'd never seen before.

I wore my yellow silk *ao dai* with the embroidered flowers, mandarin neckline, flowing black satin pants, and sandals. I'd been here long enough and lost enough weight to venture into the *ao dai* I'd had made months before. Considering the glitz, my costume was a bare minimum. Bob wore his navy blazer.

The food was limitless: largely French, but Chinese, too. The drink: abundant bottles of the best. Bob stuck to bourbon and water; I drank the imported German beer. Early in the evening, Bob and I hung out inside the antique-filled dining room, eating, drinking, and reaching out to folks we didn't know, warmly greeting those we did.

"Ennio," I said to *Time*'s Italian freelance photographer. "We got your invitation. I can't wait. Married on top of the Caravelle, pretty swank! Nervous?"

"Yeah," he said, "I'm nervous. The Caravelle was Lu's mother's choice, my expense. But this party is a hard act to follow."

After a few drinks, Bob and I tired of the social effort and headed outside where the music was loudest and spent the rest of the evening dancing under the stars on a grassy slope to classic rock and roll.

We welcomed 1971 in each other's arms, leaning against the yellow stucco garden wall under a flowering fruit tree. We overheard New Year's wishes in a half-dozen languages.

"It's 1971, Bob, new beginnings."

"1971, and we're still here."

"But this year, we leave."

"Back to the *world*. What'll it be like?"

"I don't know," I said. "But it's less than a month until our wedding anniversary. One whole year."

Bob laughed into the night. "Only a year?"

CHAPTER 14

CLAIMING HIGH GROUND

JANUARY 1971

In January, my chickens came home to roost. Jon peeled off the story from the top of the pile for me, a potential cover story with all the corporate and collegial prestige that went along with it: "Children of War."

"Here," he said. "Sink your teeth into this one."

I took it and ran.

Jon Larsen, it turned out, had recognized the potential within my prostitution story and figured that a woman just might bring something different to "Children of War." He gave me ample time and the longest possible leash. I worked on it for three weeks, and

I turned in thirty-three pages of copy.

So Jon had been enough of a certain kind of man to give me a crack at the big story—but traditional enough still to assure himself that this story would put me in no danger at all.

Children of war. There were a number of different portals and, like Alice in Wonderland, I intended to try every one of them.

I spent my first week in the orphanages. They were abhorrent in distinct and varied ways. Primarily, the very *idea* of an orphanage was antithetical to traditional Vietnamese culture and family. Ten years before, orphanages were unheard of and unneeded. Ten years before, childhood in South Vietnam was not much different than it had been a hundred years earlier. Children rode buffalo backs through an endless expanse of green rice paddies; they swam in wide clean canals and played in large muddy fields. Older children had chores, a sense of purpose and belonging. They planted rice and harvested it. They helped rear their brothers and sisters.

Everyone within sight was aunt, uncle, cousin, or grandparent. Each had a hand in rearing the children. A hamlet was simply a collection of smaller family units. If a parent died, the rest stepped in and took over. That changed with the second Indochina War, the American one. Now bombs fell from unseen planes with no warning and for no apparent reason. Sometimes, they fell in the wrong place—often, on the wrong people.

Slowly at first, then more rapidly, fragments of extended families moved from their inland ancestral lands toward the more populous coast, to refugee camps that promised safety from the capricious bombs. They left their spiritual source: the fields that fed them, the family that nourished them, and the graves of their ancestors.

They moved, because their only other choice was the unpredictable rain of terror from the sky. Relatives lost track of each other. Aunts who were like mothers were halfway across the country. Fathers were long gone, drafted into the army until the unending war ended or until they were maimed or killed.

The refugee camps I'd visited shortly after I'd arrived in Vietnam were crowded and dangerous places, breeding grounds for crime. The houses were tiny and impermanent, pushed up against one another. The camps were counterfeit hamlets, sustaining neither agriculture nor kinship. They promoted total dependence on the government for food and shelter. There was no place at all for the children to play.

From refugee camps, intended only as a temporary solution, the fragmented shrunken family moved to the cities where conditions were a magnified version of the camps—dirtier, lonelier, and more crowded. Food could no longer be grown, it needed to be bought. Mothers faced an unbearable impasse—they must abandon their children to feed them. They left them alone to find work.

And what work might be available to an uneducated, rural woman? Laundering, sewing, and ironing fatigues for the soldiers who'd dropped the bombs that exiled the family from their homes. Peddling cigarettes on street corners. Beloved children—for the first time *ever* in Vietnam—became a burden. They were no longer contributors to the whole; they'd become only mouths to feed.

Traditionally, when a parent died, children were absorbed by kin that had already behaved as parents. Now, a mother's death meant the child was completely alone. It was a violation of everything sacred.

From this utter desperation, orphanages were born: 120 registered ones housing 20,000 children; more than 150 fly-by-night operations. Outside the walls of orphanages were four times that number of children who needed them.

I spent a week in the best of the Vietnamese government-registered orphanages. Uniformly, they made my skin crawl. On one sweltering day, I sat for hours with my legs sticking to the stiff-backed chair in a large stinking warehouse. I was a reporter acting as dispassionate observer, feeling inconsolable and impotent. This orphanage, like every one of them, was frightfully understaffed.

I observed a single young aide perfunctorily prop milk bottles to babies' lips, one after another, down a row of fifty tiny mouths. She left them there until they were empty. She had no time to monitor how much an infant swallowed or to even check that the bottles stayed in place. She most certainly had no time to pat a back, hold a baby, or soothe tears.

The young aide, a skinny girl herself, spoke no English or French. She looked at me exactly as she looked at the babies—indifferently. I gestured to a baby: a dirty diaper, the bottle upside down under her. "May I?" She shrugged nonchalantly.

I sprung repeatedly from my sticky chair to fix a bottle that had fallen away, dripping milk onto the bed or floor. I reached over to touch a soft tan cheek, but I was defeated. There were so many, and I was there for just a single day. Would this baby girl be alive next week?

Seven children died each month in every government-registered orphanage. That number was touted as a decided improvement over the fifteen monthly dead, three years before. Infants died of malnutrition and untreated diarrhea. It took just a couple days to lose an unheeded infant to dehydration.

I shifted off my chair to track the lunchtime feeding routine of the older babies—the toddlers—in the next sprawling room. That room had concrete walls; the floors were swept several times a day. Still, they were littered with the debris of a hundred children's lives—food, excrement, *no* toys. These were babies on solid food, and their mealtime was a different kind of affront altogether.

At twenty-four, I did not think of myself as maternal. *Maternal* I saw as a conspiracy to turn me into my mother and eradicate my choices. But my entire body tightened at the pathetic, relentless crying and whimpering of these under-two-year-olds. The toddlers were placed side by side on long wooden benches. A plump aide—older and sterner than the first—marched from one child to the next with a single bowl and spoon. She ladled a few spoons of rice into the first child's mouth, a little boy with scabs over his body, then a few spoons into the next, a little girl whose hair was matted against her face with feces.

The single spoon went from bowl to mouth, back into the bowl and into the next mouth. If a single child were ill, every child would be. The children screeched their hunger, gestured their demand for more.

They wailed, too—it wasn't hard to imagine—for simple human touch. Doubly starved. No aide had a moment to offer it.

I wanted to grab that bowl and fill each child to the brim. I wanted to make familiar childhood sounds, "Here comes the airplane," and swoop full spoons into responsive mouths. But I did not. They were hungry and I had no food.

These were not cruel women ministering to the babies, they were hopeless ones. It came down to futility. If the collective nation of families and hamlets had given up on their own, what could a stranger in an orphanage offer? What could these poorly paid women, barely feeding their own, do?

"Most of the aides are cleaning women who know nothing about children," the American Catholic Relief Services director told me from the comfort of her air-conditioned downtown office. "Quite a number of the children who survive orphanages are emotional basket cases."

I demanded to know how she could permit it, the meager food and the inadequate staff. She, who bore the responsibility. She shrugged. It wasn't within her job description to answer such questions. "Our budget allows only so much."

"But *your* salary." I waved at the office, heavy with administrative staff. "And the others." I wouldn't let up. "Surely, the money should go to the babies, not your staff."

She smiled placidly, wholly unmoved by my fervor. Undoubtedly, she saw it as naiveté. I came perilously close to violating some journalistic boundary line, badgering this woman. I truly didn't care. "The budget was written to pay for our jobs. That's the way it works."

Ironically, only forty percent of the children in registered orphanages were orphans. The rest were economic refugees whose mothers had no resources to raise them. Their fathers were dead; their mothers were alone with perhaps eight or nine mouths to feed.

It was, for any Vietnamese woman, an inexpressible shame and grief to abandon her child to strangers. Frail young Phuoc, the mother of six children under eight years old, tried to put that concept into words for me. She was dressed in dirty black pajamas and a cast-off Oakland Raiders t-shirt. She'd given up the baby.

"I live," she said, "every single day with a hole in my heart for Nga. She is with the government. *Now* I know she will eat." Typically, mothers gave up the child who demanded the most: the newborn, the physically disabled, or the troublemaker. It was cutting off the limb to save the tree.

"Once . . ." Phuoc began. She spoke in a dirt-floor, Pabst Blue Ribbon sheet-metal hovel—her family's home. It was a sidewalk shelter, indistinguishable from strings of them, without electricity or plumbing, and only inches from Saigon's most densely trafficked thoroughfare.

"Once I had a husband, a home with my husband's mother and father, and rice fields. My mother, sisters, and brothers lived nearby. I placed flowers on my father's grave every morning. We ate what we grew and it was always enough. My husband and I rejoiced in every new child. Now I have nothing. I have emptiness inside and out. My husband is dead; my baby is gone."

Almost every mother who handed her child to an orphanage assumed she'd bring the child home when she could afford it and demanded that the arrangement be recorded as "temporary." But here lurked yet another layer of misery behind the proliferation of orphanages in Vietnam—a fraudulent one. These women were deceived.

The government distributed funds on a per head basis—the more children crammed inside an orphanage, the more piastres. The orphanage business, with government subsidies, was too lucrative not to attract scoundrels. Hoarding children became typical.

Tall, pretty, American-looking children were valued because they could be paraded before wealthy American visitors—potential donors.

"It's embarrassing. The same Amer-Asian girl is shown every time I go there," said a USAID official, one of the dozens of American and Vietnamese social workers I interviewed. These children would never be relinquished for adoption. They were too valuable to the orphanage.

But even less profitable children had a slim chance of finding adoptive homes. In December, in just a single sector of Vietnam, two dozen legitimate requests for adoption were turned down, for fatuous reasons. Eighty-one of the 120 registered orphanages were Catholic; thirteen were Buddhist. "If you're a good Catholic or Buddhist nun, the children in your orphanage are a perfect source of future nuns and true believers," a CORDS (Civil Operations and Rural Development Support) administrator told me what the others were too tactful to say.

So, a poor woman, who "temporarily" gave up her daughter to be fed, was routinely denied authorization to take her back; Phuoc had been one of them. She was blankly refused.

I had transitioned. Now, after work, I was almost always wearing black silk pajama pants and roughly made local sandals. The clothing made comfortable sense to me—or perhaps I was going native. I tried to walk off my accumulating distress—long, hard strides away from the day's discoveries to nowhere in particular.

I shared my sorrows with Nhung one evening. I told her what I'd seen and heard at the orphanages, asked her what she thought.

"Only money," she said curtly. "Orphanages, social workers, presidents, even families—they care only for money." She looked at her feet as though in shame and walked briskly away from me and my questions.

I filled Bob like pages from a diary with detailed accounts of the unspeakable. After dinner, we'd walk far and fast.

"The kids are bartered like war booty."

"All those unwelcome babies," Bob challenged me. "Sad enough to take one home?"

"Nice try."

I turned my attention, next, to the most conspicuous victims of guerilla versus air war. If there was nothing more appealing than a dark-eyed motherless war orphan, there was nothing less attractive than the badly mutilated war-damaged child. These—the most conspicuous—ironically seemed to be the easiest to ignore. They were the most hidden.

There were reasons why these children were only occasionally seen and seldom heard from in Vietnam. Many of them were grotesque to the extreme, or total invalids. They were not the children parents typically bragged about. When a child lost her leg or his eyesight, Vietnamese parents faced it with Buddhist acquiescence to the forces of nature and with the certainty that this was how the child must live out his life.

I climbed on my Honda at the start of week two and headed across town to the Center for Reconstructive Surgery. Sweat was running down my chest under the elastic of my bra. It took everything within me to begin again. The last week had left me drained. The orphans had done me in.

The hospital was an unsparingly modern and efficient facility, as physically and spiritually distant from the orphanages as I could have traveled in one week. It was clean, bright, and well-staffed; nevertheless, there was an excruciating contrast between the orderliness of the wards and the gruesome deformities of the tiny patients.

If I'd been squeamish about physical deformity before (and I most certain had been), there was no room left for that self-indulgence in this place. There was too much heartache to indulge my own queasiness. I walked past infants strapped pitifully into cribs, swaddled in bandages, held painfully immobile so they'd heal properly. I watched toddlers limp the spotless floors with faces swollen, distorted, and discolored into most un-childlike expressions. Arms grew into hips, legs didn't bend at all, and noses had ceased to exist. From the side of the sweetest face sat an enormous clump of scar tissue, the size of the child's head. I had to swallow hard and force myself not to avert my face from the wreckage of what had once been her simple smile.

Perhaps it was the complicity of silence that had permitted the Catholic Relief Services director to insist to me days later: "There has *never* been a child maimed by war. It is a myth, I tell you! The burns you see are from home fires—unfamiliar cooking fuel."

I was staggered by this woman's words. She'd been with her agency since World War II, in Saigon for two years, and had never once left her office to visit either the orphanages that she was responsible for or the hospitals. I had a hard time forgiving her that.

The Center for Reconstructive Surgery was staffed largely by young, idealistic American doctors. At that time, it was the largest children's plastic surgery hospital in the world. They had treated 3,000 war-damaged youngsters in the two years since they'd opened. Until then, there'd been no plastic surgery in Vietnam. Again, there'd been little or no need before the American war.

"Much of what we treat here should never have happened," said Dr. John Champlin—tall, thin, earnest, and just a few years past residency—as we walked through the wards. I anticipated he was about to tell me that napalm was an immoral weapon. Instead, he said, "It's the result of neglect. It's umpteen times harder to perform surgery years later than if we'd treated them at the time of the burn."

I was with Champlin one afternoon when a Vietnamese farmer brought his lithe, lovely, fifteen-year-old daughter to the hospital for treatment. I listened to the farmer's story.

"French planes flew overhead," he told the empathetic doctor quietly. "Something dropped into the air and my daughter's fingers melted until they were no longer fingers. It happened many years ago."

I looked down at the girl's hands. They were clumps of web and scar tissue.

In the man's story they were French planes, although the French were long gone in his daughter's lifetime and they had dropped no bombs. The old man didn't want to offend his American doctors; he needed them.

The hospital's doctors didn't wait for their patients to find them. They traveled to outlying hamlets in search of need. Persuading families to allow treatment was as complex as performing the surgery. First, it was necessary to instruct parents to the unknown possibilities of plastic surgery. "To convince them that they might undo the forces of nature," Champlin said. Next, they had to win their trust—these were foreign doctors.

"I'm convinced that out in the bushes, there are many, many more children who'll come in after the war," Champlin said wearily, as we wandered the immaculate operating room. "We haven't hit twenty percent of the injured yet."

The hospitalized children among whom we strolled sometimes looked less than fully human. But they refused me that absolution; I could not reduce them to faceless victims. They demanded that I remember they were kids who needed love. They chattered at me—with a Vietnamese nurse translating—garbled words through misshapen mouths. They smiled strange smiles through lidless eyes. They told the most incredible—and ordinary—stories.

"I was playing hide-and-seek with my cousin behind the trees," Mai, a ten-year-old girl without a single clearly defined feature on her face besides a lipless mouth, told me. "I was hiding. I heard the noise of planes but I didn't want to come out because then my cousin would find me."

Mai's straightforward Vietnamese passed into the nurse's stilted English, then on to me. "But my cousin never came. I looked out from behind the tree and saw my mother across the rice fields running and screaming before she fell down—dead. I heard my father scream and run to my mother's side—dead, too. I saw fire everywhere. My home, where my grandmother prepared our noon meal, burning.

"My own screams (other people tell me) I never heard. I never saw my cousin again, or my aunt, my home, or my school. I went to the hospital, and then I came back to my village to live with my sister, my brother, and my grandfather. But my grandfather doesn't speak anymore, my sister cries all the time, and I am useless. I will never see again."

When the children entered the hospital, they were often obscenely unattractive. When they left, they were seldom less so. "Typically," Champlin told me with a heavy sigh, "plastic surgery concerns itself with beauty. Here, because we're too busy with people who can't move their arms, beautification isn't done at all."

Thirteen-year-old An arrived at the hospital two months before. He'd been racing through the fields outside Nha Trang when he stumbled on what appeared to be a terrific find: a fountain pen made in China. He shouted for his friend's approval, then thoughtlessly placed the pen in his mouth and bit down. The pen was filled with plastique. It exploded and took half of An's face with it.

I listened to An, barely audible, tell his story. I took frantic notes and only occasionally looked up at his face to confirm the worst. At the orphanage, I could lift a bottle or touch a cheek. Here, I could listen, and record.

I wrote, "Fifteen-year-old Nguyen was searching for wood. He spotted a huge pile inside the fence at the Tuy Hoa Airbase. It was discarded inside a garbage heap; no American needed it. But for Nguyen and his family, it had countless uses. He reached his thin arm through the base fence and set off a protective mine. Both his legs were blown off."

At home that night, I unloaded some of the heartache on Bob.

"Tell me! What had Nguyen done to anyone? Or Mai? They're just little kids in the way of the war machine."

"America: Love it or leave it," Bob dripped sarcasm. It was the ubiquitous bumper sticker of the American patriots.

"This story is killing me."

"No. It's killing them. The war is blind to innocence."

"Actually, I think it feeds on it."

I wrote for *Time*:

> There are differences in the types of war-related burns sustained. Sometimes, cold, unadorned science packed its own wallop. Napalm is jelly-like, and splashes into the pores all over the body. It is a superficial burn, and if it

does not occur on the face or the flexing part of a limb, the doctors said, it is "just plain disfiguring."

White phosphorous, on the other hand ("Willie Pete" to the GIs) causes a much more debilitating burn. The phosphorous continues to burn on the flesh until either the oxygen or the "organic matter"—the skin—has totally dissipated.

"We've operated on 3,000 burned children," Champlin said, "and the victims are still being manufactured. Probably more children have been maimed in this war than any other." Children were particularly vulnerable to guerilla warfare where the battlefield is among the civilians, where the combat zone is their playground. On the other hand, the weapons of guerilla war don't necessarily aim to kill, but to terrorize.

"A maimed child," I wrote, and cringed at my words, "is a very successful terrorist act."

"The whole medical system is overloaded," Champlin told me. I looked up from my notepad and saw his red-rimmed, exhausted eyes. "It's like school. You have so much to do, you don't want to do any of it."

I understood him. Two weeks into this story and I was torn in half equally, by a desire to abandon the kids—to run for the hills emotionally—or to spend the rest of my life healing them. I did neither. I would use my typewriter in their defense.

Champlin refused, couldn't even begin to factor in the emotional problems of these severely disabled war victims. Discussions of psychological problems when kids were legless, sightless, or faceless seemed pointless to him.

The doctor challenged me, clearly exasperated. If I persisted in asking about emotional problems, he demanded that I try to isolate *cause*. "Kids suffer from so much other than their injuries. Many watched their parents killed, their homes burned. How do you evaluate which is the cause of their problems?"

Girls Don't!

The last day of that week was muggier than usual, 105 degrees in the shade. I drove to the National Rehabilitation Center, at the opposite side of sprawling Saigon from Mrs. An's—a forty-minute Honda ride. The administrator recited the center's statistics, numbers that numbed me past retention. They fitted 800 artificial limbs per *month*. Eighty percent of those were for civilians, more than half of those for children.

"And this will continue long after the war is over because the land mines are still out there," the USAID advisor to the rehab center insisted. "It is the nature of this war that most amputees are children—half of them, double or triple amputees."

These were the children parents often gave up to the orphanages. They simply did not know how to cope with a severely disabled child. But then, neither did the orphanage.

"And finally, there was this potentially tragic, unnumbered, unheralded source of physical harm: the damage that may have been done to yet unborn generations of Vietnamese because of the American policy of defoliation. I had traveled now full circle, to the first story I'd written for *Time* in Saigon: "The Dead Trees."

Champlin said, "I do not know a doctor in this country who doesn't believe there is a higher incidence of birth defects in this generation than the last, and who does not attribute it to herbicides."

The orphans and the physically maimed children were the concrete, overt, measurable consequences of the war. But they were, I discovered, just a slice from a much larger but less palpable pie.

The Vietnamese schoolteacher and poet, Phong Trieu, wrote in "The School on the Front Line": "If only the children could have had the moon and the stars, the flowers and the butterflies, instead of the war."

It was not only the butterflies that were lost. It was an entirely pastoral way of life, an entire culture. The children poured unloved, unlearned, and rootless into the cities that offered none of the security of the old life, and none of the affluence of the new.

I wrote:

> It is pitiful to watch an entire generation of youth turned out from the traditions that were their birthright and offered no recompense for their losses. Kids all over the world are leaving families. But it is different in Vietnam because this was the single central social structure left. Americans have tried to impose a Western sense of community, outside of the family—and it hasn't taken. In the interim: parents steal from neighbors to feed the family; no one sees any reason to obey a traffic light.

Hundreds of thousands of little boys had run away from home. Hundreds of thousands of little girls had become prostitutes, as I reprised for this story. Estimates placed the number of boys who'd left home, aged seven to sixteen, at 300,000.

To the average Vietnamese, the word *streetboy* was synonymous with thief, delinquent, liar, and unemployable. He dressed shabbily; his language was vulgar; he made his living picking pockets, begging, eating leftovers from outdoor food stalls. I spent my third week with the streetboys.

Although I could have encountered these kids on any downtown street corner panhandling, lurking in the shadows, looking for a patsy—and in fact I did daily—I decided to make my acquaintance in a different way.

I approached Richard Hughes, a lanky, thirtyish American social worker with a huge heart and an utterly realistic picture of what he'd gotten himself into. No romantic, this Richard Hughes. He welcomed me to his hostel for streetboys. It was the only place

Girls Don't!

on Earth where these kids could take a safe breath without being required to pay some emotional or moral tit for tat.

It was nothing fancy: unadorned concrete walls and floors; three largely empty rooms; benches, bedding on the floor, and a small kitchen. But it was clean and safe, and Hughes was there. "A lot of good that does," he scoffed at any proffered praise.

He harbored no illusions. He was spitting into hurricane-force winds; there were too many children; his resources were pitifully small. The pressures on these boys were substantially greater than any one man and his good works could redress.

"But what else," Hughes asked me, "is a man to do?"

Hughes was one of the very few Americans I'd encountered in this country who spoke fluent, street-colloquial Vietnamese. He willingly shared his boys and their stories with me.

It began, of course, when the kid ran away from home. The family he ran from no longer behaved like a recognizable family. He wandered the city streets with, initially, clean clothes and a shy, quiet demeanor. He found a spot on the sidewalk to sleep. With thousands of other runaways living by their wits, it hadn't been hard for him to learn the ropes.

"When a kid first comes out onto the street and he gets into trouble, can he turn to the police? To government officials? To his family?" Hughes asked me rhetorically. The answer was a firm "No. He has only the other boys."

I met Ngoc at the hostel that first morning, but I'd actually recognized his smile from the street. He was the nine-year-old shoeshine boy who camped out in front of the Saigon USO. Ngoc had big black eyes and an unforgettably beguiling grin. He invited me to follow him on the day's appointment. He welcomed my company.

He muttered a smattering of "cheap Charlie" pidgin, and I watched him endear himself to the GIs who paraded in and out of the USO.

"Hey, GI. Give you number-one shoeshine," he hailed a passing sergeant.

"Oh, it's you, Knock-knock. How you doing, fella? Sure, give me a buff."

The sergeant handed him a Baby Ruth bar from the PX. The boy rewarded him with a bigger grin.

It was a dance I watched from five feet behind Ngoc while I leaned against a door. Ngoc put some water on the soldier's already spit-polished boots and buffed with them a dirty rag. After the shine, the GI slapped some American military payment currency into Ngoc's hand. Ngoc assured him, "Hey, GI, you number one!"

The soldier had a bounce in his step when he headed inside the USO for an evening of ping-pong, bingo, or Donut Dolly diversion. He was a virtuous man; he knew he'd done good.

Ngoc walked over to me and waved his bill. "GI give Ngoc five dollars for ten cent shoeshine," he said. He sounded half triumphant, half contemptuous. He typically earned more money than the average Vietnamese family.

Hours later, I watched him pay his rake-off percentage to the man whose street he worked: a greasy-looking man who undoubtedly paid off bigger fish. Other than that, Ngoc was his own boss. Only occasionally did he stop at Hughes's place for a night's respite.

Hughes and I sat together over lunch, ham and cheese on white bread that he'd slapped together for us. I said, "Ngoc is like Dickens's Artful Dodger: self-reliant, smart, a rascal. Or maybe a younger version of a Kerouac hero. He calls his own shots."

Hughes looked me hard in the eye and answered unequivocally, "It might not be obvious to you at first, but this life is not romantic. It is brutal; there's nothing pretty about it. These children suffer extraordinary cynicism. When a child is killed, the others chalk it up to just what happens to streetboys. They've given up on their own existence."

Ngoc slept on the streets and spent his evenings gambling with his cohorts just for the hell of it. I watched him lose whatever he'd earned that day. It didn't matter to him one way or the other. When he lay awake at night on a filthy downtown sidewalk—after I'd gone home to my clean sheets—maybe he was troubled by thoughts of the family he had left behind, but he never spoke of it.

His tattoos told his story instead. On one arm, in Vietnamese, "Remember Mama." On the other, "A Meaningless Life."

There was no one, save fleetingly Hughes, who reminded Ngoc and the others of their worth. They were scum to the Vietnamese, scapegoats for the police, and dead to their families. Parents seldom made an effort to lure these boys home. There were too many other siblings to worry about.

What began in innocence and freedom seldom ended that way. Ngoc smoked cigarettes regularly at seven, picked pockets at eight, pimped for prostitutes at nine. In another year, he'd be vulnerable to the long reach of the Vietnamese mafia.

By fourteen—when his smile was no longer so dazzling, when he was no longer adorable to soft-hearted GIs—he would likely earn his keep peddling morphine for the crime syndicates, and, predictably, a slave to the drugs himself.

Ngoc, like every other streetboy, was arrested and jailed every few months, sometimes for days, sometimes for an entire month. Brutal cops beat them regularly. Streetboys were a judicial free-fire zone—utterly unprotected.

"These kids never see a human being who's honest," Hughes said. "They can't talk about anything beautiful, because no one believes in anything beautiful."

I wrote: "There really is no precedent for the total corruption and selfishness of the inhabitants of Saigon. The quantity and quality of the ugliness is unique. These little boys live immersed in the worst of it, severed from their families and removed too far from any chance of extricating themselves."

"Once he's in this life," Hughes affirmed, "he would need something very significant and promising to get him out. In Vietnam, that doesn't exist."

I wrote:

> The Ministry of Social Welfare in Vietnam calls these kids "juvenile delinquents"—but that is a misnomer. Juvenile delinquency assumes that a child had rejected a given social structure. In Vietnam, no such structure exists. These children are begging for a society, not rejecting one.
>
> These children are not suffering only because their families were wrenched from traditional rural lives and muscled into urban ones. They're suffering from a lack of anything solid and Vietnamese in this westernized, materialistic city.

A surprising number of streetboys did not come from poverty. They came from a class of nouveau riche Vietnamese who'd made their money off the copious materials being poured into the country by the Americans.

"I have one boy," Hughes said, "whose family owns four movie theaters." These boys left families where all that was spiritual and traditional was sold down the river for money and goods. It was common practice for wealthy families to formally disown their runaway sons. "I no longer assume responsibility for the actions of Dam Van An. He is no longer my son." This was an unremarkable classified ad, next to those for apartments for rent.

Hughes said, "These kids are racing full speed ahead until they burn out." And they do burn out, often from the meaningless boredom of their lives. Hughes pointed to seven-year-old Tran—fleshy, solemn, and quiet, with the kind of sweetness that could make him a poster child for streetboys.

Girls Don't!

Hughes said, "Tran woke up yesterday at 7 a.m. He washed, put on his best clothes, and spent the entire day sitting on a bench without once getting off it until eleven in the evening, when he took off his clothes and went to sleep."

At the hostel, the boys let off steam after supper; they fought among themselves. I watched one twelve-year-old thrash a much smaller boy across the cement floor, drawing blood. I watched Hughes issue a warning and then a night's expulsion for the provocateur. I wondered on which corner he'd spend the night.

Hughes had rules, and the boys knew them. The trade-off for a night at the hostel, a meal, and a shoulder to lean on was this: no drugs, no weapons, no fights, and no scams. Hughes was a demanding parent, and the kids visibly respected him. They knew he cared. But after the rowdy dinner, the curses, the raging adolescent hormones, these boys closed their eyes and, like the rest of us, were alone with their demons in the dark.

I suspected that their nighttime monsters had more immediate real-life implications than my own. Undoubtedly, they dreaded being drafted. At eighteen, with no education, these boys would be the first into the jungle—fodder for the Vietnamese Army.

"I will die; I don't care," skinny, pimply, fourteen-year-old Long told me. His lack of emotion jolted me in a way that hysterics might not have. I thought that Long was probably right. I didn't have to play God to know that most of these boys *would* die in this war. Others would desert and return to the city to solidify their criminal life: stealing Hondas and growing from the nominally cute *streetboy* into the more sinister *cowboy*, like the one who had snatched my overnight bag from the pedicab.

But it was optimistic of me to assume Long would live to see his eighteenth birthday—and when I looked at his flat, expressionless eyes, I could not. Most boys didn't look that far ahead. In the past eighteen months, *fifteen* of the ninety boys in Hughes's hostel had killed themselves, usually with an overdose of drugstore medicine—and these were the boys who'd had some degree of care.

Only fifty percent of all Vietnamese children attended the first three grades of school. There were laws that practically insured a huge percentage of poor children would never be allowed to enter school. A child could not attend school without a birth certificate. Many unsophisticated mothers left the maternity wards before the doctor-mandated, four-day stay and never received one. Others birthed their babies at home. Still others, unaware of the paper's importance, had lost it or thrown it away.

For the young girls in the Vietnamese cities, the cultural and family disintegration was much the same as the streetboys'—but the choices were slightly different. Uneducated, a girl had absolutely no chance of a government or office job. At best, she could be a servant. But if she were raised in an orphanage and untrained in the needs of a traditional home, she'd be a poor choice even as a maid.

Marriage was—I heard repeated in these exact words—"out of the question." There was a huge disproportion of young women to men. An entire generation of available husbands had been wiped out on the battlefield. A girl *lucky* enough to marry faced this. Marriage to an ARVN soldier meant permanent separation from one another. The only end to a Vietnamese soldier's term of service was death or disfigurement.

In a city where marriage, respectable jobs, and education were impossible, and starvation was the only alternative—the remaining choice was prostitution.

The Chinese, Japanese, and French had each occupied Vietnam, and still it survived intact, proudly resilient always. But among the occupying foreigners, Americans had the most effect, if only because our presence was so huge and dominating. When an entire society is permeated with foreign values, even the legendarily resilient Vietnamese could not hold on to what they'd always had.

Most children born into the drama of this unraveling culture didn't stand a chance. They had nothing to hang on to, nothing to remember, and no prevailing tools to understand and adapt to the changes.

Truc, one of Dick Hughes's streetboys, had tried to kill himself when he was only thirteen, and failed. At fifteen, he was killed in a traffic accident. In his dirty pocket was a still dirtier one-piastre bill. On the margin, in his familiar scrawl, he'd written in Vietnamese, "How many tears? How many drops of sweat?"

I worked late into Friday night at the office writing my story. Jon spent an hour looking over my shoulder as the pages poured through the typewriter—my final version.

"This looks good," he said, when I was halfway through and he could wait no longer. He was hurrying off to a dinner party. I was on absolute deadline for the week's magazine, although I knew there wasn't a chance they'd use it this week. There was too much story, too little lead time. "You've done it," Jon said, patting me on the back. "Just feed it to Luu as you finish each page. He'll telex it to New York."

"No problem."

So I sat out front in Bob Anson's old office, the hefty windows full of night. Luu sat three rooms back in front of the noisy telex machine. Sometimes he'd finish a page before I did and he'd come out to collect the next.

I never looked up from my words when he approached, but I'd nod toward my right where the next page lay. Sometimes, I'd stretch my legs by walking a single page back to him.

He never looked up from what he was doing but he always thanked me. We never said another word to one another. Luu was one of two staff tele-typists. His sole job was typing every line of copy that came out of the Saigon Bureau to *Time* in New York. He looked to be about thirty-five, with thin hair combed straight back. That evening he was wearing a blue, open-necked sports shirt with dark cotton slacks. He was quiet. He had not been hired for conversation but for his excellent typing skills and his outstanding command of English grammar and spelling. There was no knowing, or even considering, what he thought about the stories he typed.

Tonight, I was glad to be alone in the front office, glad that Jon wasn't hanging over my shoulder anymore. Glad to be secluded with the fullness of the last three weeks' work, alone with my thoughts. My thoughts ran to the mess we'd made of this country. The story ended exactly where it began. The greatest suffering to the least responsible: the children.

The story was beginning to feel like it defined everything I'd learned and lived in Vietnam and Cambodia, like a premature epitaph. I was neither too old nor too removed from my own childhood to have forgotten how it felt to trust, and to have innocence breached by an unavoidable adult incomprehension. But the *deliberate* violation of innocence in Vietnam was of another magnitude altogether—an immeasurable betrayal of an entire generation.

Luu picked up my last page and left the room. I stretched to touch my toes, shaking off the stiffness from the hours in Anson's old chair. I'd wait, I figured, until Luu finished and handed me my own copy of the telex for my files. I walked to the window and looked down on the city. I was completely absorbed in the reflections on the window.

In the reflections, I saw their shadows. Where was Ngoc

tonight? Was sightless Mai home with her silent grandfather? The soft-cheeked baby girl who could not hold a bottle, was she even alive? And the others, the faces without names, their reflections imposed on mine in the dark window.

I didn't hear Luu approach until he stood, respectfully, about four feet behind me and cleared his throat. I turned around and saw that he was crying. Eyes full, cheeks traced with tears. It was a sight I'd never once witnessed among our stoic, insistently cheerful Vietnamese staff.

"My God, Luu, what's wrong?"

He bowed ever so slightly, and he was gone.

I knew I'd written the truth.

The story sat for weeks, then months, in the New York office. Long after I'd stopped asking about it, looking for it, and obsessing over it, I found bits and pieces of my story scattered throughout a *Time* "World-Wide Look at Children of War." It was entirely unrecognizable, and I felt neither ownership nor pride.

"It might have been easier," Bob offered his consolation, "to stop the war than to influence the politics at *Time*."

I did not suspect a systematic conspiracy to ignore my opus. It just didn't fit the parameters of *Time* political thought—the same old, same old. Maybe I'd already known that when I typed it up. After the initial disappointment, I wasn't even angry. The story that I'd hoped would change the world had already changed me.

CHAPTER 15

COMING FULL CIRCLE

FEBRUARY 1971

While I had worked assiduously for those three weeks—my lens focused entirely on the ugliest face of Vietnam and the war—Saigon set out to show me her best: Tet. While I had grieved the disintegration of traditional Vietnamese culture, for three days only, it reasserted its claim.

Tet, the Lunar New Year, was a celebration of the most admirable qualities of traditional Vietnamese life. That it coincided this year with our first wedding anniversary was gravy—an entire nation celebrating our day. That it arrived just as I completed "Children of War" was serendipitous and a much-needed balm.

Girls Don't!

Bob had finagled an unheard-of two sequential midweek days off for our anniversary and Tet. We joined the street crowds. Flowers were potted on street corners, braided into garlands dangling from lamp posts, encircling arms, necks, and the handlebars of Hondas. Where had the flowers been hiding? Where were they grown?

Dressed in their finest, strangers greeted us, *"Bonjour, Monsieur, Madame."*

"Bonjour, Monsieur," we murmured over and over in unison.

We were hailed, too, in English: "I wish you the best of the New Year."

"Thank you, Sir, and to your family as well," Bob answered.

On the first of three nights, Mrs. An invited us to visit the family; she showered us with gifts. We'd arrived empty-handed. The next morning, I hurried to the PX and then gifted Mrs. An a collection of kitchen utensils. I had to explain their uses: the potato peeler, the melon baller, the fancy corkscrew. She was thrilled.

She'd baked us a dense and delicious yellow cake soaked in alcohol, with a sugared-brandy glaze drizzled over the top. We insisted she cut it then and there.

"I'm a little tipsy," Bob claimed after the first piece. Nhung translated. Mrs. An laughed. She gave us a huge melon. Nhung explained. "This fruit ripens only at Tet. It is considered good fortune to eat it now. Do you have this in America? What do you call it?"

"Watermelon," I told her.

Mrs. An cheerfully chipped away at our ignorance. The little card table set outside of *every* front door, be it villa or tin shack?

"We put fruit, flowers, and incense in front of our homes to welcome our ancestors. They come home for Tet, and we offer our best." And this, "We never sweep the floor or empty the trash during Tet— we might throw away the good fortune inside our home."

Tet, like the Jewish New Year, was sacred for the things required (and abstained from) in the hope of ensuring a flourishing new year. Vietnamese and Jewish folk alike were expected to make genuine amends to those we may have harmed.

Mrs. An explained: the Vietnamese do not argue, ever, during Tet, (which made the Viet Cong's 1968 Tet Offensive such an aberrant and shocking violation).

But now, with the daily threat of hostility removed and all of us presumed to be safe, there was room for generosity. Custom mandated visits to friends and family, endless rounds of food, conversation, and gift-giving. Tet was undoubtedly spiritual—communing with ancestral kin—but it was equally an exuberant party.

The streets were packed and bustling; streetboys and prostitutes were invisible. To me, that felt eerie and worrisome. Had the police rounded them up? Was there an agreed-upon protocol I was not privy to? I could not bring myself to ask Mrs. An.

On the eve of the final day of Tet, most Vietnamese—Buddhist, Catholic, or neither—visited one of the omnipresent pagodas. Bob and I joined the procession. We followed the crowd to the neighborhood pagoda we'd walked past for a year. Now we dared enter.

There were thirty steps that stretched across the entire façade of the building. The pagoda was plain yellow masonry with a red tile roof, but inside it was lavishly ornate. We entered one huge room with distant ceilings. The walls *were* the furnishing: frescoes of Buddhist deities encrusted in pearls and semi-precious stones and inlaid in gold.

Never in my life had I been part of such a boisterous, seemingly disorganized prayer session. It was a noisy, fabulous carnival with unusual, sometimes bizarre, offerings: food, gambling, and tests of prowess. There were scattered clumps of people having their fortunes told. Men, women, and children crowded solemnly around the seers who were seated cross-legged, quietly offering pieces of the future. To good news, there was enthusiastic applause. To the other kind, a studied equilibrium, and quiet.

"What say we find out our future?" I asked Bob.

"I think I'll pass," he said. "Aren't you the one who didn't want to know what you'd be doing next year?"

Outside the pagoda, running along the edges of the staircase like a long banister, were beggars and cripples, one below the other: legless veterans, lepers, and the homeless. No war-mutilated children, I noted. Were they invisible even at Tet? All were lined up with hats extended to the returning supplicants. The returning prayerful smiled at the beggars, wished them a prosperous New Year, and filled each hat with change and bills. We followed suit—a 1,000-piastre note in every one until we ran out of them, and then we substituted whatever Vietnamese coins we had between us.

On the night of the big parade downtown, we dressed in our best—again, Bob's blazer and my yellow *ao dai*—and we meandered slowly through the streets, carried along by the crowd of jubilant people under a full moon and a profusion of stars.

We'd eaten our anniversary dinner at a splendid French restaurant, a few degrees more extravagant than our usual.

The pulsating papier-maché dragon—a city block long, with a head the width of two pairs of outstretched arms—wended its way through the main boulevard of the Chinese sector. Children teetered on parents' shoulders, shrieking their fear and their exuberance. Their parents, beaming proudly, awaited our smiles and benediction on their children's dressed-up radiance. It was easy to bestow. These guileless children, such a contrast to those I'd recently encountered.

Tet was the magic kingdom. It was the singular moment when the war's ugliness was swallowed up in the blessings of the celebration; where the Vietnamese reclaimed—if only for three days, and in prayers for the coming year—all that they'd lost of themselves during the American war. Perhaps ten years wasn't *such* a long time, after all. It was my privilege to bear witness.

The rainy season was well past; the Christmas ceasefire had ended. The war again surged into high gear. This time, the front moved to Laos. As with Cambodia the previous year, the shift was ostensibly meant to deny the Viet Cong and North Vietnamese their sanctuaries—their supply routes along the Ho Chi Minh Trail.

This time, though, to avoid the vociferous public reaction to an American invasion into yet another sovereign nation, the American military decided to put Vietnamization to the test. ARVN soldiers were sent into Laos *without* American ground troops, with only American air support. The South Vietnamese foot soldier would be on his own.

I wilted in inactivity in Saigon's humidity. I was frustrated and forced to *read* the news reports exactly like everyone else in America. The accounts described the total failure of the South Vietnamese Army in Laos. Routed from the first, the young soldiers raced to their retreat. Few photographs from the entire war were as spectacular as the ones out of Laos—ARVN soldiers hanging by tenuous fist-holds to the runners of medical evacuation helicopters. They were swinging and falling to their deaths like flies, preferring the risks of desertion to engagement with the enemy.

Vietnamization—*years* of shifted responsibility for the war from American to Vietnamese military shoulders in preparation for our withdrawal—had been an unqualified disaster. Without American soldiers issuing commands and fighting the fight, the South Vietnamese Army lost heart and chose to run.

I knew that I needed to get out of Saigon. I was a storyteller, and the big story was eluding me in Laos. I was no less curious nor

Girls Don't!

probing than I'd been before the so-called *soft*, safe "Children of War" story. I was still happiest and most energetic when I was in the thick of things.

I wasn't the one who distinguished between the different kinds of war stories, deeming one *hard*, the other *soft*. Always, I'd been interested in the human consequences of any story. That had not changed.

By late February, I was sick and tired of being protected from danger by my bureau chief. I knew that if I waited for Jon to assign me to Laos, I'd be waiting still when the war was over. Assignment or no, I was flying into Quang Tri, the staging area for the Laotian operation.

I didn't ask Jon; I simply told him I was on my way. He could *assign* me, but he couldn't direct me. I was as independent as any other reporter, and I moved now of my own volition.

"Are you crazy, Inette?" Jon shouted. "You're *short*, you've got a little more than a month left. You want to get killed?"

"I'm going," was all I answered him. "I'll send you what I get."

Bob, on the other hand, wished me well. "Give 'em hell, girl!" He waved me off with a smile, susceptible always to my excitement.

I arrived in Quang Tri at the very northern limits of South Vietnam via a series of puddle jumpers—fixed-wing and chopper. I arrived, it seemed, with the second wave of correspondents and photographers. There was no one left from *Time*, so I had the story to myself. I would settle in for as long as it took.

First, there was the question of logistics: fifty male correspondents and photographers were staying at the heart of the base in an old World War II, tin-sided Quonset hut, a half-domed roof over a long utilitarian space. It was unbearably hot. There were two rows of army cots, parallel parked, about two feet apart, under the lowest eaves of the half-dome. A narrow plank floor ran between the rows the length of the building, leading to doors at either end.

When I arrived, I was the only woman there. Gloria Emerson had left a few days before. The US military press liaison offered me a room in the nurses' quarters at the far edge of the base near the hospital. It would have been considerably plusher and more private, no doubt, but it was a half-mile distant from the press office, the officially breaking news, the unofficial gossip, and the collegial passing along of information.

"No, thanks," I said. "I'll stay here."

"Well, okay, but—"

"I'll hang sheets around my cot. You have extras, don't you?"

"Sure, but you'd probably be more comfortable—"

"Hey, Joe," a correspondent I half recognized but couldn't name piped in. "Bring her the sheets. Here, let me help you string them up. There's an empty cot next to mine." I was grateful and cautious in one fell swoop.

It was almost noon when I arrived, and there were just a dozen or so reporters sprawled prostrate on their cots in the oppressive heat. They were the late sleepers, the less motivated, or the hungover. They uniformly chose to view my helpful colleague's motives as base. Predictably, there was a fair amount of raunchy humor as we set to work.

"Ol' Jim wants to hang sheets so can climb behind them."

"Eh, Jimbo, leaving a window open on your side?"

Jim laughed as we worked, and I did, too. I was, after all, *asking* for special attention. A couple of the men pulled themselves from their lethargy and pitched in, helping to string the sheets from the rafters, right up to the edge of the cot. There was barely enough room to stand between the cots. When I climbed onto the cot to see what it felt like—to see how our construction worked—I realized I'd be dressing and undressing in bed, and I also wondered how opaque the sheets were. But, all said and done, it felt cozy.

My decision to stay with the others turned out to be exactly the right one—although, when I climbed behind the sheets those first nights, there were a few ribald cracks.

"Need some company in there, Hon?" Or, when I was obviously undressing, "Afraid of the dark? Can I lend you my flashlight?"

After a couple of days, the men behaved as though the sheets were plaster walls—and instructed the new arrivals in the proprieties as well. When I was behind them I contentedly pretended, as a simple matter of manners, to hear nothing of what they said to one another. When I walked down the narrow center aisle in the early morning with men sprawled in various stages of undress, I stared diligently at my feet and simulated being unseeing and unseen.

Two days into my stay in Quang Tri, my name came up for a small chopper flight to Khe Sanh. I'd signed on earlier for any press trip out of Quang Tri, but I had to wait my turn. Khe Sanh was nestled inside the mountains on the very edge of the Vietnamese side of the Laotian border. Visually there was absolutely no way to distinguish where Vietnam ended and Laos began. The mountains were the mountains. They looked exactly the same on both sides of the border.

Tiny Khe Sanh, because of its position at the border—situated on a major supply route from Laos—was logistically the obvious staging area for the Laotian invasion.

But historically, it was an odd choice. The very name Khe Sanh evoked memories of an infamous three-month siege by the North Vietnamese Army on an American Marine base. It had been a major defeat for us. When the siege was finally lifted, the Marines closed down shop and abandoned Khe Sanh on April 15, 1968—just three years before. So, there was an ominousness about Americans reoccupying Khe Sanh—a nightmare remembered—and a great deal of superstition attached to it.

I flew into Khe Sanh with a couple of other reporters. We had

Coming Full Circle

the entire day ahead of us. Our flight back wouldn't leave until early evening. We scattered. I wandered the base at will for half an hour and realized, too late, that I was on the very edge of it, up against the spot where cleared ground met the jungle—and I had to go to the bathroom, badly.

There was no ducking behind these trees, all heavily mined and teeming with enemy. I was a good half mile from the nearest outhouse. I looked up next to me at a three-hundred-foot hill that had been cleared down to dust and topped with a dozen watchful American perimeter guards. Armed to the teeth, dripping grenades, and clutching M16s, twelve men stood atop the bare hill staring out from behind their dark glasses, watching with pivoting thick necks for the subtlest movement at the base's edge. There wasn't another soul around.

"Hey, guys," I screamed up the hill at them. "Know where I might find a ladies' room?"

There was immediate and unrestrained laughter. Then this: one of them balled up and pitched down a thick, green, woolen Army blanket.

"There's the ladies' room. You get to choose the spot."

My choices were limited indeed, all within a bird's-eye view of the men on the hill. I threw the heavy dark blanket over my head, my body, and about three feet of earth in every direction—and squatted. Under the unbearably hot woolen blanket it would have been hard enough to relax, but with the chorus of singsong chants from atop the hill raining down on me, it took a while.

"We *know* what you're doing! We know what you're doing! We know what you're doing!"

Heat or no, I contemplated never coming out from under the blanket again. I traveled in those five minutes beyond all previously known points I might have called embarrassment. When I finally emerged, there was no imaginable way to pretend cool—the option on that one had expired.

I left their neatly folded blanket at the foot of the hill and thanked them—tongue firmly in cheek—for their gentlemanly conduct. I headed back into the base as quickly as my heavy boots would shuffle. They hounded me with whistles and catcalls until I was out of earshot.

I chatting up nearly everyone I passed. I hoped that chance encounters would lead to stories for Jon, and they did. I was enough of an anomaly for the men to jump at the chance to speak with me.

I encountered several Cobra gunship pilots in repose. They were drinking coffee, flipping through *Playboy*, well within range of their helicopters.

"We're the crazies of this war, the certifiably insane," a curly hair, jut-jawed pilot bragged. But I knew he spoke a certain truth. Cobra pilots flew their sharp-nosed choppers fast and furiously into a targeted area—swift and low, in and out. With more propulsion than other choppers, they flew low and they could see plainly through their oversized windshields. They were uniquely able to record and memorize the specific damage they inflicted.

Among the weapons in their arsenal were explosives full of skin-penetrating pointed tacks. They unambiguously watched men, women, and children impaled on the exploding nails—stapled to the earth. These young warrant officers saw closer and clearer than most—sharp as a Saturday Night Movie—the human meaning of *antipersonnel weapons*.

They did their jobs as they were trained to do them, and they talked a very tough show. But they carried the daily horror of their visible deeds etched on their consciences. Their mothers, fathers, ministers, and teachers—their own eyes and minds—taught them that what they did was wrong. Their country, the Army, the discipline of war taught them that it was their job.

The young pilot took me inside his Cobra for a tour. I knew that when he flew his mission there'd be no place for voyeurs, no seat for me.

"Yeah," he persisted, "we're the basket cases—the hard drinkers, heavy users, the suicides. That's us. If we make it out of here alive, we'll *never* be able to make it back in the world."

I listened, appalled and utterly fascinated by the extremes to which human souls can be bent. I sat next to him behind the glass panorama to awesome destruction as he pointed out each lever on the intricate control panel and told me which ones dropped what—which buttons unbuttoned the arsenal of antipersonnel explosives and which ones unleashed the maiming array of chemicals.

And in truth, inside the sleek, fast machine, I realized that this young man from southern California—a kid who told me he'd been "one helluva surfer"—was not bragging to me at all. He was simply confessing.

The day passed like that. Random stops with young Americans; bits of stories that would weave together, I hoped, into a powerful whole. But I noticed a pattern unrelated to any story I might send to Jon. These were not guys who were fantasizing about my body, only partly disguised under my tapered fatigues. They were entirely intent on using my shoulder. I was their older sister.

The truth of that day was that I was a much rarer commodity than someone to take to bed. I was a woman you could speak English with. There was an emotional openness that I felt certain was denied my male colleagues. With me, these boys could cry.

Late in the afternoon, I was sprawled in the sun with a nineteen-year-old grunt from New York. Gary was stretched out, stripped to bare chest and boxers, working on an already terrific tan. He was draped over the top of sandbags surrounding a

Girls Don't!

series of three-foot-deep underground bunkers—his home when the enemy got aggressive. Gary was round-faced and cherubic; he looked no more than sixteen. He'd been telling me about his family.

"My mom, she doesn't want to hear too much about what's going on here. She just wants to tell her friends that I'm some kind of hero—a regular American patriot.

"Dad keeps telling me that I need to be a man. That I'm going to have to live with myself after this is all over. That I better not shame myself. 'Course it's *him* he's worried I'll shame.

"My little brother Joe is a goof-off. He's against the war because he's afraid. I can't say that I blame him. He took off out of high school for San Francisco. The draft board can't find him, and my dad says he's dead to us. Well, maybe to *him*—but not to me.

"I'm close to my sister Janet; she's two years older than me. You remind me of her."

I asked, "Do you write her what you're doing here?"

"Yeah, I write Janet. But you know, it's really tough to explain this place to anybody." Here, Gary's eyes filled up and he rubbed them quickly with the back of his fist.

"I mean," he said, "how do *you* write what this is like?"

"I don't know," I said. "Sometimes, I just stare at a page and try to figure out what it is they want to hear, like you. But sometimes I get to tell the truth. I get to say this isn't at all like they told us it would be. "

"Shit," he said. "Shit."

He screened his eyes from the sun with his forearm and his floppy-brimmed hat and he was silent. Gary had been humping the boonies in Vietnam for six-and-a-half months, three weeks in Khe Sanh. He was one of the small slice of American enlisted men in Vietnam who actually fought the daily ground war.

We imagined, back in the United States, that all 500,000

soldiers were engaged in battle at any given moment. That all two-and-a-half million men who'd been processed through here had walked through the jungles and fallen face down in the mud. The facts were different.

Only fifteen or twenty percent at any given time were in the field. The rest were in *support*: in hospitals, supply arsenals, offices, motor pools. Gary was one of the unlucky few.

A screeching siren broke our reverie and screamed, *Incoming!* Incoming artillery and rockets spilled over the perimeter of vulnerable Khe Sanh from the thickly vegetated hillsides. I heard the siren seconds before I heard the first explosion. Gary grabbed his fatigue shirt in one hand, my arm in the other, and dove head-first into the bunker. I was pulled behind him into the pitch blackness.

The bunker, one of scores strung around the base, looked from the outside like this: a mound of sandbags piled around a trench in the earth, maybe eight feet by four. The roof over the trench was camouflaged canvas, held in place by the top row of sandbags. When the canvas flap was dropped over the opening, there wasn't a trace of daylight.

I was the last into the bunker; eight men had preceded me. We sat hip to hip, legs curled tight, wedged snug against each other's hot bodies. My head touched the canvas roof of the bunker unless I bent my neck. The first sensations for me—after the total darkness—were the heat, the unbreathable thick air, and the putrid smell of sweat. It wasn't a murky locker-room sweat after a hard workout—it was the far more acrid smell of fear. I thought in those first few seconds that I might suffocate.

Gary sensed my panic. "Here." He breached the utter darkness with a glowing cigarette and passed the last bit of a lit joint to me. "This'll help."

I didn't hesitate. I sucked deeply off the roach and thanked him for it. I began to pass it on to the next, but Gary said, "No, finish it up—there's more."

By now the heat in the bunker was the least of it. The ground was rumbling around us. It was shaking with the noise and reverberation of artillery exploding, of bunkers being blown to bits. This was a new kind of impotence, this sitting in a dark hole in the ground protected from shrapnel off explosives by a sheet of canvas and a few sandbags, knowing that none of it would mean a thing in a direct hit. We sat like that for a couple hours, listening intently to the rumblings at first—then not listening at all.

"If you can hear it," Gary advised me, "then you're okay. If you can't hear it—it don't matter no more."

The dope helped. It helped me focus, like grass sometimes did. The dope relieved me of the burden of listening to what was going on outside the bunker. I was riveted instead to the boys inside, listening just to them.

In that solid wall of blackness, one faceless kid told me he'd left school in the tenth grade, expecting the war would be his one chance to make good. School sure hadn't been. "Excuse my French. But this fucking hellhole ain't no place to build your future."

Another voice, cracking like in puberty, spewed bewilderment. The people he'd come to help exploited him: "Shit—no *friendlies* here—every one of them hate our American asses."

Another deeper voice in the dark vented frustration that the good guys and the bad guys looked exactly alike. "Hell, they're all gooks."

Every boy in that bunker wanted *Time* magazine and his family back home to know what this place was really like, and they wanted me to take responsibility for telling them. I knew I was destined to disappoint them; their truth would never make it through the corporate translation.

But I would try to write some words in good faith and from

deep feeling about this bunker and the boys inside—about the Cobra pilot too. I knew that Jon, at least, would welcome them.

Inside that bunker, Gary wanted to tell me a story—and he told it *very* softly.

"Gimme a toke," he demanded to someone down the line before he began.

"In a hamlet over that mountain," he gestured with the lit joint about an inch above my nose, "a young Vietnamese woman gave birth to a boy." She gave birth bravely, he told me, and without medical intervention. She pushed a perfect little boy from her body.

"She laid her newborn son on the ground in front of her and lifted a butcher's knife," Gary said. "She swore in a firm voice, '*Never* a fighter; never a soldier. Never!'"

"The mother," Gary told me quietly, "sliced off her son's toes—every one, every toe. 'Cut off his toes,' she said, 'to save his soul.'"

I had no way of knowing whether this story was merely a battlefield legend. But for the grunts in that bunker, it was incontestably true. They needed to believe in the existence of an implacable morality.

The rumbling earth stilled. A siren signaled "All clear." Gary told me to toss back the heavy canvas flap, that it was okay to get out now.

Bent in half, I led Gary and the seven other men I hadn't yet seen but whom I'd definitely heard, from inside the canvas cave out into the brilliant sunshine. For a few shocking seconds, we all were blind.

CHAPTER 16

RISING AND FALLING (REDUX)

MARCH 1971

For a week, I traipsed between my tented cot in the Quonset hut in Quang Tri and the medical evacuation choppers heading into Laos. On the eighth day, my helicopter was hit.

The chopper was hoisted horizontally with the force of an unseen punch to the jaw—then just as violently thrust down like a fist pummeling the nape of the neck. Hurled up, then recklessly forced back down.

Again, an immediate head count, each of us checking: gunners, pilots, civilians. Everyone in his or her place—or nearly there.

Launched a couple of feet into the air, we three journalists were sprawled like in a childhood game of frozen statues in various unnatural positions over the cold chopper floor. I was on my knees grabbing at some sharp edge on the wall. The distinguished Brit was flat on his back and scrambling to get up. The bulky network guy was balancing on his buttocks, arms flailing in the air.

I heard words—sharp, excited, demanding words—between the pilots. They were taking inventory of what was still whole on the Huey, what was not. We were inside, and there was no way to imagine what we looked like from the outside.

Helplessly, we moved now in very slow motion. Not a soul spoke. Without words, we got the picture. We were cruising over the landscape in spitting distance from the valley floor, seemingly unable to gain an inch of altitude, with the speed of a much-maligned tortoise.

The soft comfort, soothing security, and musing reverie that I routinely felt in a chopper aloft was gone. The jungle belonged, without serious challenge, to the enemy. That he *was* my enemy (or saw me as his) was transparently evident.

This jungle, although alive still with miraculous flora and fauna, was more pressingly alive with Viet Cong. I could actually feel their proximity in the hairs on the back of my neck. I'd seen artillery fire strike us at a greater distance than the twenty-five feet we were doomed now to coast.

I began to see myself inside this ungainly target with the enormous rotor on top through the scope of somebody's rifle. I could watch myself from the ground. We were, at best, easy pickings—assuming, in any case, that this chopper still had it in her to navigate these narrow mountain passes and V-shaped canyons, the distance to Khe Sanh—forget Quang Tri.

My thoughts ran like quicksand. *If* I lean over the side of this helicopter and keep an eye out for enemy fire, if I keep my adrenaline up and my whole self alert, then maybe I can keep this tub afloat and we'll make it.

Some people come from deeply religious families. I grew up in a deeply superstitious one. *If* we didn't walk under ladders, break mirrors, let a black cat cross our path or spill salt, then and only then would our world be safe.

It was like that for me now: the illusion of safety, where there was none at all. I can't speak for the others. The pilots were occupied. The gunners too, staring down their barrels at the same nearby swatches of green I watched for signs of crouching black pajama pants or flashing metal. We jointly watched for signs of who was watching us.

But we three reporters were momentarily jobless, separated from the completion of our responsibilities. Our jobs had meaning only so long as we could transmit our stories. This story—the flight, the landing zone, the artillery fire—was just introspection and diddling if we didn't write it down and hand it off to someone who'd print it or broadcast it beyond this helicopter.

At this moment, that part of our job didn't look so promising.

So I made up a job for myself. I never lifted my eyes from the passing woodland. I was thirty-five feet from the side of the tree-covered cliff, floating along in a dream of attentiveness. The chopper whittled its way through the thick air inside the narrow crevice of the canyon, following the gentle bend of the mountain face. I sucked in my breath and held it until the holding became who I was.

If I watched, *if* I were vigilant, I'd prevent the preventable. I agreed to leave the navigating of this injured helicopter to the blond, athletic-looking pilot. *And why wasn't he in prep school somewhere?!* I'd take care of the rest.

I could not have said for sure how long we hobbled along those corridors of potential enemy fire, weaving past the mountainsides in our faces, scraping close to the ground. But I'd guess an hour; it seemed a day. We kept afloat; we kept moving. Really slow, or just counting-my-heartbeats slow?

I knew there was no entering Khe Sanh without going up and over a small mountain, just a five-hundred-foot climb in elevation. But the young pilot didn't seem sanguine about our chances of rising those five hundred feet.

"Jesus," he mumbled into his mouthpiece. "Jesus and Mary." He radioed his last communiqué to the ground, conserving his strength and everything else his chopper had in her for the last big push.

But push we did. Something miraculous goosed us over that last hurdle. I never asked how and I never understood why. But we lifted—somehow we lifted—over that granite hill into Khe Sanh. Not with the buoyant, meditative grace I'd associated with choppers on the rise—this one was more like hoisting and cranking.

So I haven't the faintest idea what that lean, twenty-one-year-old warrant officer pulled off to get us up and over that last obstacle, and in fact I can no longer remember his name. But at the time, my superstition kicked in and I believed that the nice young man simply *wished* us over—with some meaningful incantations of my own. It was far too early in my life to consider faith or prayer, to imagine miracles.

I do remember that fine, first glimpse of sunny Khe Sanh. All the camouflage and tinny ugliness of American military architecture—gone. In its place, a faint but unequivocal glow blanketing the entire base, magnifying its intensity at the otherwise indistinguishable dirt clearing where we finally touched down.

We sat stock-still for a few moments and felt the implacably solid earth before any of us stirred. The pilot shifted first. He walked around to our side to help us down.

He smiled broadly into my face. "I told you that you were in good hands." He offered me his hand, and I took it.

We were greeted like this: a couple dozen military men and a dozen reporters cheering wildly, clapping riotously, and slapping us on the back. Then a colleague grabbed me by the shoulders and spun me around—my first look at the chopper.

It was riddled. Big chunks of metal peeled open around three-foot-wide craters. Here, the tail was brutally wrenched apart. There, ragged edges were shredded just inches from where I'd sat. Like the top of a monstrous can of tuna that someone ripped off with a dull knife—like that everywhere. It was the most dramatically destroyed helicopter I'd ever seen bring its crew and passengers back alive.

Alive! And here was one of many ironies of man and war. The very thing that threatened to kill us promised to make us heroes. As though nearly dying was a commendable deed in its own right. With correspondents, it was the dramatic near miss that earned our colleagues' respect. Yes, the story filed—but, even more praiseworthy, the story lived to be filed.

But there was another irony. If, by all established macho standards, I'd just chalked up a good one, it mattered a great deal less to me now than it would have a year before. The approval I'd been seeking all along, of course, had been my own.

Only afterwards, after a lunch that I could not swallow; after listening to the story regurgitated a dozen times; after a quick and uneventful—but not routine—chopper flight back to Quang Tri; with applause still ringing in my ears and the wrecked chopper still stranded in all its glory—not yet dramatically hauled to oblivion suspended from the bottom of a much larger helicopter—only *then* did I begin to have second thoughts.

Finally alone, on a quiet spot, fifty yards from the Medevac launching pad where I'd lifted off that morning, I sat down in the dirt. I stared up at the blue sky, then down at the brown earth that was dusting my fatigue pants, and finally over at two helicopters waiting their turn.

Momentarily—it couldn't have lasted more than seconds—I felt a rush of nausea and I began to shake, shivering as if I were freezing in the 100-degree sunshine. Choking back my vomit, I felt utterly exposed, raw, and vulnerable.

Like some apocalyptic nightmare held up to broad daylight, I could distinctly imagine myself zipped inside a body bag, face pressed against the canvas—no breath left to hold.

Bob had one month left of his conscripted fourteen. He was out of here in April, and I was following him. If there was any choice in that matter, I didn't know it. My acceptable excuse for being at war would be going home with Bob.

"I don't want to die here," I said aloud for the first time in a year. "I'm ready to go home."

CHAPTER 17

AFTERWARDS

Within six months, Bob was a graduate student; I was a graduate student wife and loathing it. I had a daily byline in the Cleveland newspaper; I was a hotshot *former* Vietnam correspondent. But inside our apartment, a single line of rooms off a crowded hallway in Cleveland Heights, I was the wife. My inescapable identity, and my reason for being there, a reflection of Bob's. Our friends were a dozen graduate students and their wives. The wives griped about "putting my husband through school." Within four years, more than half the couples were sleeping with one another or divorced—but not us.

Every single day, Bob yearned to quit. He was sick and tired of being a student, and I wasn't suffering silently. I squirmed that Bob was unavailable, locked up in his backroom office, studying. I detested Cleveland.

But what I really hated were the expectations within a marriage. Because of the woman I was *reared* to be, I was bound to marry. Because of the woman I was *born* to be, I was bound to struggle with it. How much to give? How much to keep for myself?

Bob asked none of that from me. There were greater forces at work, silent messages demanding that wives be self-sacrificing—the hidden muscle behind accomplished men.

Four-and-a-half years after we'd met, almost a year and a half after we'd married, six weeks back from Saigon, on the front stairs of my parents' home, I exploded. "Damn it, Bob, that's not where it goes! I can't do this all by myself!" Then, a mountain of fury.

It was our first real fight.

Bob, habituated since childhood around the dinner table to unpredictable rage, withdrew into impenetrable silence. There passed over his shocked heart and face a shadowy message: "What have I gotten myself into?" But he didn't tell me that for fifteen years.

We'd stopped in Baltimore for just three weeks, and I was choking. I needed only look up at my mother—studying us from her upstairs balcony while we packed the van at the curb below—to know my choices had narrowed. Unguarded for even a minute, *domesticity*—all my mother's and father's plans for their girl-child—would slip into my dreams, my marriage, and my soul. I screamed at Bob because I was desperately afraid of it.

I had wandered freely the clustered streets of Hong Kong and the dusty bases at Long Binh and Quang Tri feeling alive. Now there was the threat of extinction, absorption into my parents' plan: a daughter, a wife, a mother in the blink of an eye.

Traveling, a stranger in a foreign land, I'd been able to invent myself. Roaming Pleiku or Phnom Penh, I was without a past or future, entirely of the moment. But the closer I stood to what childhood asked, the more obstructed the view.

So we had our first real fight. Vietnam had guaranteed a united front—Bob and me against the world. But away from the suffocating war, the oppressive military, and the very real external dangers, we were free to feud.

After fifteen years of steadfast opposition, at thirty-four I agreed to have a baby.

Afterwards

I pushed out our first son ten years after Khe Sanh, and I counted: one nose, two eyes, two hands, ten toes. I remembered that other mother and her story told to me under fire in the pitch-black bunker. At thirty-seven, I gave birth to our second. At thirty-nine, I was divorced, with custody of two small boys. Not a single thing about losing Bob, my very best friend, was easy. Almost everything felt hard outside of our shared story.

Bob had been the one who had always wanted to have children, but it turned out that I was the one who needed them. I couldn't have known that at the time, either.

In 1997, at my youngest son's bar mitzvah reception, my oldest son laughed at my incorrigible *adultness*. "Mom," six-foot Sam wrapped an arm around my shoulder and told me, "You're a geezer. You don't remember what it's like to be a kid."

Had I ever been one? Had I ever known that freedom? Or was I the ripe fruit off the tree of a loving Jewish home, dwarfed by its expectation?

There's ample irony to this story, perhaps even a small personal tragedy. In Vietnam—at war—my partnership with Bob truly *worked*. His pride in my exploration and accomplishment was authentic. My empathy for his military entrapment and support for his capacious intellect were real.

At the edges of the earth's map—inside a foreign conflagration—the gender roles in my marriage had enormous latitude, for both of us. A young wife wasn't denied her opportunity for extreme risk. A young husband wasn't required to compete with his wife's ambitions. Neither was measured by the other's dispositions—or choices. There was an effortless balance. Convention, in the form of loving parents, wasn't looking over my shoulder. Of course, Bob and I couldn't live out our entire lives in the Vietnam War.

Undoubtedly, there were conflicting motives driving any ambitious woman of that era—the schizophrenic struggle between the forces of powerful feminist language and the contrarian forces of the world-as-it-still-was.

Perhaps this sounds to younger women, reared in other times to other messages, strangely archaic, peculiarly quaint.

To my own much older ears, what I have lived and now written could sound much the same. But I feel a deep affection for the girl who lived it—all of it. For her energetic innocence, for the verve with which she lived her every unconscious jerk and twitch.

In truth, even now, women who identify as feminists—as I most certainly did and do—occupy competing universes: fulfill expectations and please or drop breadcrumbs on a path of our own creation. Obviously, that gymnastic pursuit for gender equilibrium persists.

This story remains the epic tale we live and relive while we try to imagine our piece of, and our place in, this world we inhabit. Still, neither men nor women appear to make singular choices for singular reasons.

But *then*—the magnetic pull to be a supportive wife in service to a partner's ambitions constrained the struggle for balance. *Then*, ironically, the most adventurous of women were in other settings, the most traditional. This is their story.

I thought it remarkable: Anyone could have taken the Pan Am flight I took to Saigon in mid-February 1970, but of course not everyone did. People go where they need to go.

When I set out on that plane from Baltimore toting three polyester dresses and one red pantsuit, I carried some baggage and I refused the rest. But there is no way that I am able to imagine, even now, that I could have turned back

WITH GRATITUDE

This project was guided twenty-five years ago by the wise and experienced hands of my Portland, Oregon, writing group. They were five intelligent, committed women—novelists all—who met once a month for two years, shaped this story, and made me a much better writer: Emily Horowitz; Jenny Jacobs; Stella Lillicrop; Maya Muir; Perla Peszkin. I send each of you my gratitude and benediction on your own books and other life projects.

Thanks to The Proprioceptive Writing Center—Linda Trichter Metcalf and Tobin Simon—for the safest possible place that a seed could be sown: "*Saigon was a girl, not a city.*" Thanks, too, for the support of the Virginia Center for the Creative Arts, where that seed took root those many years ago. And to playwright/novelist Frank George Reilly for a genuine eye-opening critique, at the exact moment when I thought I'd written my last draft.

Without a lifetime of friendship and authorial advice from Hamilton Gregory (his memory *is* a blessing), whose friends he insisted become mine, I'd never have met Skip Isaacs. Without the generous collegiality of Skip, an accomplished former *Baltimore Sun* Vietnam correspondent, this book might never have found its welcoming home. And that home, welcoming indeed, was Texas Tech University Press—with its dream of an acquisitions editor, Travis Snyder; its gifted senior graphic designer, Hannah Gaskamp; and Christie Perlmutter, a copy editor with the ear of a poet.

I send an outpouring of gratitude to Diane and Bill Elliot, who asked nothing and offered everything. Thank you for far more than "A Room of My Own."

Finally, and from my deepest. I have had two meaningful, life-shaping marriages. The first began with this book. The next continues to fill me to this day.

INDEX

A Deadly Shade of Gold, 107
A Purple Place for Dying, 107
Abrams, Creighton (Gen.), 88, 171, 209
adjutant general, 185
Advanced Infantry Training, 21, 187
advisor, 124, 125, 162, 230
Agent Orange, 81
Air Force, 82, 149, 180, 189
air support, 12, 245
AK-47s, 7, 96
Aleutian Island, 25
Alger, Horatio, 92
altar boy, 22
Amer-Asian, 223
American Embassy, 66
Amsterdam, 52
Annapolis, Maryland, 22, 24, 27, 34, 44, 88, 97, 147, 161
"Another Alleged Massacre," 83
Anson, Bob, 60, 79, 88, 91, 166, 170, 177, 238
Anson, Diane, 170
antipersonnel weapons, 250
anti-war, 21, 43, 61, 89, 108, 159, 177, 179, 184

ao dai, 36, 75, 152, 155, 215, 244
Apollo 13, 108
Armed Forces Radio, 70, 191, 107
Army of the Republic of Vietnam (ARVN), 12, 117, 125, 237, 245
Arnett, Peter, 95–96
Article 15, 184–85
artillery, incoming, 253
artillery shells, 7, 97
Associated Press, 42
Athens, Greece, 52, 73
Atlantic Monthly, 167
Atlantic Ocean, 192
Australians, 50
AWOL, 20
B-52s, 5
Bachelor Enlisted Men's Quarters (BEQ), 141, 143
Baltimore, Maryland, 19, 31, 48, 86, 102, 135, 190, 264, 266,
Baltimore Sun, 34, 267
Bangkok, Thailand, 48–49, 53, 60–61, 149, 178–79, 190
bao chi (journalist), 5, 115
bar mitzvah, 265
Basic Training, 21–22, 28, 186–87
bat mitzvah, 70

Index

Beirut, Lebanon, 42, 178–79
Bench, Johnny, 209
Big Red One (1st Infantry Division), 88
birth certificate, 237
black market, 37, 68, 80, 131
body bags, 8–9, 14, 106
body count, 105
book burnings, 27, 57
boonie, 65, 96, 137, 252
Brides magazine, 145
British Commonwealth, 50
British Embassy, 58
Broadway Fish Market, 86
Brodard's (Saigon café), 35, 107
Buddhism, 174
Buddhist temple, 35
Bunker, Ellsworth, 88, 171
bunkers, 252, 254
bureau chief, 42, 48, 159, 165, 168, 170, 172, 182, 246
C-130, 95, 158
California, 20, 22, 26–27, 143, 178, 186, 251
Cambodia, 30, 47–50, 54, 56, 61–62, 94, 96–98, 108, 112, 115–18, 121–24, 126–-29, 131–33, 145, 147, 150, 166, 169, 171, 177, 178, 239, 245
Cambodian Army checkpoints, 126
cameraman, 12
Camus, Albert, 200
can sa (marijuana), 109
Canada, 24, 27
capital city, 59
Caravelle (hotel), 92, 216
Carolina coast, 181
Catholic Mass, 29
Catholic Relief Services, 221, 225

Catholicism, 174
Center for Reconstructive Surgery, 225
Central Highlands, 3, 40
Central Market, 85-87
Central Office for South Vietnam (COSVN), 94–95
Cercle Sportif, 145
Champlin, John, 226–27, 229–30
Chi Phu, Cambodia, 122–23, 130
Chiang Kai-shek, 113
Chicago, Illinois, 22
chief of correspondents 170, 173
"Children of War," 217–18, 240–41, 246
Chinese junk, 141
Chinese rifles, 95
Chinooks, 40, 77, 97
Cholon, 153
chopper, 3–4, 6–7, 9–10, 12–14, 77, 97, 158, 246, 248, 250, 257–61
Christian Brothers' monastery, 230
Christmas, 26–27, 193, 207–8, 210, 215, 245
CIA, 62
citron pressé, 42, 90
Clark, Marsh, 42–43, 45, 47–48, 50, 55, 61, 79–80, 89–93, 112–13, 165, 167, 169–71, 173, 177–79, 181, 196
Clark, Pippa, 43, 89, 91, 165, 171
Cleveland, Ohio, 44, 263
Coast Guard, 21
Cobra gunships, 40, 109, 250–51, 255
Cody, Wyoming, 22
Cold War, 179
Colonial architecture, 54
conscientious objector, 21–22
Continental Palace Hotel, 42, 90

Index

coup d'état, 61, 94
C-rations, 62, 97–98
Cu Chi, Vietnam, 121, 124
Da Nang, Vietnam, 157–58, 160–62, 165
Daily Cardinal, The, 158
Darker Than Amber, 113
Date of Estimated Return from Overseas (DEROS), 104–5, 149, 188
Defoliation, 82, 230
Dead (Grateful), 70
Delta, 40, 162–63
Denver, Colorado, 22
dependents, military 32, 71, 136, 141
Do Cao Tri (Gen.), 10, 117–19, 125
double-digit midget, 105
Donut Dolly, 121, 233
Dow Chemical riot, 158–59
Dowell, Bill, 34–36, 106–7, 111–20, 122–26, 128, 130, 132, 148, 188
Dr. Seuss, 86, 152
draft board, 22, 252
draft lottery, 26
draftee, 66, 68, 145, 149, 162, 172, 187, 207
Dudman, Richard, 112, 147
dust off, 11
early out, 187
Emerson, Gloria, 40–41, 67, 147, 247
Erawan Hotel, 50–51, 53
Esper, George, 42
Esquire, 195
establishment rag, 83
European cities, 36
Evans, Phil, 34, 38, 42–44, 89, 147
Evening Capital (Annapolis), 27, 34, 61, 147, 165
Falana, Lola, 208–9
Fawcett, Denby, 93
54th Military Police Unit, 65, 77–78
firefight, 7, 105-6
First Amendment, 185
1st Infantry Division, 88–89
Five o'clock Follies, 105
Florence, Italy, 18–19, 73, 102, 193
Flower People, 215
Flynn, Sean, 133, 147
Fontainebleau Hotel (Miami), 30
Fort Gordon, Georgia, 20, 26
Fowler, Harry, 162
fragging, 209
freelance, 43, 79–80, 145, 166, 216
"friendlies," 67, 254
Fulbright, J. W., 215
Gaddi's (restaurant), 198–99
Gart, Murray, 170–71
Genoa, 193
Georgia, 20, 63
Germany, 21
GI, 21, 37, 51, 72, 104, 106, 109, 113–15, 141, 153, 156–57, 185, 190, 211, 229, 232, 234
GI Bill, 201
Go Dau Ha, Vietnam, 118–19, 130
Golden Gate Park, 30
"gooks," 254
Graduate Record Exam (GRE), 201, 207
"green," 37
Greene, Graham, 44, 90
Greenway, David, 48–50
"Greetings," 22
grunt, 8, 104, 109, 115, 139, 190, 251, 255
Guam, 31

Index

guard duty, 69–71, 77
guerilla war, 8, 122, 190, 229
Gulf Stream, 181
gunners, 4, 10, 14–15, 257, 259
Haifa, Israel, 193
hard news, 44
Harris Tweed, 195–96
Harvard, 49, 185
helicopter, 4, 6, 8,10, 12, 15, 39–40, 97, 112, 132, 245, 250, 257–59, 261
Hendrix, Jimi, 110
Hero of the People's Armed Forces, 166
Hilton, 190, 197
hitchhike, 22, 112
Hitler, 184
Ho Chi Minh Trail, 5, 245
Holy Land, 193
Honda 50, 38, 45, 66, 69,76, 86,103, 113, 115, 123, 142, 146, 151–52, 164, 176, 205, 210–13, 225, 230, 236, 242
Hong Kong, 89, 91, 113, 135, 140, 149–50, 165–66, 188–92, 194–99, 203–4, 206, 264
Honolulu, Hawaii, 31, 149, 190
Honolulu Advertiser, 93
hookah, 154
Hope, Bob, 208–9
Hotel Le Royal, 54, 130
Huey, 4–5, 10, 13, 258
Hughes, Richard, 231–36, 238
Iacobucci, Ennio, 80, 216
I Corps, 65, 77
Imperial Hotel, 60
Indonesian Embassy, 49, 51
intelligence officer, 34
Irish American, 137
Irishman, 100

Israel, 171
Italy, 18, 138, 192
Ivy League, 49, 61
Japanese, 81, 237
Jerusalem, 42
Jesuits, 23, 52, 71, 196
Jewish, 19–20, 29, 100–101, 185, 243, 265
Jewish New Year, 243
joint (marijuana), 109–10, 253, 255
Joint US Public Affairs Office (JUSPAO), 39, 41, 84
Joplin, Janis, 110
juvenile delinquents, 235
Kafka, Franz, 167
Kent State University, 107–10
Kesey, Ken, 107
Khe Sanh, Vietnam, 248, 252–53, 258, 260, 265
Khmer Rouge, 30, 147
killing fields, 30
Kodak Instamatic, 48
Korean, 33, 120–21, 176
land mines, 99, 128, 130, 152, 230
land reform, 80
landing zones, 4, 6, 39
Laos, 4, 10, 12, 178. 245–46, 248, 257
Larsen, Jonathan, 170–72, 178, 181–82, 210, 215, 217–18, 238–39, 246, 250–51, 255
Larsen, Wendy, 172, 181, 210
Lexington Market, 86
Li'l Abner, 8
Light at the End of the Tunnel, The, 215
Light Observation Helicopter (LOH), 132
Lon Nol, 62, 94, 145
Long Binh, 32, 51, 63, 65, 72–73,

272

Index

109, 208–9, 264
M16, 7, 66, 70, 249
MACV (Military Area Command, Vietnam), 39–40, 68, 71, 84, 206–7
Madame Bovary, 107
Madison, Wisconsin, 83, 158
mafia (Vietnamese), 234
malaria, 44, 161
Manhattan, 198
Manila, Philippines, 149
Marine Corps Press Center, 160
Marines, 67, 83, 160, 248
marriage, 25, 28, 41, 43, 103, 175, 192, 202, 237, 263–65, 268
marriage license, 28
*M*A*S*H*, 206
Matriarchs, 20
MacDonald, John, 107, 113, 124
Medevac, 4–5, 7–8, 14, 106, 261
Mediterranean, 64, 193
Mekong River, 98, 130, 163
Mikimoto, 196–97
military court, 185–86
military payment currency (MPC), 37, 154
military police (MP), 63, 65–67, 69–71, 78, 77–78, 121, 140–41, 182
Miller, Buddy (author's brother), 38, 103
Miller, Harmon (author's brother), 32, 103, 172
Ministry of Social Welfare, 235
Minnesota, 183
monsoons, 150, 153
Morrow, Mike, 112, 147
Moto Guzzi, 111
motorcycle helmet, 141
Mrs. An, 36–37, 44–45, 64, 73, 100, 113, 151, 167, 173, 175–76, 230, 242–43
Mrs. Loppheimer, 103
Mt. Rushmore, 184
Murray, Arthur, 19, 193
My Lai, Vietnam, 39, 83
Mykonos, Greece, 180
Napalm, 68, 81, 109, 158, 226, 228
National Assembly Building, 80
National Guard, 107
National Liberation Front (NFL), 47
National Rehabilitation Center, 230
Naval Academy, 24–25, 27, 57
Navy captains, 40
NBC Radio correspondent, 34
Neak Loeung, Cambodia, 98, 130
New Year's, 193, 207, 214–16, 241–44
New York, 18, 43, 50, 58, 59–61, 79–84, 89, 97, 157, 159, 166, 169–70, 178–79, 192, 238–40, 251
New York Times 40, 147
New Zealanders, 50
Newsweek, 42
Nguyen Cao Ky, 98, 130
Nguyen Van Thieu, 171, 177
Nha Trang, Vietnam, 176–77, 179–80, 228
Nhung (An), 37, 173–77, 179–81, 224, 242
90th Provost Marshal's Office, 78, 94, 137, 168, 182
Nixon, Richard, 41, 94, 98, 209
North Vietnamese, 7, 30, 91–92, 166, 169–70, 173, 177, 245, 248
O positive (blood type), 39
Oakland, California, 22, 30, 108,

Index

187, 222
officers' club, 67, 84, 121, 142, 177
Olympia typewriter, 44
opium den, 153
orphanages, 218–25, 228, 230
Pabst Blue Ribbon hovels, 36, 222
pacified, 118
Page, Tim, 133, 147
pagoda, 76, 124–26, 174, 243–44
Pale Gray for Guilt, 107
Pan Am, 31, 48, 189, 266
Paradise Lost, 105
Paris, France, 40, 47
Patriarchs, 20
Patton, George S., 206
pedicabs, 73, 151, 157, 163–64, 210, 236
Peninsula Hotel, 198
Pentagon, 39, 60, 80, 81, 94, 206
Pentax, 48, 55, 113
Perot, H. Ross, 92–93
Peugeot, 126, 129–30
Pham Xuan An, 165–66, 177
Phnom Penh, Cambodia, 45, 47, 50, 53–54, 57, 61–62, 97, 112, 122–23, 126–27, 129–31, 169–70, 178, 264
Phong Trieu, 230
Photojournalists, 133, 147
piastres, 37, 73, 117, 155, 163, 166, 169, 223, 238, 244
pilots, 3–6, 9–12, 14–15, 109, 250–51, 255, 257–60
Pines, Burt, 79
Plain Dealer (Cleveland), 44
Pleiku, Vietnam, 105, 264
Pond, Elizabeth, 112, 147
post office, 22, 131
POW (prisoner of war), 91, 92
Prasaut, Cambodia, 122, 124

Pratt Street meat market, 86
press attaché, 41
press pass, 39–40, 116, 142, 208
private first class (PFC), 84, 114, 186
prostitution, 155–57, 217, 231, 234, 237, 243
provost marshal's office, 78, 94, 137, 168, 182
Pulitzer Prize, 96
Pump House Gang, The, 107
PX, 66–67, 69, 101, 197, 205, 233, 242
Quang Tri, Vietnam, 3–4, 6, 10–12, 246, 248, 257–58, 261, 264
(RMS) *Queen Elizabeth*, 18
Quiet American, The, 44
Quonset hut, 4, 6, 11, 246, 257
R&R, 91, 140, 149–50, 188, 204
rabbi, 28–29
Red Cross, 121, 213
Reed, Walter, 147
refugee camps, 218–19
Republic of South Vietnam, 33, 158
Republican, 43, 61, 159, 172
Reserves, Army, 21
Reuters, 42
Rolling Stone, 183, 185
Rome, Italy, 36, 73
Rotterdam, Netherlands, 18
Route One, 112, 116, 121, 123, 127, 129
Royal Palace (Cambodia), 56
Royal Thai Airlines, 49
Russian artillery, 95
Saar, John, 80, 172
Saigon, Vietnam, 11, 22, 26, 30–31, 33–36, 38–40, 42, 44,

49–51, 53–54, 58–61, 63–65, 67, 71–73, 77–81, 83, 85–86, 89–94, 100, 102, 104, 107–9, 111–12, 116–18, 120–21, 130, 137, 141–42, 145, 147, 151–54, 156–57, 162–67, 170–72, 176, 178, 181–82, 186, 189, 198, 203–4, 207–8, 210–11, 215, 222, 225, 230, 232, 234, 239, 241, 245, 264, 266–67
Saigon bureau, 58, 157, 165, 178, 239
Saigon bureau chief, 42, 159, 165, 168, 170, 182, 246
Saigon River, 36, 141, 170
San Francisco, California, 31, 35, 44, 197, 211, 252
San Francisco Examiner, 44
San Francisco Steak House, 197
Sartre, Jean-Paul, 200
"Sat Cong Badges," 83
Sayle, Murray, 111–28, 130–32
school integration battles, 57
School on the Front Line, The, 230
716th Military Police Detachment, 182
Severn River, 24, 161
Shell Oil, 129
shoeshine boy, 232
"short," 11
shrapnel, 147, 254
Sihanouk, Norodom, 47, 54–56, 61–62, 94
Simon and Garfunkel, 102
Sinatra, Frank, 167
Singapore, 149, 155, 166, 170, 178
skid row, 22
Skoun, Cambodia, 169, 177
smoke grenades, 7
Sometimes a Great Notion, 107

Son Thang, 83
South Africans, 50
South China Sea, 160
South Vietnamese Army, 30, 245. *See also* Army of the Republic of Vietnam
South Vietnamese Embassy, 34
Southeast Asia, 47, 49
St. Augustine, 200
St. Thomas Aquinas, 200
standard operating procedure (SOP), 68
Statue of Liberty, 184
Stone, Dana, 133, 147
street girls, 155
streetboys, 71, 147, 167, 231, 233–35, 237–38, 243
stringer, 79, 84
sugarcane, 44
Sunday Times (London), 113
Svay Rieng, Cambodia, 122, 126
Swanson, Dick, 80, 172
Swanson, Germaine, 172
Sweden, 24, 27
Swiss military, 195–96
Sydney, Australia, 149
tail gunners, 4, 14
Tay Ninh, Vietnam, 117, 119, 121
tear gas, 20
Tet, 241–44
Tet Offensive, 30, 66–67, 71, 166
Thailand, 31, 49
Third World country, 43, 142
Time Inc., 43, 79, 106, 166, 170, 178
Time-Life, 79
Times Paris bureau, 40
Tokyo, Japan, 149
tomboy, 18
Ton Son Nhut Airport, 32, 69, 105,

157, 163
top sergeant, 68
tracer bullet, 146
Tran Hung Dao, 146
Tu Do Street, 156–57, 190
25th Infantry Division, 121
United Press International (UPI), 42
United States Agency for International Development (USAID), 161, 223, 230
University of California, Berkeley, 20
University of Saigon, 172
University of Wisconsin, 20, 43, 48, 158
US military press, 97, 247
US press office, 39, 44, 97, 247
USO, 107, 205, 232–33
USS *Aurelia*, 18, 47, 54, 192
Viet Cong (VC), 7, 30, 66, 83–84, 94–95, 106, 115, 117, 153, 243, 245
Vietnam War Moratorium, 21

Vietnamization, 30, 98, 245
war correspondent, 34, 43, 147, 182, 187, 202
war veterans, 87
warrant officer, 6, 109, 250, 260
Washington Beltway, 153
Washington, DC, 21, 24, 34, 153
"Wedding March," 29
West Coast, 19
Western correspondents, 47, 61
Westinghouse Radio, 61
white phosphorous, 229
Whitesides, Bruce M., 82
Wild Bunch photojournalists, 147
"Willie Pete." *See* white phosphorus
Willwerth, Jim, 80, 170
withdrawal (of US troops from Vietnam), 41, 88, 245
Wolfe, Tom, 107
World War II, 25, 81, 88, 121, 137, 158, 179, 206, 208, 225, 246
Yom Kippur, 19
Zumwalt (Elmo), 209

ABOUT THE AUTHOR

Inette Miller was an award-winning national and international journalist for twenty years: a war correspondent for *Time* magazine in Vietnam and Cambodia and a Capitol Hill and State Department reporter. She is a widely published author, an exhilarating public speaker, and an enthusiastic writing workshop teacher. She is the recipient of Associated Press awards and Virginia Center for the Creative Arts fellowships and is a long-standing member of the Authors Guild.